# From God to Us

# From God to Us

## How we got our Bible

### Norman L. Geisler
### &
### William E. Nix

moody press
chicago

To

*H. Chester Woodring, Jr.*

*and*

*Charles H. Shaw*

*Beloved mentors in the faith*

© 1974 by
THE MOODY BIBLE INSTITUTE
OF CHICAGO

The Bible quotations used in this book are from the Authorized King James Version, the American Standard Version of 1901, and, unless otherwise stated, the Revised Standard Version.

The use of selected references from various versions of the Bible in this publication does not necessarily imply publisher endorsement of the versions in their entirety.

ISBN: 0-8024-2878-9

Third Printing, 1976

*Printed in the United States of America*

# CONTENTS

# 1

# THE CHARACTER OF THE BIBLE

THE BIBLE is a unique book. It is one of the oldest books in the world, and yet it is still the world's best seller. It is a product of the ancient Eastern world, but it has molded the modern Western world. Tyrants have burned the Bible, and believers revere it. It is the most quoted, the most published, the most translated, and the most influential book in the history of mankind.

Just what is it that constitutes this unusual character of the Bible? How did the Bible originate? When and how did the Bible take on its present form? What is meant by the "inspiration" of the Bible? These are the questions which occupy our interest in this introductory chapter.

## THE STRUCTURE OF THE BIBLE

The word *Bible* (Book) came into English by way of French from the Latin *biblia* and the Greek *biblos*. It was originally the name given to the outer coat of a papyrus reed in the eleventh century B.C. By the second century A.D., Christians were using the word to describe their sacred writings.

## THE TWO TESTAMENTS OF THE BIBLE

The Bible has two major parts: the Old Testament and the New Testament. The Old Testament was written and preserved by the Jewish community for a millennium or more before the time of Christ. The New Testament was composed by disciples of Christ during the first century A.D.

The word *testament*, which is better translated "covenant," is taken from the Hebrew and Greek words designating a compact or agreement between two parties. In the case of the Bible, then,

7

we have the old contract between God and His people, the Jews, and the new compact between God and Christians.

Christian scholars have stressed the unity between these two Testaments of the Bible in terms of the person of Jesus Christ who claimed to be its unifying theme.[1] St. Augustine said the New Testament is veiled in the Old Testament, and the Old Testament is unveiled in the New Testament. Or, as others have put it, "The New is in the Old concealed, and the Old is in the New revealed." Again, Christ is enfolded in the Old Testament but unfolded in the New. Believers before the time of Christ looked forward in expectation, whereas present-day believers see the realization of God's plan in the Christ.

| BOOKS OF THE OLD TESTAMENT | | |
|---|---|---|
| The Law (Pentateuch)—5 books | Poetry—5 books | |
| 1. Genesis <br> 2. Exodus <br> 3. Leviticus <br> 4. Numbers <br> 5. Deuteronomy | 1. Job <br> 2. Psalms <br> 3. Proverbs <br> 4. Ecclesiastes <br> 5. Song of Solomon | |
| History—12 books | Prophets—17 books | |
| 1. Joshua <br> 2. Judges <br> 3. Ruth <br> 4. I Samuel <br> 5. II Samuel <br> 6. I Kings <br> 7. II Kings <br> 8. I Chronicles <br> 9. II Chronicles <br> 10. Ezra <br> 11. Nehemiah <br> 12. Esther | A. Major <br> 1. Isaiah <br> 2. Jeremiah <br> 3. Lamentations <br> 4. Ezekiel <br> 5. Daniel | B. Minor <br> 1. Hosea <br> 2. Joel <br> 3. Amos <br> 4. Obadiah <br> 5. Jonah <br> 6. Micah <br> 7. Nahum <br> 8. Habakkuk <br> 9. Zephaniah <br> 10. Haggai <br> 11. Zechariah <br> 12. Malachi |

1. See Norman L. Geisler, *Christ, the Theme of the Bible* (Chicago: Moody Press, 1968).

## THE SECTIONS OF THE BIBLE

The Christian Bible is commonly divided into eight sections, four in the Old Testament and four in the New.

| BOOKS OF THE NEW TESTAMENT | |
|---|---|
| Gospels | History |
| 1. Matthew<br>2. Mark<br>3. Luke<br>4. John | 1. Acts of the Apostles |
| Epistles | |
| 1. Romans<br>2. 1 Corinthians<br>3. 2 Corinthians<br>4. Galatians<br>5. Ephesians<br>6. Philippians<br>7. Colossians<br>8. 1 Thessalonians<br>9. 2 Thessalonians<br>10. 1 Timothy<br>11. 2 Timothy | 12. Titus<br>13. Philemon<br>14. Hebrews<br>15. James<br>16. 1 Peter<br>17. 2 Peter<br>18. 1 John<br>19. 2 John<br>20. 3 John<br>21. Jude |
| Prophecy | |
| 1. Revelation | |

The fourfold division of the Old Testament is based on a topical arrangement of books stemming from the translation of the Hebrew Scriptures into Greek. This translation known as the Septuagint (LXX), was begun in the third century B.C. The Hebrew Bible does not follow this fourfold, topical classification of books. Instead, a threefold division is employed, possibly based on the official position of the author. Moses, the lawgiver, has his five books listed first; these are followed by the books of men who held the prophetic office. Finally, the third section contained books by men who were believed to have had a prophetic gift but who did not hold a prophetic office. Hence, the Hebrew Old Testament has the following structure:

| THE HEBREW OLD TESTAMENT ARRANGEMENT | | |
|---|---|---|
| The Law (Torah) | The Prophets (Nebhiim) | The Writings (Kethubhim) |
| 1. Genesis<br>2. Exodus<br>3. Leviticus<br>4. Numbers<br>5. Deuteronomy | A. Former Prophets<br>  1. Joshua<br>  2. Judges<br>  3. Samuel<br>  4. Kings<br>B. Latter Prophets<br>  1. Isaiah<br>  2. Jeremiah<br>  3. Ezekiel<br>  4. The Twelve | A. Poetical Books<br>  1. Psalms<br>  2. Proverbs<br>  3. Job<br>B. Five Rolls (Megilloth)<br>  1. Song of Songs<br>  2. Ruth<br>  3. Lamentations<br>  4. Esther<br>  5. Ecclesiastes<br>C. Historical Books:<br>  1. Daniel<br>  2. Ezra-Nehemiah<br>  3. Chronicles |

Source: This is the arrangement in modern Jewish editions of the Old Testament. Cf. *The Holy Scriptures, According to the Masoretic Text;* and Rudolf Kittel and Paul E. Kahle (eds.), *Biblia Hebraica.*

The basis for this threefold division of the Hebrew Scriptures is found in Jewish history. The earliest possible testimony to it is the prologue to the book of Sirach, or Ecclesiasticus, during the second century B.C. The Jewish Mishnah (Teaching), the first-century Jewish historian Josephus, and subsequent Jewish tradition have also continued this threefold categorization of their Scriptures. The New Testament makes one possible allusion to a threefold division of the Old Testament when Jesus said, "All things must be fulfilled, which were written in the law of Moses, and in the prophets, and in the psalms concerning me" (Lk 24:44).

Regardless of the fact that Judaism has maintained a threefold division to date, Jerome's Latin Vulgate and subsequent Christian Bibles have followed the more topical fourfold format of the Septuagint. Combining this division with the natural and widely accepted fourfold categorization of the New Testament, the Bible may be cast into the following overall Christocentric structure:

| Old Testament | Law | Foundation for Christ |
| | History | Preparation for Christ |
| | Poetry | Aspiration for Christ |
| | Prophecy | Expectation of Christ |
| New Testament | Gospels | Manifestation of Christ |
| | Acts | Propagation of Christ |
| | Epistles | Interpretation and Application of Christ |
| | Revelation | Consummation in Christ |

Although there is no divinely authoritative basis for viewing the Bible in an eightfold structure, the Christian insistence that the Scriptures be understood Christocentrically is firmly based on the teachings of Christ. Some five times in the New Testament, Jesus affirmed Himself to be the theme of Old Testament Scripture (Mt 5:17; Lk 24:27, 44; Jn 5:39; Heb 10:7). In view of these statements, it is natural to view the eightfold topical arrangement of Scripture in terms of its one theme—Christ.

## CHAPTERS AND VERSES IN THE BIBLE

The earliest Bibles have no chapter and verse divisions. These were added for convenience in quoting the Scriptures. Stephen Langton, a professor at the University of Paris and later Archbishop of Canterbury, divided the Bible into chapters in 1227. Verses were added in 1551 and 1555 by Robert Stephanus, a Paris printer. Happily, Jewish scholars since that time have adopted the same chapter and verse divisions for the Old Testament.

## THE INSPIRATION OF THE BIBLE

The most significant characteristic of the Bible is not its formal structure but its divine inspiration. The Bible's claim to be divinely inspired must not be misunderstood. It is not poetic inspiration but divine authority that is meant when we speak of the inspiration of the Bible. The Bible is unique; it is literally "God-breathed." Now let us examine what this means.

## INSPIRATION DEFINED

Although the word *inspiration* is used only once in the New Testament (2 Ti 3:16) and once in the Old Testament (Job 32:8), the process by which God communicates His authoritative message to man is described in many ways. An examination of the two great passages on inspiration in the New Testament will aid in understanding the meaning of biblical inspiration.

### BIBLICAL DESCRIPTIONS OF INSPIRATION

Paul wrote to Timothy, "All scripture is inspired by God and is profitable for teaching, for reproof, for correction, and for training in righteousness" (2 Ti 3:16). That is, the Old Testament Scriptures or writings are "God-breathed" (Gk. *theopneustos*) and, therefore, authoritative for the thought and life of the believer. A kindred passage in 1 Corinthians 2:13 stresses the same point. "And we impart this," wrote Paul, "in words not taught by human wisdom but taught by the Spirit, interpreting spiritual truths to those who possess the Spirit." Words taught by the Holy Spirit are divinely inspired words.

The second great passage in the New Testament on the inspiration of the Bible is 2 Peter 1:21. "No prophecy ever came by the impulse of man, but men moved by the Holy Spirit spoke from God." In other words, the prophets were men whose messages did not originate with their own impulse but were "Spirit-moved." By revelation God spoke *to* the prophets in many ways (Heb 1:1): angels, visions, dreams, voices, and miracles. Inspiration is the way God spoke *through* the prophets to others. The fact that the prophets searched their own writings to see "what person or time was indicated by the Spirit of Christ within them when predicting the sufferings of Christ and the subsequent glory" (1 Pe 1:11), is a further indication that their words were not ultimately self-initiated.

Combining the classical passages on inspiration, we find that the Bible is inspired in the sense that Spirit-moved men wrote God-breathed words which are divinely authoritative for Christian faith and practice. Let us now analyze these three elements of inspiration more closely.

THEOLOGICAL DEFINITION OF INSPIRATION

The single time the New Testament uses the word *inspiration,* it is applied only to the writings and not to the writers. It is the Bible which is inspired and not the human authors. Properly speaking, it is only the product which is inspired, not the persons. The writers spoke and undoubtedly wrote about many things, such as those in the mundane affairs of life, which were not divinely inspired. However, since the Holy Spirit did, as Peter said, move upon the men who produced the inspired writings, we may by extension refer to inspiration in a broader sense. This broader sense includes the total *process* by which Spirit-moved men uttered God-breathed and hence divinely authoritative words. It is this total process of inspiration which contains three essential elements: divine causality, prophetic agency, and written authority.

*Divine Causality.* God is the Prime Mover in the inspiration of the Bible. It is the divine which moved the human. God spoke to the prophets first and then through them to others. God revealed, and men of God recorded the truths of faith. That God is the ultimate source and original cause of biblical truth is the first and most fundamental factor in the doctrine of inspiration. Nevertheless, it is not the only factor.

*Prophetic Agency.* The prophets who wrote Scripture were not automatons. They were more than recording secretaries. They wrote with full intent and consciousness in the normal exercise of their own literary styles and vocabularies. The personalities of the prophets were not violated by a supernatural intrusion. The Bible which they wrote is the Word of God, but it is also the words of men. God used their personalities to convey His propositions. The prophets were the immediate cause of what was written, but God was the ultimate cause.

*Written Authority.* The final product of divine authority working through the prophetic agency is the written authority of the Bible. The Scriptures are "profitable for teaching, for reproof, for correction, for training in righteousness." The Bible is the last word on doctrinal and ethical matters. All theological and moral disputes must be brought to the bar of the written Word. The Scriptures derive their authority from God through His prophets.

Nevertheless, it is the prophetic writings and not the writers as such which possess and retain the resultant divine authority. The prophets have died; the prophetic writings live on.

In brief, an adequate definition of inspiration must have three fundamental factors: God the Prime Mover, men of God as the instruments, and a divinely authoritative writing as the final result.

### SOME IMPORTANT DISTINCTIONS

#### INSPIRATION DISTINGUISHED FROM REVELATION AND ILLUMINATION

Two related concepts which help to clarify by contrast what is meant by inspiration are revelation and illumination. The former deals with the *disclosure* of truth, the latter the *discovery* of that truth. Revelation involves the *unveiling* of truth, illumination the *understanding;* but inspiration as such involves neither. Revelation concerns the origin and giving of truth; inspiration the reception and recording of it; illumination the subsequent apprehension and understanding of it. The inspiration which brings a written revelation to men is not in itself a guarantee that they will understand it. Illumination of the mind and heart is necessary. Revelation is an objective disclosure; illumination is the subjective understanding of it; inspiration is the means by which the revelation became an objective disclosure. Revelation is the fact of divine communication, inspiration is the means, and illumination is the gift of understanding that communication.

#### INSPIRATION OF THE ORIGINAL, NOT THE COPIES

The inspiration and consequent authority of the Bible does not automatically extend to every copy and translation of the Bible. Only the original manuscripts, known as autographs, were inspired. Mistakes and changes made in copy and translation cannot claim this original inspiration. Second Kings 8:26, for example, says that Ahaziah was twenty-two years old at his coronation, whereas 2 Chronicles 22:2 says he was forty-two years old. Both cannot be correct. Only the original and not the scribal error is authoritative. Other examples of this type can be found in present copies of the Scriptures (e.g., cf. 1 Ki 4:26 and 2 Ch 9:25). A translation or copy, then, is authoritative only to the extent that it accurately reproduces the autographs.

Exactly how accurately the Bible has been copied will be discussed later (chap. 15) under the science of textual criticism. For now it is sufficient to note that the great doctrinal and historical content of the Bible has been transmitted down through the centuries without substantial change or loss. Twentieth-century copies and translations of the Bible do not possess *original* inspiration but they have a *derived* inspiration insofar as they are faithful copies of the autographs. Technically speaking, only the autographs are inspired, but for all practical purposes the present-day English Bible, in that it is an accurate transmission of the original, is the inspired Word of God.

Since the autographs are not extant, some critics have objected to inerrant autographs which have never been seen. They ask how it can be held that the originals were errorless if they have never been seen. The answer is that inerrancy is not an empirically known fact but a belief based on the teaching of the Bible about its own inspiration, the highly accurate nature of the vast majority of transmitted Scripture, and the lack of any disconfirming evidence. The Bible claims to be an utterance of God who cannot make mistakes. And even though no infallible originals have ever been discovered, neither has anyone ever discovered a fallible autograph. What we do have are very accurately copied manuscripts which have been adequately translated into English. Hence, for all matters of doctrine and duty, today's Bible is an adequate representation of the authoritative Word of God.

INSPIRATION OF THE TEACHING BUT NOT ALL THE CONTENTS OF THE BIBLE

It is also essential to note that only what the Bible *teaches* is inspired and without error; not everything the Bible *contains* is errorless. For example, the Scriptures contain the record of many evil and sinful acts but do not commend any of these. Instead, they condemn such evils. The Bible even records some of the lies of Satan (e.g., Gen 3:4). It is not thereby teaching that these lies are true. The only thing that inspiration guarantees here is that this is a true record of a lie Satan actually told.

Sometimes it is not perfectly clear whether the Bible contains merely a record of what someone else said or did, or whether it teaches that we ought to do it too. For instance, is the Bible teaching that everything Job's friends said is true? Are all the conclusions of the man "under the sun" in Ecclesiastes the teaching of God or merely a true record of such vain thoughts? Whatever the case, a student of the Bible is admonished not to take everything the Bible *says* at face value. He must seek what the Bible is *teaching* and not just everything about which the Bible is speaking. The Bible records many things which it does not recommend, such as the assertion "there is no God" (Ps 14:1). In each case what the Bible contains must be studied in order to determine what it commands. Only what the Bible teaches is inspired and not everything referred to in its contents.

In summation, the Bible is an unusual book. It is composed of two testaments which contain sixty-six books claiming divine inspiration. By inspiration is meant that the original manuscripts of the Bible were given by revelation of God and are thereby invested with absolute authority for Christian thought and life. This means that whatever is taught in the Bible is for the Christian the final court of appeal. The precise nature of biblical inspiration is the next topic for examination.

# 2

# THE NATURE OF INSPIRATION

THE FIRST GREAT LINK in the chain of communication "from God to us" is inspiration. There are several theories about inspiration, some of which fall short of the biblical teaching on the subject. Our purpose in this chapter will be twofold: first, to examine these theories about inspiration and, second, to determine precisely what is implied in the teaching of the Bible as to its own inspiration.

## SEVERAL THEORIES ABOUT INSPIRATION

Historically, theories about the inspiration of the Bible have varied with the essential characteristics of the three theological movements: orthodoxy, modernism, and neoorthodoxy. Although these three views are not limited to one time period only, their primary manifestation is characteristic of three successive periods in the Christian church.

For most of church history the orthodox view held sway, namely, the Bible *is* the Word of God. With the rise of modernism many came to believe that the Bible merely *contains* the Word of God. Even more recently, under the influence of contemporary existentialism, neoorthodox theologians have held the Bible *becomes* the Word of God when one personally encounters God through it.

### ORTHODOXY: THE BIBLE IS THE WORD OF GOD

For some eighteen centuries of church history the orthodox view of inspiration prevailed. With only minor dissenting voices, the great fathers of the church held firmly that the Bible is the Word of God written down. Orthodox theologians through the centuries

17

have agreed that the Bible is verbally inspired, i.e., the written record came by God's inspiration. However, attempts to seek an explanation as to just how the written record can be God's Word when it was obviously composed by human authors with differing styles has led to two opposing views among orthodox thinkers. On the one hand, some have held to "verbal dictation," arguing that the biblical authors wrote only what God dictated word for word. On the other hand, some have opted for the "inspired concept" theory that God only gave the thoughts which the prophets were free to put into their own words.

*Verbal dictation.* A clear and articulate presentation of verbal dictation is found in John R. Rice's *Our God-Breathed Book—The Bible.*[1] Disclaiming that verbal dictation is mechanical, the author argues that God gave the dictation through the personality of the author. For God by his special province formed the very personalities upon which the Holy Spirit was later to call for His word-for-word dictation. Thus, argues Rice, God had prepared in advance the particular styles he desired in order to produce His exact words by using the predetermined vocabularies and styles of the different human authors. The final result, then, is a word-for-word verbal dictation of God in Holy Scripture.

*Inspired concepts.* In his *Systematic Theology,* A. H. Strong takes a view which has been called conceptual inspiration.[2] God inspired only the concepts and not the particular literary expression into which each biblical author cast them. God gave the thoughts to the prophets who were at liberty to put them into their own terms. In this way Strong hoped to avoid any mechanical implications of verbal dictation and still preserve the divine origin of the Scriptures. God provided the conceptual inspiration and the men of God gave it a verbal expression characteristic of their own styles.

MODERNISM: THE BIBLE CONTAINS THE WORD OF GOD

Along with the rise of German idealism and biblical criticism (see chap. 14) a new view of biblical inspiration evolved with theological modernism or liberalism. In contrast to the traditional

1. John R. Rice, *Our God-Breathed Book—The Bible* (Murfreesboro, Tenn.: Sword of the Lord, 1969).
2. A. H. Strong, *Systematic Theology* (Grand Rapids: Revell, 1907).

orthodox view that the Bible *is* the Word of God, the modernists contend that the Bible merely *contains* the Word of God. Certain parts of the Bible are divine and true, but other parts are clearly human and in error. They feel the Bible is a victim of its times like any other book. They say that many of the legends, myths, and false beliefs about science were incorporated into the Bible. They argue that since these are not inspired of God they must be rejected by enlightened men as remnants of a primitive mentality unworthy of Christian belief. Only the divine truths contained within this admixture of ancient ignorance and error are truly inspired of God.

*Illumination view.* Some argue that the "inspired sections" of the Bible result from a kind of divine illumination wherein God granted deep religious insight to pious men. These insights were enjoyed with varying degrees of understanding and were recorded with admixtures of erroneous religious lore and scientific belief common to their day. Hence, the Bible expresses degrees of inspiration dependent on the depth of religious illumination which the author experienced.

*Intuition view.* On the other end of the modernistic camp are those who deny any divine element in the Bible whatsoever. To them the Bible is merely a Jewish scrapbook of legends, stories, poems, etc., with no essential historical value.[3] What others call divine inspiration is nothing but intensive human intuition. Within this Jewish folklore known as the Bible may be found some significant examples of heightened moral and religious genius. But these spiritual insights are purely naturalistic. In no sense are they anything more than human intuition; there is no supernatural inspiration or illumination.

### NEOORTHODOXY: THE BIBLE BECOMES THE WORD OF GOD

At the beginning of this century the turn of world events and the influence of the Danish father of existentialism, Soren Kierkegaard, gave rise to a new reformation within European theology. Many began to turn again to the Scriptures to hear the voice of God. Without giving up their critical views of the Bible, they began to take seriously the Bible as the *locus* of God's revelation

3. Henrik W. Van Loon, *Story of the Bible* (Garden City, N. Y.: Garden City, 1941), p. 227.

to man. In a kind of new orthodoxy they affirmed that God speaks to them through the Bible; the Scriptures *become* the Word of God to them in a personal encounter.

Like the other theories on the inspiration of the Bible, neo-orthodoxy developed two wings. On the more critical extreme are the demythologists who deny any religiously significant historical or factual content in the Bible and hold only to the existential religious care beneath the myths. On the other hand, the more evangelical thinkers try to preserve much of the historical and factual data of Scripture but argue that the Bible as such is not God's revelation. Rather, God reveals Himself through the Bible in personal encounter, but not in a propositional way.

*Demythological view.* Rudolf Bultmann and Shubert Ogden are characteristic representatives of the demythological view. They differ chiefly in that the latter sees no historical core beneath the myths of the Bible although the former sees some. Both agree that the Bible is written in the mythological language of its day which is passé. The task of the modern Christian is to demythologize the Bible, i.e., to strip it of this legendary form and to find the existential core beneath it. Bultmann says that once the Bible is divested of these religious myths, one arrives at the real message of God's self-giving love in Christ. It is not necessary to hold to an objective, historical, and propositional revelation in order to experience this subjective and personal truth. Hence, the Bible *becomes* God's revelation to us when by a proper (i.e., demythological) interpretation one is confronted with absolute love as set forth in the myth of God's selfless love in Christ. Thus, the Bible in itself is no revelation at all; it is a primitive, mythological expression through which God is personally revealed when it is correctly demythologized.

*Personal Encounter.* The other wing of neoorthodoxy, represented by men like Karl Barth and Emil Brunner, takes a more orthodox view of Scripture. Acknowledging that there are some imperfections in the written record (even in the autographs), Barth nevertheless contends that the Bible is the *locus* of God's revelation.[4] He says that God speaks to us through the Bible; it is

4. Karl Barth, *Church Dogmatics,* vol. 1, *Doctrine of the Word of God* (Naperville, Ill.: Allenson, 1956), pp. 592-95.

the vehicle of His revelation. Just as the dog hears his master's voice through the imperfect phonograph recording, so the Christian can hear God speak through Scripture. Brunner asserts that God's revelation is not propositional (i.e., *in* the words) but always personal (*through* the words).[5] The Bible as such is not a revelation but only a record of God's personal revelation to men of God in other ages. However, when modern men encounter God through the Scriptures the Bible has *become* the Word of God to them. In contrast to the orthodox view, the Bible is not an inspired record for the neoorthodox theologians. Instead, it is an imperfect record which, nonetheless, is the unique witness to God's revelation. When God breaks through the written record in a personal way to speak to the reader, then the Bible at that moment *becomes* the Word of God to him.

## THE BIBLICAL TEACHING ABOUT INSPIRATION

Many objections have been leveled at the various theories of inspiration from different viewpoints with varying degrees of legitimacy, depending on the vantage point taken. Since the purpose of this study is to understand the character of the Bible, the criterion here will be to evaluate all these theories in the light of what the Scriptures reveal about their own inspiration. Let us begin with what the Bible formally teaches and then look at what is logically implied in this teaching.

### WHAT THE BIBLE TEACHES ABOUT ITS OWN INSPIRATION

In the preceding chapter we have already examined in general the teaching of the two great texts of the New Testament on the subject of inspiration (2 Ti 3:16 and 2 Pe 1:21). The Bible claims to be a divinely authoritative book resulting from a process whereby Spirit-moved men wrote God-breathed words. Now let us examine in detail what is meant by this claim.

*Inspiration is verbal.* Whatever else may be claimed about the Bible, it is clear that the Bible claims a *verbal* inspiration for itself. The classical text in 2 Timothy 3:16 declares that it is the *graphā* or writings which are inspired. "Moses wrote all the *words* of the Lord" (Ex 24:4). Isaiah was told to inscribe in a book

5. Emil Brunner, *Theology of Crisis* (New York: Scribner, 1929), p. 41.

God's everlasting message (Is 30:8). David confessed, "The Spirit of the Lord speaks by me, his *word* is upon my tongue" (2 Sa 23:2). It was the *word* of the Lord which came to the prophets hundreds of times in the Old Testament. Jeremiah was told, "diminish not a *word*" (Jer 26:2, KJV).

In the New Testament Jesus and the apostles stressed the recorded revelation by the oft repeated phrase, "*it is written*" (see Mt 4:4, 7, 10; Lk 24:27, 44). The apostle Paul testified that he spoke in "*words* . . . taught by the Spirit" (1 Co 2:13). John warned not to subtract from the "*words* of . . . the prophecy" of his revelation (Rev 22:19). The Scriptures (i.e., *writings*) of the Old Testament are continually referred to as the *Word* of God. In the famous Sermon on the Mount Jesus declared that not only the very words but even the smallest part of a Hebrew word was from God: "For truly I say to you, till heaven and earth pass away, not an iota, not a dot, will pass from the law until all is accomplished" (Mt 5:18). Whatever may be theorized about the inspiration of Scripture notwithstanding, it is clear that the Bible claims for itself verbal or written authority. Its very words are said to be from God.

*Inspiration is plenary.* The Bible claims to be inspired in all its parts. Inspiration is plenary or full. "*All* scripture is inspired by God" (2 Ti 3:16). No part of Scripture is without full doctrinal authority. For the whole Old Testament, wrote Paul, "is profitable for doctrine, for reproof, for instruction in righteousness" (2 Ti 3:16, KJV). Again, he wrote, "*Whatever* was written in former days was written for our instruction" (Ro 15:4). Jesus and New Testament writers amply illustrate their belief in the full and complete inspiration of the Old Testament by quoting from every part of the Scriptures as authoritative, including some of its most disputed teachings. The creation of Adam and Eve, the destruction of the world by a flood, the miracle of Jonah and the whale, and many other incidents are quoted authoritatively by Jesus (see chap. 3). No part of Sacred Writ claims less than full and complete authority. Biblical inspiration is plenary.

Of course plenary inspiration extends only to the teachings of the autographs, as has already been discussed (chap. 1). But everything the Bible teaches, whether in Old or New Testaments, is fully and completely authoritative. No teaching of Scripture is without divine origin. God inspired the very written expression of all prophetic teaching. Inspiration is plenary, that is, full and complete, extending to every part.

*Inspiration gives authority.* Already apparent is the fact that inspiration conveys final authority of the written document. Jesus said, "The scripture cannot be broken" (Jn 10:35). On numerous occasions our Lord appealed to the written Word of God as final arbitrator for faith and practice. He claimed Scripture as His authority for cleansing the temple (Mk 11:17); for rebuking the tradition of the Pharisees (Mt 15:3, 4); for settling doctrinal disputes (Mt 22:29). Even Satan was resisted by Christ on the authority of the written Word, "It is written . . . It is written . . . It is written . . . ," Jesus responded to Satan's temptations (Mt 4:4, 7, 10).

On occasion Jesus would say, "Everything written . . . *must be fulfilled*" (Lk 24:44). But an even stronger affirmation of the final authority of Scripture is found in His pronouncement, "It is easier for heaven and earth to pass away than for *one dot* of the law to become void" (Lk 16:17). The written Word is unbreakable. It comes from God and it has the authority of God invested in it.

SOME IMPLICATIONS OF THE BIBLICAL DOCTRINE OF INSPIRATION

There are several things not formally presented in the doctrine of inspiration which are nonetheless clearly implied in it. Three of these will be discussed here: the equality of the New Testament with the Old, the variety of literary expression, and the inerrancy of the record.

*Inspiration refers to the New Testament and the Old.* Most of the passages cited above on the plenary nature of inspiration refer directly only to the Old Testament. On what basis can they be extended to the New Testament? The answer to this question is that the New Testament, like the Old, claims to be Scripture and prophetic writings, and all Scripture and prophetic writings are held to be inspired of God.

According to 2 Timothy 3:16, all Scripture is inspired. Although the explicit reference here is to the Old Testament, it is true that the New Testament is also considered Scripture. Peter, for example, classes the epistles of Paul along with the "other scriptures" of the Old Testament (2 Pe 3:16). First Timothy 5:18, in quoting the gospel of Luke (10:7), refers to it as "scripture." This is even more significant when one considers that neither Luke nor Paul were among the twelve apostles. Since the epistles of Paul and writings of Luke (Luke and Acts; see Ac 1:1, Lk 1:1-4) were classified as Scripture, then by direct implication the rest of the New Testament written by the apostles was also considered to be inspired Scripture. In brief, if "all Scripture is God-breathed," and the New Testament is considered to be Scripture, then by clear implication the New Testament is considered to be on an equal level of authority with the Old Testament. Indeed, this is precisely how Christians since the times of the apostles have viewed the New Testament. They have regarded it as equally authoritative with the Old.

Furthermore, according to 2 Peter 1:20-21, all prophetic writings are God-given or inspired. And since the New Testament claims to be a prophetic writing, then it follows that it too is claiming to be of equal authority with the Old Testament prophetic writings. John, for example, referred to the Book of Revelation as "the words of the prophecy of this book" (22:18). Paul claimed that the church is built upon the foundation of the New Testament apostles and prophets (Eph 2:20; 3:5). Since the New Testament is, like the Old, a writing of God's prophets, it possesses the same authority as the Old Testament inspired Scriptures.

*Inspiration includes variety of literary sources and styles.* The fact that inspiration is verbal or written does not exclude the use of literary documents and differing literary styles. The Scriptures are not dictated word for word in the usual sense of that phrase. To be sure, there were small sections of the Bible, such as the Ten Commandments, which were given through direct words from God (see Deu 4:10), but nowhere is it either stated or implied that the Bible is a word-for-word dictation. The writers of Holy Scripture were authors and composers, not merely secretaries or stenographers.

There are several factors in the makeup of Scripture which support this contention. First, there is a marked difference in vocabulary and style from writer to writer. Compare the powerful literary expressions of Isaiah to the mournful tones of Jeremiah. Compare the complex literary construction of Hebrews to the simple style of John. The more technical language of Luke the physician is easily distinguished from the pastoral images of James.

Second, the Bible makes use of nonbiblical documents such as the book of Jasher (Jos 10:13), the book of Enoch (Jude 14) and even the poet Epimenides (Ac 17:28). We are informed that many of the proverbs of Solomon were edited by the men of Hezekiah (Pr 25:1). Luke acknowledges the use of many written sources of Jesus' life in the composition of his own gospel (Lk 1:1-4).

Third, the biblical authors employed a variety of literary devices not characteristic of a wooden word-for-word dictation. Much of the Scripture is poetry (for example, Job, Psalms, Proverbs). The gospels are filled with parables. Jesus used satire (see Mt 19:24), Paul employed an allegory (Gal 4) and even hyperbole (Col 1:23), and James wrote with many metaphors and similes.

Finally, the Bible uses the common-sense, everyday language of appearance as opposed to a technical or scientific language. This is not to say that it is unscientific, but that it is nonscientific. It is no more unscientific to speak of the sun standing still (Jos 10:12) than of the sun rising (Jos 1:15). To say the Queen of Sheba came "from the end of the earth" or the people at Pentecost came "from every nation under heaven," is not to speak with scientific exactness. The writers used common, grammatic modes of expressing their topic.

So whatever else is implied in the doctrine of inspired writings, the data of Scripture clearly indicates that it includes the usage of a variety of literary sources and styles of expression. Not everything came directly from God by dictation. And not everything was expressed in a uniform and literal way. Inspiration is to be understood historically and grammatically. It is not to be understood as a uniform, divine dictation exclusive of human sources, personalities, and varieties of expression.

*Inspiration implies inerrancy.* Not only is the Bible inspired, but by means of this inspiration it is inerrant, or without error. Whatever God utters is the truth without error. In fact, the Scriptures claim to be the utterance, indeed the very words, of God. Whatever the Bible teaches is inerrant, since inerrancy is logically entailed in inspiration. God cannot lie (Heb 6:18); His Word is truth (Jn 17:17). Hence, whatever subject the Bible speaks upon, it speaks truly. There are no historical nor scientific errors in the teaching of Scripture. Everything the Bible teaches is of God and, therefore, without error.

It is not possible to evade the implications of factual inerrancy by claiming that the Bible has nothing to say about factual or historical matters. Much of the Bible is presented as history. The very tedious genealogies alone attest to this fact. Some of the great teachings of the Bible, such as creation, the virgin birth of Christ, the crucifixion and the bodily resurrection, clearly involve factual matters. There is no way to "spiritualize" away the factual and historical nature of these biblical truths without doing violence to an honest cultural and grammatical analysis of the text.

The Bible is not a scientific textbook, but when it touches upon scientific matters in its teaching, it does so without error. The Bible is not a secular history book, but where secular and sacred history meet in its pages, the Bible speaks inerrantly. If the Bible is not correct in factual and empirical matters which are verifiable, then how could it be trusted in spiritual matters which are not subject to such tests? Or, in Jesus' words to Nicodemus, "If I have told you earthly things and you do not believe, how can you believe, if I tell you heavenly things?" (Jn 3:12).

# 3

# THE INSPIRATION OF THE
# OLD TESTAMENT

DOES THE BIBLE really claim inspiration for itself or is this merely a claim that believers have made for the Bible? More specifically, do each of the sections and books of the Bible claim to be inspired? These are the questions before us in the next two chapters. First, let us examine the claim for inspiration in the Old Testament.

## THE OLD TESTAMENT CLAIM FOR INSPIRATION

The general claim for inspiration in the Old Testament is based on the fact that it presented itself to and was received by the people of God as a prophetic utterance. Books written by God's prophets were preserved in a holy place. Moses placed his law by the ark of God (Deu 10:2). Later it was preserved in the tabernacle for teaching future generations (Deu 6:2). Each prophet after Moses added his inspired writings to this collection. In fact, the *key* to the inspiration of the Old Testament is the prophetic function of its writers.

### THE OLD TESTAMENT AS A PROPHETIC WRITING

A prophet was the mouthpiece of God. His function is clarified by the various descriptions given him. He was called a man of God (1 Ki 12:22), revealing that he was chosen of God; a servant of the Lord (1 Ki 14:18), indicating his occupation; a messenger of the Lord (Is 42:19), designating his mission for God; a seer or beholder (Is 30:10), revealing apocalyptic source of his truth; a man of the Spirit (Hos 9:7), showing by whose promptings he spoke; a watchman (Eze 3:17), manifesting his alertness to do

the work of God. By far and away, the most common expression
was "prophet," or spokesman for God.

By his very calling, a prophet was one who felt as did Amos,
"The Lord God has spoken; who can but prophesy?" (Amos 3:8);
or, as another prophet who said, "I could not go beyond the command of the LORD my God, to do less or more" (Num 22:18). As
Aaron was a prophet or mouthpiece for Moses (Ex 7:1), speaking "all the words which the LORD had spoken unto Moses" (Ex
4:30), even so God's prophets were to speak only what He commanded them. God said of His prophets, "I will put my words in
his mouth, and he shall speak to them all that I command him"
(Deu 18:18). Further, "You shall not add to the word which I
command you, nor take away from it" (Deu 4:2). In summation,
a prophet was one who declared what God had disclosed to him.

False prophets were detected by their false prophecies and by
the lack of miraculous confirmation. Deuteronomy declares,
"When a prophet speaks in the name of the LORD, if the word
does not come true, that is a word which the LORD has not
spoken" (18:22). Whenever there was any other question of
contest or confirmation, God designated His own by miracles.
The earth opened up and swallowed Korah and those with him
who contested Moses' call (Num 26:10). Elijah was vindicated
over the prophets of Baal by fire from heaven (1 Ki 18:38). Even
the Egyptian magicians finally conceded of Moses' miracles, "This
is the finger of God" (Ex 8:19).

It is clear from the function of a prophet of God that what he
uttered was the word of God. It remains for us to see that the
Old Testament Scriptures were considered to be prophetic utterances. There are several ways to determine this.

*Prophetic utterances were written.* Many prophetic utterances
were given orally, but we are concerned here with the fact that
some of them were written and that the written words were considered to be the prophetic utterance of God. There is no question that Moses' written words were considered as divinely
authoritative. "This *book* of the law shall not depart out of your
mouth" (Jos 1:8), the children of Israel were exhorted. Joshua,
his successor, also wrote words "in the *book* of the law of God"
(Jos 24:26). When the king burned Jeremiah's first written mes-

sage to him, the Lord ordered the prophet to "take another *scroll* and write on it all the former words that were in the first scroll" (Jer 36:28). Isaiah the prophet was commanded, "Take . . . a large *tablet* and write upon it" (Is 8:1). Similarly, Habakkuk was told by God, "Write the vision; make it plain upon *tablets*, so he may run who reads it" (Hab 2:2).

Later prophets used the writings of prophets before them as the written Word of God. Daniel knew from the prophecy of Jeremiah that the Babylonian exile of his people was ending. He wrote, "I, Daniel, perceived by the *books* the number of years which, according to the word of the Lord to Jeremiah the prophet, must pass" (Dan 9:2).

*The Old Testament writers were prophets.* All the traditional authors of the Old Testament are designated prophet by either title or function. Not all of them were prophets by training, but all possessed a prophetic gift. Amos confessed, "I am no prophet, nor a prophet's son . . . and the LORD said to me, 'Go, prophesy to My people Israel'" (Amos 7:14). David, credited with writing almost half of the Psalms, was a king by occupation. Nevertheless, he testified, "The Spirit of the Lord speaks by me, his word is upon my tongue" (2 Sa 23:2). The New Testament plainly calls him a prophet (Ac 2:30). Likewise, King Solomon, the traditional author of Song of Solomon, Proverbs, and Ecclesiastes, received visions from the Lord (1 Ki 11:9). According to Numbers 12:6, a vision was God's way of designating to His people those who were His prophets. Although Daniel was a statesman, he was called Daniel the prophet by Jesus (Mt 24:15).

Moses, the great lawgiver and deliverer of Israel, is called a prophet (Deu 18:15; Ho 12:13). As the successor of Moses, Joshua was considered a prophet of God (Deu 34:9). Samuel, Nathan, and Gad were all writing prophets (1 Ch 29:29), as were Isaiah, Jeremiah, Ezekiel, and the twelve minor prophets.

*An official register of prophetic writings was kept.* Evidence indicates no nonprophetic writing was preserved with the sacred collection which was started with the Mosaic Law. And it appears that there was a continuity of prophets, each adding his book to his prophetic predecessors. Moses put his books by the ark. Joshua is said to have added his to the collection (Jos 24:26).

Following him, Samuel added his words to the collection when "he wrote them in a book and laid it up before the Lord" (1 Sa 10:25).

Samuel founded a school of the prophets (1 Sa 19:20) which later had students who were called the "sons of the prophets" (2 Ki 2:3). There is ample testimony in the books of Chronicles that histories were kept by the prophets. David's history was written by the prophets Samuel, Nathan, and Gad (1 Ch 29:29). The history of Solomon was recorded by Nathan, Ahijah, and Iddo (2 Ch 9:29). This was also the case with the histories of Rehoboam, Jehoshaphat, Hezekiah, Manasseh, and other kings (see 2 Ch 9:29; 12:15; 13:22; 20:34; 33:19; 35:27).

By the time of the Babylonian exile in the sixth century B.C., Daniel referred to the collection of prophetic writings as "books" (Dan 9:2). According to Ezekiel (13:9), there was an official register of the true prophets of God. Anyone who uttered false prophecies was excluded from the official roll. Only the true prophet of God was officially recognized and only the writings of these prophets were kept among the inspired books. From the earliest known times, all thirty-nine books of the Old Testament constituted these prophetic writings. More will be said about this later (see chaps. 7 and 8).

SPECIFIC CLAIMS FOR INSPIRATION WITHIN THE OLD TESTAMENT

The inspiration of the Old Testament does not rest merely on a general analysis of it as a prophetic writing. There are numerous specific claims within the individual books as to their divine origin. Let us examine the claims according to the currently recognized categorization of the Hebrew Old Testament into law, prophets, and writings.

*Inspiration of the law of Moses.* According to Exodus 20:1: "God spake all these words." That God spoke to Moses is repeated dozens of times in Leviticus (e.g., 1:1; 8:9; 11:1). Numbers repeatedly records, "The LORD spoke to Moses" (e.g., 1:1; 2:1; 4:1). Deuteronomy adds, "Moses spoke to the people of Israel according to all that the LORD had given him in commandments to them" (1:3).

The rest of the Old Testament in one accord declares the

Mosaic books as given by God. Joshua immediately imposed the books of the law on the people of Israel (1:8). Judges refers to the Mosaic writings as the "commandments of the Lord" (3:4). Samuel acknowledged that God had appointed Moses (1 Sa 12:6, 8). In Chronicles his writings are spoken of as the "book of the law of the LORD given by Moses" (2 Ch 34:14). Daniel refers to the curse written in the law of Moses as "His [God's] words which He spoke against us" (Dan 9:12). Even in Ezra and Nehemiah there is recognition of the law of God given to Moses (Ezra 6:18; Neh 13:1). That the books of Moses were divinely given is the unanimous consent of the Old Testament.

*Inspiration of the prophets.* According to present Jewish division of the Old Testament, the books of the prophets include the former prophets (Joshua, Judges, Samuels, and Kings) and the latter prophets (Isaiah, Jeremiah, Ezekiel, and the twelve minor prophets). These books also claim divine authority. "Joshua wrote these words in the book of the law of the Lord" (Jos 24:26). God spoke to men in Judges (1:1, 2; 6:25) and Samuel (3:11) who spoke and wrote to all Israel (4:1, cf. 1 Ch 29:29). The latter prophets abound in claims of divine inspiration. The familiar "Thus says the LORD" with which they introduce their message occurs hundreds of times. From Isaiah to Malachi the reader is literally bombarded with divine authority.

Chronologically the Old Testament ends with this section known as the prophets, and there is no subsequent Old Testament testimony to their inspiration. However, there are references within the prophets to other prophetic writers who composed their books at an earlier time. Daniel considered Jeremiah's book inspired (Dan 9:2). Ezra recognized the divine authority of Jeremiah (Ezra 1:1) as well as that of Haggai and Zechariah (Ezra 5:1). In a very important passage Zechariah refers to the divine inspiration of Moses and the prophets who preceded him, calling their works "the law and the words which the LORD of hosts had sent by his Spirit through the former prophets" (7:12). These passages leave little doubt that the books contained in the section of the Jewish Scriptures known as the prophets bear the claim of divine inspiration.

*Inspiration of the writings.* The original Old Testament probably had only two basic divisions, the law and the prophets (see chap. 7). This last section was later divided into the prophets and the writings. Perhaps this is based on the official position of the author as to whether he was a prophet by occupation or simply by gift. Those falling into the latter category were put in the section called writings. Psalms, the first book in this collection, was written largely by David who claimed that his Psalms were Spirit-given to the very words (2 Sa 23:2). Song of Solomon, Proverbs, and Ecclesiastes have been traditionally ascribed to Solomon as the record of God-given wisdom (see 1 Ki 3:9-10). Proverbs contains specific claims to divine authority. Ecclesiastes (12:13) and Job (chap. 38) both end as an authoritative teaching. Daniel's book is based on a series of visions and dreams from God (Dan 2:19; 8:1 etc.).

Several books have no explicit claim to divine inspiration such as Ruth, Esther, Song of Solomon, Lamentations, Ezra-Nehemiah, and Chronicles. If Ruth were written by the prophet Samuel as a part of Judges, then it would come under the general claim of a prophetic writing. By the same token, Lamentations, the work of Jeremiah, is prophetic. The Song has already been noted as a work of the God-given wisdom of Solomon. Jewish tradition ascribes Chronicles, Ezra, and Nehemiah to Ezra the priest and to Nehemiah who functioned with prophetic authority in the repatriation of Israel from the Babylonian captivity (cf. Ezra 10 and Neh 13). The author of Esther is not stated, perhaps to preserve his anonymity in the hostile Persian setting. The point of view in Esther is notably Jewish, and the book provides the written authority for the celebration of the Jewish feast of Purim. This amounts to an implicit claim to divine authority.

In summary then, virtually every book of the Old Testament offers some claim to divine inspiration. Sometimes it is the implied authority, but it is usually the explicit claim of "thus says the Lord." From beginning to end the inspiration of the Old Testament is solidly built on numerous passages, all of which allege their divine origin.

## New Testament Support for the Old Testament Claim for Inspiration

There are three lines of approach in examining the New Testament teaching on the inspiration of the Old Testament. There are the passages which refer to the divine authority of the Old Testament *as a whole*. There are the references to the inspiration of given *sections* of the Old Testament. Finally, there are authoritative quotes of *specific books* in the Jewish canon.

### NEW TESTAMENT REFERENCE TO THE INSPIRATION OF THE WHOLE OLD TESTAMENT

The New Testament recognizes the inspiration of the Old Testament in many ways. Sometimes it uses such expressions as "Scripture," "the Word of God," "the law," "the prophets," "the law and the prophets," and "the oracles of God."

*The Scriptures* is by far the most common title used in the New Testament for the Old. According to Paul, "All [Old Testament] *scripture* is inspired of God" (2 Ti 3:16). Jesus said, "The *scripture* cannot be broken" (Jn 10:35). Often the New Testament uses the plural, *Scriptures*, to denote the authoritative collection of Jewish writings. Jesus responded to the Pharisees, "Have you never read in the *scriptures* . . . ?" (Mt 21:42), or "You are wrong, because you know neither the *Scriptures*, or the power of God" (Mt 22:29). The apostle Paul "argued with them from the *scriptures*" (Ac 17:2) and the Bereans "searched the *scriptures* daily" (Ac 17:11, KJV). In these and numerous other references the New Testament acknowledges the whole of the Old Testament canon as divinely inspired writings.

*The Word of God* is a less common but perhaps more forceful description of the Old Testament's inspiration. In Mark 7:13 Jesus charged that the Pharisees made void "the word of God" through their traditions. John 10:35 uses the phrase "the word of God" as synonymous to "the Scripture." There are numerous other references to "the word of God," but not all of them clearly identify with the Old Testament. Paul argued, "not as though the word of God had failed" (Ro 9:6). In another place he speaks of his refusal to tamper with the word of God (2 Co 4:2). The writer of Hebrews states that "the word of God is living and active" (Heb 4:12). Peter's statement that "To him [i.e., of Christ] all of the prophets bear witness" (Ac 10:43) could scarcely be limited to less than the whole Old Testament in view of Luke 24:27, 44. The passages which do clearly identify the whole Old Testament as the Word of God leave no doubt as to the assertion of divine inspiration.

*The law* usually refers to the Old Testament as a shortened form for the law of Moses, and denotes only the first five books of Jewish Scripture. On some occasions, however, the word *law* describes the whole Old Testament. John 10:34 is probably a case in point. Since the quote is from Psalm 82:6, it is clear that the law of Moses is not intended. That "law" is used here in connection with both "scripture" and "the word of God" would indicate the whole Old Testament is in view. In John 12:34, the people mention "the law," although elsewhere Jesus calls it "their law" (Jn 15:25), and in Acts Paul identifies it as "the law of the Jews" (Ac 25:8). Paul introduced a quotation of the Old Testament with the phrase "in the law it is written" (1 Co 14:21). In His famous Sermon on the Mount Jesus used the term *law* as synonymous with "the law and the prophets," a phrase which we shall see clearly refers to the divinely inspired documents of the Old Testament (Mt 5:18).

*The law and the prophets* or "Moses and the prophets" is the second most common title of the Jewish Scriptures. These designations occur a dozen times in the New Testament. Jesus used the phrase twice in His famous sermon (Mt 5:17; 7:12), claiming He came to fulfill "the law and the prophets" and that they would never pass away. Luke 16:16 presents "the law and the prophets" as all the divine revelation up to the time of John the Baptist. In his defense before Felix, Paul acclaimed the "law and the prophets" to be the whole counsel of God which he as a devout Jew had practiced from his youth (Ac 24:14). It was "the law and the prophets" which was read in the synagogues (Ac 13:15) and of which the Golden Rule was considered the moral summation (Mt 7:12).

*The prophets* occasionally referred to all of the Old Testament. Since the whole Old Testament is a prophetic utterance it is not surprising that it is sometimes called "the prophets." That it is sometimes called "*scriptures* of the prophets" indicates that a group of books is intended (Mt 26:56). The all-inclusive "everything written of the Son of man" would seem to point to the whole Old Testament (Lk 18:31). Indeed, the title "prophets" is used in parallel with the phrase, "the law and the prophets" (Lk 24:25, 27); and it clearly refers to the entire Old Testament.

*The oracles of God* is no doubt intended to convey this notion. It appears twice, and refers to the Old Testament Scriptures. Paul said that the Jewish people were "entrusted with the oracles of God" (Ro 3:2). Elsewhere, the need for someone to teach "the first principles of the oracles of God" is stated (Heb 5:12, ASV). The written word of the Old Testament is God's Word.

*It is written* is used on more than ninety occasions in the New Testament. Most of these statements introduce specific quotations, but some have a more general application to the Old Testament as a whole. Examples of this latter usage include the following: "How *is it written* of the Son of Man, that he should suffer many things and be treated with contempt?" (Mk 9:12; cf. 14:21). This is a summary of the general teaching about Christ's death in the Old Testament rather than a specific quotation from it. An even more definitive reference is Luke 18:31: "Everything that *is written* of the Son of man by the prophets will be accomplished." Along with others like "these are days of vengeance, to fulfil all that *is written*" (Lk 21:22), there is sufficient support for the thesis that writings of the Old Testament as a whole were considered divinely inspired. They were predictive of Christ and were under the divine necessity of fulfillment.

*That it might be fulfilled* is a phrase frequently used with reference to the Old Testament in general. Jesus indicated that the law, prophets, and psalms "must be fulfilled" (Lk 24:44). On another occasion he said, "I have not come to abolish them [the laws and prophets] but to fulfill them" (Mt 5:17). This formula introduces a specific quotation from or reference to the Old Testament over thirty times. It always indicates the prophetic nature of Scripture as given by God, and of necessity it must be fulfilled.

NEW TESTAMENT REFERENCES TO SPECIFIC SECTIONS OF THE
OLD TESTAMENT

A second indication in the New Testament that the Old Testament was considered divinely inspired are the references to the authority of given sections of the Hebrew Scriptures (viz., the law, the prophets, and the writings).

*The law and the prophets,* as was indicated above, refers to a two-fold division of the Old Testament and occurs a dozen times in the New Testament. It indicates all the inspired writings from Moses to Jesus (Lk 16:16) which are considered to be the imperishable word of God (Mt 5:18). Besides the combined references there are some which treat the law and the prophets separately.

*The law* usually designates the first five books of the Old Testament, as in Mt 12:5. Sometimes it is called "the law of Moses" (Ac 13:39; Heb 10:28). On other occasions these books are simply entitled "Moses" (2 Co 3:15), "the books of Moses," (Mk 12:26) or "the books of the law" (Gal 3:10). In each case there is an appeal to the divine authority of Mosaic teaching. The whole Pentateuch of Moses was held to be from God.

*The prophets* usually identifies the second half of Old Testament Scripture (see Jn 1:45; Lk 18:31). The phrases "the scriptures of the prophets" (Mt 26:56) and "the book of the prophets" (Ac 7:42) are also used. It is not always clear that these titles refer only to the books written subsequent to Moses, although sometimes it does, as the separation of the two titles reveals. As far as the title *prophets* is concerned, its very meaning as a spokesman for God indicates the divine inspiration of the books so entitled (2 Pe 1:20-21).

*The writings* is not a term used in the New Testament. This is a nonbiblical description which divides the prophetic writings into two sections: those which were written by professional prophets ("the prophets") and those writings which were not ("the writings"). There is only one allusion in the New Testament to a possible threefold division of the Old Testament. Jesus spoke of "The law of Moses, and the prophets, and the psalms" (Lk 24:44). It is not clear here whether He is singling out the book of Psalms, because of its special messianic significance, as part of "the law

and the prophets" to which He referred earlier in the chapter
(v. 27), or to the first book of the section which is known as "the
writings." Whatever the case, the Messianic and prophetic nature
of this supposed third division of the Old Testament marks it
clearly as inspired of God. And if there are only two sections to
the Old Testament canon (as we will argue in chap. 7), then the
remainder of the inspired Scriptures have already been treated
under the designation "the prophets."

NEW TESTAMENT REFERENCES TO SPECIFIC BOOKS OF THE OLD
TESTAMENT

Of the twenty-two books in the Jewish canon referred to by
Josephus (*Against Apion* I. 8), some eighteen are cited as authoritative by the New Testament. No citations of Judges, Chronicles,
Esther, or the Song of Solomon are to be found, although there are
references to events in Judges (Heb 11:32) and Chronicles (Mt
23:35; 2 Ch 24:20). Allusion to the Song of Solomon 4:15 may
be found in Jesus' reference to "living water" (Jn 4:10), but this
would not be a support of the book's authority. Likewise, the
possible reference to the feast of Purim from Esther 9 in John
5:1, or the similarity of Revelation 11:10 to Esther 9:22, would
fall short of a support of the inspiration of Esther. The divine
authority of the book of Esther is adequately attested elsewhere
(see chap. 8) but not by New Testament quotations.

Virtually all the eighteen remaining books of the Hebrew canon
are cited with authority in the New Testament. The creation of
man in Genesis (1:27) is quoted by Jesus in Matthew 19:4-5. The
fifth commandment of Exodus (20:12) is cited as Scripture in
Ephesians 6:1. The law for a leper's cleansing from Leviticus
14:2-32 is referred to in Matthew 8:4. Numbers is not quoted as
such, but 1 Corinthians refers to events recorded in the book as
written for Christian admonition (1 Co 10:11). Numbers (12:7)
records Moses' faithfulness and is cited authoritatively in Hebrews
3:5. Deuteronomy is one of the most quoted books in the Old
Testament. Jesus quoted it twice in His temptation (Mt 4:4 and
4:7; cf. Deu 8:3 and 6:16).

Joshua received the promise from God, "I will not fail you or
forsake you" (Jos 1:5) and is quoted in Hebrews 13:5. Jesus cited

the incident from 1 Samuel 21:1-6 of David eating bread from the tabernacle as the authority for his activity on the sabbath. God's reply to Elijah from 1 Kings 19:18 is quoted in Romans 11:4. Ezra-Nehemiah is probably quoted in John 6:31 (cf. Neh 9:15), although God's provision to Israel of "bread from heaven" is also referred to elsewhere (Ps 78:24; 105:40).

The book of Job (5:12) is distinctly quoted as authoritative by Paul, "It is written, 'He catches the wise in their craftiness' " (1 Co 3:19). Psalms is another of the most-quoted Old Testament books. It was a favorite of Jesus. Compare Matthew 21:42. "The very stone which the builders rejected has become the head of the corner," with Psalm 118:22. Peter quoted from Psalm 2 in his sermon at Pentecost (Ac 2:34-35). Hebrews abounds in references to the Psalms; the first chapter quotes Psalms 2, 104, 45, and 102. Proverbs 3:34, "God opposes the proud, but gives grace to the humble," is clearly quoted in James (4:6). There is no verbatim quotation of Ecclesiastes, but there are some passages which seem to be doctrinally dependable. Paul's statement, "Whatever a man sows, that he will also reap" (Gal 6:7), resembles Ecclesiastes 11:1. The challenge to avoid youthful lust (2 Ti 2:22) reflects Ecclesiastes 11:10. That death is divinely appointed (Heb 9:27; cf. Ec 3:2); that the love of money is the source of evil (1 Ti 6:10; cf. Ec 5:10) and that we should not be wordy in prayer (Mt 6:7; cf. Ec 5:2) are also examples.

Isaiah is another of the Old Testament books most quoted in the New Testament. John the Baptist, in Matthew 3:3, introduced Jesus with a quotation from Isaiah 40:3. In His hometown synagogue Jesus read from Isaiah 61:1-2: "The Spirit of the Lord is upon me" (cf. Lk 4:18-19). Paul frequently quoted from Isaiah (cf. Ro 9:27; Ac 28:25-28). Jeremiah 31:15 is quoted in Matthew 2:17-18, and Jeremiah's new covenant (chap. 31) is cited twice in Hebrews 8:8; 10:16. Lamentations, which is appended to Jeremiah in the twenty-two books of the Hebrew Bible, is alluded to in Matthew 27:30 (cf. Lam 3:30). Ezekiel is cited on several occasions in the New Testament, although none are word-for-word quotes. Jesus' teaching on the new birth (Jn 3:5) may come from Ezekiel 36:25-26. Romans 6:23 states "the wages of sin is death," which reflects Ezekiel 18:20: "The soul that sins shall surely die."

John's use of the four living creatures (Rev 4:7) is clearly taken from Ezekiel 1:10. Daniel is identified by name in our Lord's Mount Olivet discourse (Mt 24:15; cf. Dan 9:27; 11:31), and Matthew 21:30 encompasses Daniel 7:13. The twelve minor prophets were grouped together in the Hebrew Old Testament. There are many quotations from this group of writings. Habakkuk's famous, "The just shall live by his faith" (Hab 2:4) is quoted on three occasions in the New Testament (Ro 1:17; Gal 3:11; Heb 10:38). Matthew 2:15 quotes Hosea 11:1: "Out of Egypt I called my son."

This leaves only Judges-Ruth, Chronicles, Esther, and Song of Solomon which are not clearly cited by the New Testament. However, Judges provides historical events which the New Testament refers to as authentic (Heb 11:32) and Chronicles is probably intended by Jesus' reference to the blood of Zechariah (Mt 23:35). This leaves only Esther and Song of Solomon without explicit reference in the New Testament, no doubt because the New Testament writers had no occasion to cite them. Esther is the basis for the Jewish feast of Purim and Song was read at the great Feast of the Passover, which reflects its esteem by the Jewish community.

The New Testament substantiates the claim of inspiration for the whole Old Testament, all of its sections, and almost every one of its books in particular. In addition to this, there is direct and authoritative reference to many of the great persons and events of the Old Testament, including the creation of Adam and Eve (Mt 19:4), the flood of Noah's time (Lk 17:27), the miraculous call of Moses (Lk 20:37), supernatural provision for Israel in the wilderness (Jn 3:14; 6:49), the miracles of Elijah (Lk 4:24-25) and Jonah in the belly of the great fish (Mt 12:41).

## AFFIRMATION OR ACCOMMODATION?

Despite the volume and authoritative nature of New Testament citations, some have suggested that Jesus and the apostles were not really affirming the inspiration and authenticity of the Old Testament. Rather, they assert, the New Testament writers were accommodating themselves to the accepted Jewish beliefs of the day. This suggestion is subtle but not substantial. It does not square with the facts of Scripture nor with the claims of Christ. The most numerous and emphatic references to the inspiration and authenticity of the Old Testament are from the lips of Jesus who showed no tendency toward accommodation. Chasing the money changers from the temple (Jn 2:15), denouncing "blind guides" (Mt 23:16) and "false prophets" (Mt 7:15), and rebuking leading teachers (Jn 3:10) are scarcely evidences of accommodation.

In fact, Jesus clearly rebuked those who held to traditions rather than to the word of God (cf. Mt 15:1-6). Six times in a single chapter (Mt 5), Jesus contrasted the truth about the Scripture with false beliefs which had grown up about it when he charged, "It was *said*," not "it is written," but "I say unto you." Jesus did not hesitate to assert, "You are wrong" (cf. Mt 22:29), when men erred. And when they understood the truth, He would encourage them by saying, "You have answered right" (Lk 10:28). Jesus' teaching on the divine authority of the Old Testament is so unconditional and so uncompromising that one cannot reject it without rejecting His words. If one does not accept the authority of the Old Testament as Scripture, then he impugns the integrity of the Saviour. Whatever else may be said about the inspiration of the Old Testament, this much is clear: the Old Testament claimed inspiration for itself, and the New Testament overwhelmingly confirms that claim.

# 4

# THE INSPIRATION OF THE NEW TESTAMENT

THE APOSTLES AND PROPHETS of the New Testament did not hesitate to classify their writings as inspired along with the Old Testament. Their books were revered, collected, and circulated in the early church as sacred Scripture. What Jesus claimed about the Old Testament inspiration He also promised His disciples for the New. Let us examine this promise of inspiration and its fulfillment in the pages of the New Testament.

## THE NEW TESTAMENT CLAIM OF INSPIRATION

There are two basic movements in understanding the New Testament claims about its own inspiration. First is the promise of Christ that the Holy Spirit would guide them in the teaching of His truth as the foundation of the church. Then there is the acclaimed fulfillment of this in the apostolic teaching and in writing of the New Testament.

### THE PROMISE OF CHRIST ABOUT INSPIRATION

Jesus did not write any books. He did, however, commend the authority of the Old Testament (see chap. 3) and promise to inspire the New. On several occasions Jesus promised divine authority for the apostolic witness to Himself.

*The commission of the twelve.* When Jesus first sent out His disciples to preach the kingdom of heaven (Mt 10:7), He promised them the direction of the Holy Spirit. "For what you are to say will be given to you in that hour; for it is not you who speak, but the Spirit of your Father speaking through you" (Mt 10:19-20;

41

cf. Lk 12:11-12). Their proclamations for Christ were prompted by the Spirit of God.

*The sending of the seventy.* The promise of divine unction was not limited to the twelve. When Jesus sent out the seventy to preach "the kingdom of God" (Lk 10:9) He told them, "He who hears you hears me, and he who rejects you rejects me" (Lk 10:16). They returned acknowledging the authority of God on their ministry even over Satan (Lk 10:17-19).

*The Mount Olivet discourse.* In His sermon on the Mount of Olives, Jesus reaffirmed His original promise to the disciples. "Do not be anxious beforehand, what you are to say," He exhorted them. "But say whatever is given you in that hour, for it is not you who speak, but the Holy Spirit" (Mk 13:11). Their words were to come from God by the Spirit and not merely from themselves.

*The Last Supper teachings.* The promise of the guidance of the Holy Spirit was more clearly defined at the Last Supper. Jesus promised them, "But the Counselor, the Holy Spirit, whom the Father will send in My name, He will teach you all things, and bring to your remembrance all that I have said to you" (Jn 14:26). Here is the key to why Jesus did not write His teachings. The Spirit would quicken the memories of those who heard Him; they would be Spirit-directed in all that Christ had taught them. For, "When He, the Spirit of truth, comes, He will guide you into all truth" (Jn 16:13). "All truth" or "all things" Christ taught would be Spirit-guided. Apostolic teaching would be inspired of God's Spirit.

*The Great Commission.* When Jesus at last commissioned His disciples to "make disciples of all nations . . . *teaching* them to observe all I have commanded you" (Mt 28:19-20), it was with the promise that they had *all authority* in heaven and earth to do so. Whatever they taught would be invested with the authority of God. Their words would be God's Word.

### THE PROMISE OF CHRIST CLAIMED BY THE DISCIPLES

The followers of Christ did not forget His promise. They claimed for their teaching precisely what Jesus promised, the authority of God. This they did in several distinct ways: by claiming to continue Christ's teaching ministry, by claiming equality with the Old Testament, and by making specific claims in their writings for divine authority.

*The claim to be continuing Christ's teaching.* Luke claims to give an accurate account of what "Jesus began to do and teach" in his gospel. He implies that Acts records what Jesus continued to do and teach through the apostles (Ac 1:1; cf. Lk 1:3-4). Indeed, the first church is said to have been characterized by devotion to "the apostle's teaching" (Ac 2:42). Even the teachings of Paul, based as they were on direct revelations from God (Gal 1:11-12), were subjected to apostolic approval (Ac 15). The New Testament church itself is said to be "built upon the foundation of the apostles and [New Testament] prophets" (Eph 2:20; cf. 3:5).

Whereas it is true that the oral pronouncements of the living apostles were as authoritative as their written ones (1 Th 2:15), it is also true that the books of the New Testament are the only authentic record of apostolic teaching which we have today. The qualification that a member of the twelve apostles must be an eyewitness of the ministry and resurrection of Christ (Ac 1:21-22) eliminates any succession of apostles beyond the first century. And the fact that no authentic apostolic teaching exists which is not found in the New Testament limits all that the apostles taught to the twenty-seven books of the New Testament. Along with the Old Testament, these books alone are considered inspired or divinely authoritative because only these have been found to be truly apostolic or prophetic (see chap. 10).

In brief, Christ promised that all apostolic teaching would be Spirit-directed. The New Testament books are the only authentic record we have of apostolic teaching. Hence, the New Testament alone can lay claim to be an authoritative record of Christ's teachings.

*Comparison of the New Testament to the Old.* The promise of Christ to inspire the teachings of the apostles and the fulfillment of that promise in the writings of the New Testament is not the only indication of its inspiration. Another indication is its direct comparison to the Old Testament. Paul distinctly recognized the inspiration of the Old Testament (2 Ti 3:16) by calling it "scripture." Peter classed Paul's epistles right along with "the other

scriptures" (2 Pe 3:16), and Paul quotes Luke's gospel, calling it
"scripture" (1 Ti 5:18, quoting Lk 10:7). Indeed, elsewhere the
apostle gives his own writings equal authority with "scripture"
(1 Ti 4:11, 13).

The book of Hebrews declares that the God who spoke of old
through prophets has in these last days spoken to us about salvation through His Son (Heb 1:2). The author goes on to say, "It
was declared at first by the Lord, and it was attested to us by
those [apostles] who heard" (Heb 2:3). The apostles were the
channel of God's truth in the New Testament just as the prophets
were in the Old. It is not strange then, to observe that the apostolic books should be placed on the same authoritative level as the
inspired books of the Old Testament. Both are prophetic.

As a matter of fact, Peter wrote that prophetic writings came by
divine inspiration (2 Pe 1:21), and New Testament writings distinctly claim to be prophetic. John calls his book a prophecy and
classes himself among the prophets (Rev 22:18-19). New Testament prophets are listed along with the apostles as the foundation
of the church (Eph 2:20). Paul probably includes his own writings when he speaks of "the revelation of the mystery which was
kept secret for long ages but is now disclosed and through the
prophetic writings is made known to all nations" (Ro 16:25-26).
He claimed in Ephesians 3:3, 5 that "the mystery was made
known to me by revelation . . . which was not made known to
the sons of men in other generations as it has now [in New Testament times] been revealed to His holy apostles and [New Testa-
ment] prophets by the Spirit" (cf. Eph 2:20). So the prophetic
writings of the New Testament reveal the mystery of Christ who
was predicted in the prophetic writings of the Old Testament.
Like the Old, the New Testament is a prophetic utterance of God.

*Direct claims for inspiration in New Testament books.* Within
the books of the New Testament are numerous indications of their
divine authority. These are both explicit and implicit. The gospels
present themselves as authoritative accounts of the fulfillment of
Old Testament prophecies about Christ (cf. Mt 1:22; 2:15, 17;
Mk 1:2). Luke wrote in order that the reader could know the
truth about Christ which was "delivered to us by those who from
the beginning were eyewitnesses and ministers of the word [of

God]" (Lk 1:1). John recorded his words that men "may believe that Jesus is the Christ, the Son of God, and that believing . . . may have life in his name" (Jn 20:31). He adds that his testimony is true (Jn 21:24).

The Acts of the Apostles, also written by Luke, presents itself as an authoritative account of what Jesus continued to do and teach through the apostles (Ac 1:1). This too was seen as a fulfillment of Old Testament prophecy (cf. Ac 2 and Joel 2). Since Paul quoted Luke's gospel as "scripture" (1 Ti 5:18), it is evident that both he and Luke considered continuation of that account in Acts to be divinely authoritative as well.

Each of Paul's epistles, Romans through Philemon, lays claim to inspiration. In Romans Paul establishes his divine call to apostleship (Ro 1:1-3). He concludes this letter with a claim that it is a prophetic writing (Ro 16:26). The apostle completes 1 Corinthians saying, "What I am writing to you is a command of the Lord" (1 Co 14:37). He introduces 2 Corinthians by repeating the claim to apostleship (2 Co 1:1-2). In that letter he defends his apostleship more completely than anywhere else in the New Testament (2 Co 10-13). Galatians offers the strongest defense of Paul's divine credentials. Speaking of the revelation of the gospel of grace to him, he wrote, "I did not receive it from man, nor was I taught it, but it came through a revelation of Jesus Christ" (Gal 1:12). In Ephesians he further declares, "the mystery was made known unto me by revelation" (Eph 3:3). Philippians twice admonishes the believers to follow the apostolic pattern of life (Phil 3:17; 4:9). In Colossians, like Ephesians, Paul argues that his apostolic office came directly from God, "to make the word of God fully known" (Col 1:25). First Thessalonians concludes with the admonition, "I adjure you by the Lord to have this letter read to all the brethren" (1 Th 5:27). Earlier he had reminded them, "It was the word of God which you heard from us" (1 Th 2:13). Second Thessalonians also concludes with an exhortation: "If anyone refuses to obey what we say in this letter, note that man, and have nothing to do with him, that he may be ashamed" (2 Th 3:14). About the message of 1 Timothy the apostle wrote, "Command and teach these things . . . Till I come, attend to the public reading of scripture, to preaching, to

teaching" (1 Ti 4:11, 13). Here Paul places his own epistle on par
with the Old Testament. Both were to be read in the churches
with binding authority (cf. Col 4:16). Second Timothy contains
the classical passage on inspiration (2 Ti 3:16), as well as the
exhortations to follow the pattern of the sound words received
from Paul (2 Ti 1:13). "I charge you," he wrote, "preach the
word" (2 Ti 4:1-2). Likewise, Paul commanded Titus, "Declare
these things; exhort and reprove with all authority" (Titus 2:15).
Although the tone in Philemon is intercessory, Paul makes it clear
that he could command what is requested in love (Phile 8).

Hebrews 2:3-4 make it evident that this book—whoever wrote
it—is based on the authority of God through the apostles and
eyewitnesses of Christ. Its readers are told to remember their
leaders, those "who spoke the word of God" (Heb 13:7). The
writer then adds, "I appeal to you, brethren, bear with my word of
exhortation" (Heb 13:22). James, the brother of our Lord (Gal
1:19) and leader of the Jerusalem church (Ac 15:13) writes with
apostolic authority to the twelve tribes in the dispersion (Ja 1:1).
First Peter claims to be from "an apostle of Jesus Christ" (1 Pe
1:1), and contains typical apostolic exhortations (1 Pe 5:1, 12).
Second Peter comes from "Simon Peter, a servant and apostle of
Christ" and reminds the readers that "the commandments of the
Lord through your apostles" are of the same authority with the
predictions of the prophets in the Old Testament (2 Pe 3:2).
First John comes from one who has "heard . . . seen . . . looked
upon . . . and touched" Christ (1 Jn 1:1). In this book John presents the test for truth and error (1 Jn 4:1-2), designates the
apostolic community as from God (1 Jn 2:19) and writes to confirm the faith of true believers (1 Jn 5:13). Second and 3 John
come from the same apostle with the same authority (cf. 2 Jn 5,
7; 3 Jn 9, 12). Jude writes a record of "our common salvation" in
defense of "the faith which was once for all delivered to the
saints" (Jude 3). "The Revelation of Jesus Christ, which God
gave" (Rev 1:1), describes the origin of the last book in the New
Testament. "I was in the Spirit on the Lord's day," wrote John,
"and I heard behind me a loud voice like the sound of a trumpet
saying, "Write what you see in a book and send it to the seven
churches" (Rev 1:10-11). No book in the Bible contains a more

explicit claim to divine inspiration than the Revelation. The warning not to tamper with its words is placed under a threat of divine judgment which is the strongest such threat in Scripture. It is an appropriate conclusion to the claim that the entire New Testament is the inspired Word of God, on a par with the sacred writings of the Old Testament.

## SUPPORTING CLAIM FOR THE INSPIRATION OF THE NEW TESTAMENT

There are two lines of evidence which indicate support of the New Testament claim of divine inspiration. One is within the New Testament itself, and the other begins with church Fathers who followed the apostles.

### SUPPORTING CLAIM FOR INSPIRATION WITHIN THE NEW TESTAMENT

The first-century church was not naïve in its acceptance of inspired writings. Jesus had warned of false prophets and deceivers coming in His name (Mt 7:15; 24:10-11). Paul exhorted the Thessalonians not to accept erroneous teaching from any letter pretending to be from him (2 Th 2:2). John urged the believers, "Beloved, do not believe every spirit, but test the spirits to see whether they are of God" (1 Jn 4:1). There were incorrect and false teachings about Christ circulating in the first century (cf. Lk 1:1-4). Hence, the New Testament church had to be discriminating from the very beginning. Any books received without apostolic signature (2 Th 3:17) were to be refused. The fact that books were read, quoted, collected, and circulated within the New Testament church gives assurance that they were received as prophetic or divinely inspired from the very beginning.

*Public reading of New Testament books.* It was a Jewish custom to read the Scriptures on the Sabbath (cf. Lk 4:16). The church continued this practice on the Lord's day. Paul urged Timothy to "attend to the public reading of the scripture" (1 Ti 4:13). In the Colossian epistle Paul wrote, "And when this letter has been read among you, have it read also in the church of the Laodiceans; and see that you read also the letter from Laodicea" (Col 4:16). The public reading of these letters as Scripture in the churches verified their initial acceptance as divine authority by the New Testament church.

*Circulation of New Testament books.* The Colossian passage cited above reveals another very important fact. The books written to one church were intended to be of value for other churches, and they were circulated in order to accomplish this purpose. Perhaps this procedure of trading inspired books led to the earliest copies of the New Testament. One thing indicated by this circulation is that churches other than the one addressed in the epistle recognized and read as Holy Scripture the various letters.

*Collection of New Testament books.* Not only were New Testament books read and circulated in the churches, but Peter informs us that they were collected as well. Peter apparently possessed a collection of Paul's letters which he plainly classed with the inspired writings of the Old Testament. He wrote, "So also our beloved brother Paul wrote to you according to the wisdom given him, speaking of this as he does in all his letters . . . which the ignorant and unstable twist to their own destruction, as they do the other *scriptures*" (2 Pe 3:15-16). These books were read, circulated, and collected by the New Testament church along with the canon of Old Testament, and without question they were considered inspired writings.

*Quotation of New Testament books.* The books of the Old Testament were written over a much longer time span than the New. Hence, there is more quotation of earlier prophets by later ones in the Old Testament. Nevertheless, the fact that quotations from earlier New Testament books are found in later ones reveals that these books were considered inspired writings by their contemporaries. Paul quoted Luke's gospel as Scripture in 1 Timothy 5:18. "The laborer deserves his wages" (cf. Lk 10:7). Jude clearly cites 2 Peter 3:2-3, saying, "But you must remember, beloved, the predictions of the apostles of our Lord Jesus Christ; they said to you, 'In the last time there will be scoffers, following their own ungodly passions'" (Jude 18). Luke refers to his previous book (Ac 1:1) and John alludes to his own gospel (1 Jn 1:1). Paul mentions another letter he wrote to the Corinthians (1 Co 5:9). While some of these examples provide no formal quotations, they do help illustrate the fact that within the New

Testament itself there is recognition of one inspired writing by another. And the total process of reading, circulating, collecting, and quoting of New Testament books in New Testament times amply illustrates the recognition of their claim of divine inspiration.

SUPPORTING CLAIM FOR INSPIRATION WITHIN THE EARLY CHURCH

Every one of the New Testament writers is quoted with divine authority by an apostolic Father. These leaders of the church lived within a generation or two of the close of the New Testament (i.e., before A.D. 150). In effect they provide an unbroken continuity to the New Testament claim of inspiration from apostolic time into the early church, and for that matter down through the centuries following.

*The earliest church Fathers.* The earliest writings in Christendom contain numerous references to New Testament Scripture. Many of these citations have the same authoritative designations as those used when the New Testament quotes the Old. The *Epistle of Pseudo-Barnabas* (c. 70-130), a work falsely ascribed to Paul's associate, cites Matthew 26:31 as what "God saith" (5:12). Later it calls Matthew 22:14 "Scripture" (4:14). Clement of Rome, in his *Epistle to the Corinthians* (c. 95-97), calls the synoptic gospels (Matthew, Mark, Luke) "Scripture." He also employs the phrases "God saith" and "it is written" to designate passages from the New Testament (cf. chap. 36 and 46). Ignatius of Antioch (d. c. 110), wrote seven epistles in which he made numerous citations from the New Testament Scriptures. Polycarp (c. 110-35), a disciple of the apostle John, made many quotations from New Testament books in his *Epistle to the Philippians.* Sometimes he introduced them with expressions like "the Scriptures saith" (cf. chap. 12). The so-called *Shepherd of Hermas* (c. 115-40) was written in the apocalyptic style (visions) of the book of Revelation and contains numerous references to the New Testament. *The Didache* (c. 100-120), or *Teaching of the Twelve,* as it is sometimes called, records many loose quotations of the New Testament. Papias (c. 130-40) includes the New Testament in a book entitled *Exposition of the Oracles of the Lord,* the same phrase used to denote the Old Testament in Romans 3:2. The

so-called *Epistle to Diognetus* (c. 150) makes many allusions to
the New Testament without title.

What is apparent in the use of the New Testament by the
apostolic Fathers is this: the New Testament, like the Old, was
considered a divinely inspired book. Often the quotations are
loose and usually undesignated as to source. But anyone reading
the Fathers cannot fail to see what the works of the New Testament apostles were given the same high esteem as the inspired
books of the Old Testament.

*Later church Fathers.* From the latter part of the second century there is a continuing support for the claim of New Testament
inspiration. Justin Martyr (d. 165) regarded the gospels as "the
voice of God" (*Apology* 1: 65). "We must not suppose," he
wrote, "that the language proceeds from men who were inspired,
but from the Divine Word which moves them" (1.36). Tatian
(c. 110-80), a disciple of Justin, quotes John 1:5 as "scripture" in
chapter 13 of his *Apology*. Irenaeus (c. 130-202) in his *Against
Heresies* wrote, "For the Lord of all gave the power of the Gospel
to his apostles, through whom we have come to know the truth.
. . . This Gospel they preached. Afterwards, by the will of God,
they handed it down to us in the Scriptures, to be 'the pillar and
ground' of our faith" (5. 67).

Clement of Alexandria (c. 150-215) classes both Testaments as
equally divine authority saying, "the Scriptures . . . in the Law,
in the Prophets, and besides by the blessed Gospel . . . are valid
from their omnipotent authority" (*Stromata* 2. 408-9). Tertullian
(c. 160-220) maintained that the four gospels "are reared on the
certain basis of Apostolical authority, and so are inspired in a far
different sense from the writings of the spiritual Christian."[1]
Hippolytus (c. 170-236), a disciple of Irenaeus, offers one of the
most definitive statements on inspiration in the early Fathers. In
*de Antichristo*, speaking of the New Testament writers, he
affirmed,

> These blessed men . . . having been perfected by the Spirit of
> prophecy are worthily honored by the Word Himself, were
> brought to an inner harmony, . . . like instruments, and having

1. Brooke Foss Westcott, *An Introduction to the Study of the Gospels*
(New York: Macmillan, 1902), p. 421.

the Word within them, as it were, to strike the notes . . . by Him they were moved, and announced that which God wished. For they did not speak of their own power; . . . they spake that which was [revealed] to them alone by God.[2]

Origen (c. 185-254), teacher in Alexandria, was also strong on inspiration. He held that the "Spirit inspired each one of the saints, whether prophets or apostles; and there was not one Spirit in the men of the old dispensation, and another in those who were inspired at the advent of Christ" (from *De Principiis*). For in its entirety "the Scriptures were written by the Spirit" (16:6). The bishop Cyprian (c. 200-258) clearly affirmed the inspiration of the New Testament, declaring it to be "Divine Scripture" given by the Holy Spirit. Eusebius of Caesarea (c. 265-340), noted as a church historian, expounded and catalogued the inspired books of both testaments in his *Ecclesiastical History*. Athanasius of Alexandria (c. 295-373), known as the "father of orthodoxy" because of his defense of the deity of Christ against Arius, was the first to use the word *canon* of the New Testament books. Cyril of Jerusalem (c. 315-316) speaks of "the divinely inspired Scriptures of both the Old and the New Testaments." After listing the twenty-two books of the Hebrew Scriptures and twenty-six of the New Testament (all but Revelation), he adds, "Learn also diligently, and from the Church, what are the books of the Old Testament, and what are those of the New. And, pray, read none of the apocryphal writings" (*Of the Divine Scriptures*).

It is unnecessary to proceed further. It will suffice at this point to note that the orthodox doctrine of the inspiration of the New Testament continued down through the Middle Ages into the Reformation and on into the modern period of church history. Louis Gaussen has the situation well summarized as he writes,

> With the single exception of Theodore of Mopsuestia [c. 400], . . . it has been found impossible to produce, in the long course of the EIGHT FIRST CENTURIES OF CHRISTIANITY, a single doctor who has disowned the plenary inspiration of the Scriptures, unless it be in the bosom of the most violent heresies that have tormented the Christian Church."[3]

2. Quoted in ibid., p. 418-19. Westcott's brackets.
3. L. Gaussen, *Theopneustia: The Plenary Inspiration of the Holy Scriptures*, trans. David Scott (Chicago: BICA, n.d.), pp. 139-40.

In summary then, the inspiration of the New Testament is based on the promise of Christ that His disciples would be directed by the Spirit in their teachings about Him. His disciples claimed this promise, and there is clear indication that the writers of the New Testament themselves, as well as their contemporaries, recognized it as accomplished. They believed that the New Testament was divinely inspired, and from the time of the very earliest Christian records on, there has been an almost unanimous support for the inspiration of the New Testament along with the Old.

# 5

# THE EVIDENCES FOR THE
# INSPIRATION OF THE BIBLE

THROUGH THE CENTURIES Christians have been called upon to give a reason or defense for their faith (1 Pe 3:15). Since the Scriptures lay at the very foundation of their faith in Christ, it has been incumbent upon Christian apologists to provide evidence for the inspiration of the Bible. It is one thing to *claim* divine inspiration for the Bible and quite another to provide evidence to *confirm* that claim. Before examining the supporting evidence for the inspiration of Scripture, let us summarize precisely what it is that inspiration claims.

## A SUMMARY OF THE CLAIM FOR THE INSPIRATION OF THE BIBLE

The inspiration of the Bible is not to be confused with a poetic inspiration. Inspiration as applied to the Bible refers to the God-given authority of its teachings for the thought and life of the believer.

### BIBLICAL DESCRIPTION OF INSPIRATION

The word *inspiration* means God-breathed, and it refers to the process by which the Scriptures or writings were invested with divine authority for doctrine and practice (2 Ti 3:16-17). It is the writings which are said to be inspired. The writers, however, were Spirit moved to record their messages. Hence, when viewed as a total process, inspiration is what occurs when Spirit-moved writers record God-breathed writings. Three elements are contained in this total process of inspiration: the divine causality, the prophetic agency, and the resultant written authority. (See chaps. 1 and 2.)

*The three elements in inspiration.* The first element in inspiration is *God's causality.* God is the Prime Mover by whose promptings the prophets were led to write. The ultimate origin of inspired writings is the desire of the Divine to communicate with man. The second factor is the *prophetic agency.* The Word of God comes through men of God. God employs the instrumentality of human personality to convey His message. Finally, the written prophetic utterance is invested with *divine authority.* The prophet's words are God's Word.

*The characteristics of an inspired writing.* The first characteristic of inspiration is implied in the fact that it is an inspired writing; namely, it is *verbal.* The very words of the prophets were God-given, not by dictation but by the Spirit-directed employment of the prophet's own vocabulary and style. Inspiration also claims to be *plenary* (full). No part of Scripture is without divine inspiration. Paul wrote, "All scripture is inspired by God." In addition, inspiration implies the *inerrancy* of the teaching of the original documents (called autographs). Whatever God utters is true and without error, and the Bible is said to be an utterance of God. Finally, inspiration results in the divine *authority* of the Scriptures. The teaching of Scripture is binding on the believer for faith and practice.

THE BIBLICAL CLAIM TO DIVINE INSPIRATION

Inspiration is not something merely attributed to the Bible by Christians; it is something the Bible claims for itself. There are literally hundreds of references within the Bible about its divine origin (see chaps. 3 and 4).

*The claim for the inspiration of the Old Testament.* The Old Testament claims to be a prophetic writing. The familiar "thus says the Lord" fills its pages. False prophets and their works were excluded from the house of the Lord. Those prophecies which proved to be from God were preserved in a sacred place. This growing collection of sacred writings was recognized and even quoted by later prophets as the Word of God.

Jesus and the New Testament writers held these writings in the same high esteem; they claimed them to be the unbreakable, authoritative, and inspired Word of God. By numerous references to the Old Testament as a whole, to its basic sections, and to almost every Old Testament book, the New Testament writers overwhelmingly attested to the claim of divine inspiration for the Old Testament.

*The claim for the inspiration of the New Testament.* The apostolic writings were boldly described in the same authoritative terms which denoted the Old Testament as the Word of God. They were called "scripture," "prophecy," etc. Every book in the New Testament contains some claim to divine authority. The New Testament church read, circulated, collected, and quoted the New Testament books right along with the inspired Scriptures of the Old Testament.

The contemporaries and immediate successors of the apostolic age recognized the divine origin of the New Testament writings along with the Old. With only heretical exceptions, all of the great Fathers of the Christian church from the earliest times held to the divine inspiration of the New Testament. In brief, there is continuous claim for the inspiration of both Old and New Testaments from the time of their composition to the present. In modern times this claim has been seriously challenged by many from inside and outside Christendom. This challenge calls for a substantiation of the claim for inspiration of the Bible.

### SUPPORT FOR THE BIBLICAL CLAIM FOR INSPIRATION

Defenders of the Christian faith have responded to this challenge in sundry ways. Some have transformed Christianity into a rational system, others have claimed belief in it because it is "absurd," but the great mass of informed Christians through the centuries have avoided either rationalism or fideism. Claiming neither absolute finality nor complete skepticism, Christian apologists have given "a reason for the hope that is in them." The following is a summary of evidence for the biblical doctrine of inspiration.

#### INTERNAL EVIDENCE OF THE BIBLE'S INSPIRATION

There are two lines of evidence to be considered on the inspiration of the Bible: the evidence flowing from within Scripture itself (called internal evidence) and that coming from outside of it (known as external evidence). There are several lines of internal evidence which have been presented.

*The evidence of self-vindicating authority.* Some have claimed that the Bible speaks, like a lion's roar, with its own convincing authority. As Jesus astonished the crowds, "for he taught them as one who had authority" (Mk 1:22), even so the "thus says the Lord" of Scripture speaks for itself. When the voice spoke to Job out of the whirlwind, it was evident to him that it was the voice of God (Job 38). The words of Scripture need not be defended; they need only to be heeded to know they are the words of God. The most convincing way to demonstrate the authority of a lion is to let it loose. Likewise, the inspiration of the Bible does not need to be defended; rather, the teachings of the Bible need to be expounded. It is argued that God can speak most effectively for Himself. The Bible can vindicate its own authority once its voice is heard.

*Evidence of the testimony of the Holy Spirit.* Closely allied with the evidence of the self-vindicating authority of Scripture is the witness of the Holy Spirit. The Word of God is confirmed to the children of God by the Spirit of God. The inner witness of God in the heart of the believer as he reads the Bible is evidence of its divine origin. The Holy Spirit not only bears witness to the believer that he is a child of God (Ro 8:16) but that the Bible is the Word of God (2 Pe 1:20-21). The same Spirit who communicated the truth of God also confirms to the believer that the Bible is the Word of God. From the earliest centuries it has been the consensus of the Christian community in which the Spirit operates that the books of the Bible are the Word of God. God's Word is thus confirmed by God's Spirit.

*Evidence from the transforming ability of the Bible.* Another so-called internal evidence is the ability of the Bible to convert the unbeliever and to build up the believer in the faith. Hebrews says, "The word of God is alive and active, sharper than a two-edged sword . . ." (4:12). Untold thousands have experienced this power. Drug addicts have been cured by it; derelicts have been transformed; hate has been turned to love by reading it. Believers grow by studying it (1 Pe 2:2). The sorrowing are comforted, the sinners are rebuked, and the negligent are exhorted by the Scriptures. God's Word possesses the dynamic, transforming power of God. God vindicates the Bible's authority by its evangelistic and edifying powers.

*The evidence of the unity of the Bible.* A more formal evidence of the Bible's inspiration is its unity. Comprised as it is of sixty-six books, written over a period of some fifteen hundred years by nearly forty authors in several languages containing hundreds of topics, it is more than accidental that the Bible possesses an amazing unity of theme—Jesus Christ. One problem—sin—and one solution—the Saviour—unify its pages from Genesis to Revelation. Compared to a medical manual written amid such variety, the Bible shows marked evidence of divine unity. This is an especially valid point in view of the fact that no one person or group of men put the Bible together. Books were added as they were written by the prophets. They were then collected simply because they were considered inspired. It is only later reflection, both by the prophets themselves (e.g., 1 Pe 1:10-11) and later generations, which has discovered that the Bible is really one book whose "chapters" were written by men who had no explicit knowledge of the overall structure. Their role could be compared to that of different men writing chapters of a novel for which none of them have even an overall outline. Whatever unity the book has must come from beyond them.

EXTERNAL EVIDENCES OF THE BIBLE'S INSPIRATION

The internal evidence of inspiration is mostly subjective in nature. It relates to what the believer sees or feels in his experience with the Bible. With the possible exception of the last mentioned evidence, the unity of the Bible, these internal evidences are available only on the inside of Christianity. The nonbeliever does not hear the voice of God, nor sense the witness of His Spirit, nor feel the edifying power of Scripture in his life. Unless he steps by faith to the inside, these evidences will have little if any convincing effect on his life. This is where the external evidence plays a crucial role. It serves as signposts indicating where the "inside" really is. It is public witness to something very unusual, which serves to draw attention to the voice of God in Scripture.

*The evidence from the historicity of the Bible.* Much of the

Bible is historical and as such is subject to verification. There are two main lines of support for biblical history: archaeological artifacts and specifically written documents. With respect to the first, no archaeological find has ever invalidated a biblical teaching. On the contrary, as Donald J. Wiseman wrote, "The geography of Bible lands and visible remains of antiquity were gradually recorded until today more than 25,000 sites within this region and dating to Old Testament times, in their broadest sense, have been located."[1] In fact, much of the earlier criticism of the Bible has been decisively overturned by archaeological discoveries which have demonstrated the existence of writing in Moses' day, the history and chronology of the kings of Israel, and even the existence of the Hittites, a people once known only from the Bible.

The more widely publicized discovery of the Dead Sea Scrolls illustrates a point less well known; namely, that there are thousands of manuscripts for both Old and New Testaments, compared with a handful of many great secular classics. This makes the Bible the best documented book from the ancient world. While no historical find is a direct evidence of any spiritual claim in the Bible, such as the claim to be divinely inspired, yet the historicity of the Bible does provide indirect verification of the claim of inspiration. For confirmation of the Bible's accuracy in factual matters lends credibility to its claims when speaking on other subjects. Jesus said, "If I have told you earthly things and you do not believe, how can you believe if I tell you heavenly things?" (Jn 3:12).

*Evidence from the testimony of Christ.* In connection with the foregoing evidence for the historicity of the biblical documents is the evidence of the testimony of Christ. Since the New Testament has been documented as historical, and since these same historical documents provide us with the teaching of Christ about the inspiration of the Bible, one needs only to assume the truthfulness of Christ in order to argue for the inspiration of the Bible. If Christ possesses any kind of authority or integrity as a religious teacher, then the Scriptures are inspired. For He taught that they were God's Word. In order to falsify this contention, one must

1. Donald J. Wiseman, "Archaeological Confirmation of the Old Testament" in *Revelation and the Bible,* ed. Carl F. H. Henry (Grand Rapids: Baker, 1958), pp. 301-2.

reject the authority of Jesus to make pronouncements on the subject of inspiration. The evidence from Scripture conclusively reveals that Jesus held to the full divine authority of the Scriptures (see chap. 3). Indications from the gospel record, with ample historical backing, show that Jesus was a man of integrity and truth. The argument, then, is this: if what Jesus taught is true, and Jesus taught that the Bible is inspired, then it follows that it is true that the Bible is inspired of God.

*The evidence from prophecy.* Another forceful external testimony to the inspiration of Scripture is the fact of fulfilled prophecy. According to Deuteronomy 18, a prophet was false if he made predictions which were never fulfilled. No unconditional prophecy of the Bible about events to the present day has gone unfilled. Hundreds of predictions, some of them given hundreds of years in advance, have been literally fulfilled. The time (Dan 9), city (Mic 5:2) and nature (Is 7:14) of Christ's birth were foretold in the Old Testament, as were dozens of other things about His life, death, and resurrection. Other prophecies, such as the education and communication explosion (Dan 12:4), the repatriation of Israel, and the rebuilding of Palestine (Is 61:4) are being fulfilled today. There are other books which claim divine inspiration, such as the Koran and parts of the Veda. But none of these books contain predictive prophecy. As a result, fulfilled prophecy is a strong indication of the divine authority of the Bible.

*The evidence from the influence of the Bible.* No book has been more widely disseminated and has more broadly influenced the course of world events than has the Bible. The Bible has been translated into more languages, has been published in more copies, has influenced more thought, inspired more art, and motivated more discoveries than any other book. The Bible has been translated into over one thousand languages representing more than ninety percent of the world's population. It has been published in some billions of copies. There are no close seconds in the all-time best-seller list. The influence of the Bible and its teaching in the Western world is clear for all who study history. And the influential role of the West in the course of world events is equally clear. Civilization has been influenced more by the

Judeo-Christian Scriptures than by any other book or combination of books in the world. Indeed, no great moral or religious work in the world exceeds the depth of morality in the principle of Christian love, and none has a more lofty spiritual concept than the biblical view of God. The Bible presents the highest ideals known to men which have molded civilization.

*Evidence from the apparent indestructibility of the Bible.* Despite its importance (or maybe because of it), the Bible has suffered more vicious attacks than would be expected to be made on such a book. But the Bible has withstood all its attackers. Diocletian attempted to exterminate it (c. A.D. 303), and yet it is the most widely published book in the world today. Biblical critics once regarded much of it as mythological, but archaeology has established it as historical. Antagonists have attacked its teaching as primitive, but moralists urge that its teaching on love be applied to modern society. Skeptics have cast doubt on its authenticity, and yet more men are convinced of its truth today than ever. Attacks continue to arise from science, psychology, and political movements, but the Bible remains undaunted. Like the wall four-feet high and four-feet wide, blowing at it seems to accomplish nothing. The Bible remains just as strong after the attack. Jesus said, "Heaven and earth will pass away, but my words will not pass away" (Mk 13:31).

*Evidence from the integrity of the human authors.* There are no good reasons to suppose that the authors of Scripture were not honest and sincere men. From everything that is known of their lives, and even their deaths for what they believed, they were utterly convinced that God had spoken to them. What shall we make of men—over five hundred of them (1 Co 15:6)—who claim as evidence for the divine authority of their message that they saw the Jesus of Nazareth, crucified under Pontius Pilate, alive and well? What shall we make of the claim that they saw Him on about a half-dozen occasions over a period of a month and a half? That they talked with Him, ate with Him, saw His wounds, and handled Him, and even the most skeptical among them fell at His feet and cried, "My Lord and my God!" (Jn 20:28)? It stretches one's credulity to believe that they were all drugged or deluded, especially in view of the number and nature of the encounters and its lasting effect on them. But granting their basic integrity, we are confronted with an unusual phenomenon of men—hundreds of them—facing death with the claim that God had given them the authority to speak and write. When men of sanity and noted integrity claim divine inspiration and offer as evidence that they have communicated with the resurrected Christ, then men of good will who seek the truth must take notice. In brief, the honesty of the biblical writers vouches for the divine authority of their writings.

Other arguments have been offered for the Bible's inspiration, but the main weight of the case here will rest on these. Do these arguments *prove* that the Bible is inspired? No, these are not proofs with rationally inescapable conclusions. Even an amateur philosopher can devise ways to avoid the logic of the arguments. And even if they did prove the inspiration of the Bible, it would not necessarily follow that they would *persuade* it to the satisfaction of all. Rather, they are evidences, testimonies, or witnesses. As witnesses they must be cross-examined and evaluated as a whole. Then, in the jury room of one's own soul a decision must be made—a decision which is based not on rationally inescapable proofs but on evidence which is "beyond reasonable doubt."

Perhaps all that need be added here is that if the Bible were on trial and we were part of a jury called upon for a verdict, based on a comprehensive examination of the claim and alleged credentials of the Bible to be inspired, we would be compelled to vote that it is "guilty of being inspired as charged." The reader too must decide. For those who tend to be indecisive, one is reminded of the words of Peter: "Lord, to whom shall we go? You have the words of eternal life" (Jn 6:68). In other words, if the Bible—with its clear-cut claim to be inspired, with its incomparable characteristics and multiple credentials— is not inspired, then to what else can we turn? It has the words of eternal life.

# 6

# THE CHARACTERISTICS OF
# CANONICITY

WHICH BOOKS BELONG in the Bible? What about the so-called missing books? How did the Bible come to have sixty-six books? These are the kinds of questions covered in the next few chapters. This subject is called canonicity. It is the second great link in the chain from God to us. Inspiration is the means by which the Bible received its *authority;* canonization is the process by which the Bible received its final *acceptance.* It is one thing for prophets to receive a message from God but another for that message to be recognized by the people of God. Canonicity is the study which treats the recognition and collection of the books given by God's inspiration.

## DEFINITION OF CANONICITY

The word *canon* is derived from the Greek *kanon* (a rod, ruler) which in turn comes from the Hebrew *kaneh,* an Old Testament word meaning "measuring rod" (cf. Eze 40:3). Even in pre-Christian usage the word was broadened to indicate a standard or norm other than a literal rod or rules. The New Testament employs the term in its figurative sense to indicate a rule for conduct (Gal 6:16).

### EARLY CHRISTIAN USAGE OF THE WORD "CANON"

In early Christian usage the word *canon* came to mean the "rule of faith" or the normative writings (i.e., the authoritative Scriptures). By the time of Athanasius (fl. c. 350) the concept of a biblical canon or normative Scriptures was developing. The word *canon* was applied to the Bible in both active and passive senses. In the active sense the Bible is the canon by which all else is to be judged. In the passive sense, canon meant the rule or standard by which a writing was judged to be inspired or authoritative. This double usage causes some confusion which we will attempt to clarify. First, let us look at what is meant by a canon of Scripture in the active sense. Then we will look at its meaning in the passive sense.

SOME SYNONYMS OF CANONICITY

The existence of a canon or collection of authoritative writings antedates the use of the term *canon*. The Jewish community collected and preserved their Holy Scriptures from the time of Moses.

*Sacred Scriptures.* One of the earliest concepts of a canon was that of sacred writings. That the writings of Moses were considered sacred is indicated by the holy place in which they were stored beside the ark of the covenant (Deu 31:24-26). After the temple was built, these sacred writings were preserved in it (2 Ki 22:8). The special accord granted to these select books alone indicates that they were considered to be canonical or sacred writings.

*Authoritative writings.* The divine authority of Scripture is another designation of its canonicity. The authority of the Mosaic writings was impressed on Joshua and Israel (Jos 1:8). Each king of Israel was exhorted to "write for himself in a book a copy of this law, . . . and he shall read in it all the days of his life, that he may learn to fear the LORD his God" (Deu 17:18-19). Since the books came from God they were invested with His authority. As authoritative writings they were canonical or normative for the Jewish believer.

*Books that defile the hands.* In the teaching tradition of Israel there arose the concept of books so holy or sacred that those who used them had "defiled their hands." The Talmud says, "The Gospel and the books of the heretics do not make the hands unclean; the books of Ben Sira and whatever books have been written since his time are not canonical" (Tosefta Yadaim 3:5). The books of the Hebrew Old Testament, by contrast, do make the hands unclean because they are sacred. Hence, only those

books which demand that the user undergo a special ceremonial
cleansing were regarded as canonical.

*Prophetic books.* As previously discussed (chap. 3), a book
qualified as inspired only if it had been written by a prophetic
spokesman of God. The works of false prophets in nonprophetic
books were rejected and not collected in a holy place. In fact,
according to Josephus (*Contra Apion* 1:8), only those books
which were composed during the prophetic period from Moses to
Artaxerxes could be canonical. He wrote, "From Artaxerxes until
our time everything has been recorded, but has not been deemed
worthy of like credit with what preceded, because the exact succession of the prophets ceased." Only the books from Moses to
Malachi were canonical since only these were written by men in
the prophetic succession. During the period from Artaxerxes
(fourth century B.C.) to Josephus (A.D. first century) there was
no prophetic succession; hence, it was not part of the prophetic
period. The Talmud makes the same claim, saying, "Up to this
point [fourth century B.C.] the prophets prophesied through the
Holy Spirit; from this time onward incline thine ear and listen to
the sayings of the wise" (Seder Olam Rabba 30). In order to be
canonical, then, an Old Testament book must come from the
prophetic succession during the prophetic period.

### DETERMINATION OF CANONICITY

These descriptions of canonicity will help clarify what is meant
by canonical Scripture. The confusion between the active and
passive senses of the word *canon* have occasioned ambiguity in
the issue of what determines the canonicity of a book.

#### SOME INADEQUATE VIEWS ON WHAT DETERMINES CANONICITY

Several views of what determines the canonicity of a writing
have been suggested. All of these positions confuse the canons or
rules by which one discovers a book to be inspired (passive sense
of the term *canon*) with the canon of normative writings which is
discovered (active sense of the term *canon*). As such, these
theories are inadequate in their notions of what determines the
canonicity of a book. Let us examine them briefly.

*The view that age determines canonicity.* The theory that the canonicity of a book is determined by its antiquity, that it came to be venerated because of its age, misses the mark for two reasons. First, many very old books, as the Book of Jasher and the Book of the Wars of the Lord (Jos 10:13 and Num 21:14) were not accepted into the canon. Further, the evidence is that books were received into the canon immediately, not after they had aged. This was true of the books of Moses (Deu 31:24-26), of Jeremiah (Dan 9:2) and the New Testament writings of Paul (2 Pe 3:16).

*The view that Hebrew language determines canonicity.* Also insufficient is the view that those books written in the "sacred" language of the Hebrews were considered sacred books and those not written in Hebrew were not put in the canon. The fact of the matter is that not all books written in Hebrew were accepted, as some of the rejected Hebrew apocryphal books as well as other earlier nonbiblical writings indicate (see Jos 10:13). In addition, there are sections of books which were accepted into the canon that were not written in Hebrew (Dan 2:4b–7:28 and Ezra 4:8–6:18; 7:12-26 are in Aramaic).

*The view that agreement with the Torah determines canonicity.* Another inadequate view is that a book's canonicity was determined by whether or not it agreed with the Torah (Law of Moses). It goes without saying that books known to contradict the Torah would be rejected, since it was believed that God would not contradict Himself in subsequent revelations. But this theory misses two important points. First, it was not the Torah which determined the canonicity of everything after it. Rather, it was the same factor determining the canonicity of the Torah which determined the canonicity of all Scripture, namely, the fact that all of them were divinely inspired. In other words, the view that agreement with the Torah determines canonicity is inadequate because it does not explain what determined the canonicity of the Torah. Secondly, the theory is too broad. Many other books which agreed with the Torah were not accepted as inspired. The Jewish fathers believed their Talmud and Midrash agreed with the Torah but never pronounced them canonical. The same is true of many Christian writings and the New Testament.

*The view that religious value determines canonicity.* Still another suggestion is that the religious value of a book was determinitive of its position in the canon. Here again the cart is before the horse. It is axiomatic to say that a book without some kind of spiritual value would be rejected from the canon. It is also true that not every book with spiritual value is automatically canonical, as a wealth of both Jewish and Christian literature, including the Apocrypha, evidences. The important thing, however, is that this theory confuses cause and effect. It is not religious value which determines canonicity; it is canonicity which determines the religious value. More precisely, it is not the value of a book which determines its divine authority; it is the divine authority which determines its value.

### CANONICITY IS DETERMINED BY INSPIRATION

The books of the Bible are not considered God-given because they are found to have value in them; they are valuable because they are given of God—the source of all value. And the process by which God gives His revelation is called inspiration. It is the inspiration of a book which determines its canonicity. God gives the divine authority to a book and men of God receive it. God reveals and His people recognize what He reveals. Canonicity is determined by God and discovered by man. The Bible is the "canon" or rule by which all else is to be measured because it possesses God-given authority. Whatever rules (canons) may be used by the church to discover precisely which books have this canonical or normative authority should *not* be said to "determine" their canonicity. To speak of the people of God, by whatever rules of recognition, as "determining" which books are divinely authoritative confuses the issue. Only God can give divine authority and, hence, canonicity to a book.

The primary notion of the word canon as applied to Scripture is the active sense, i.e., that the Bible is the ruling norm of faith. The secondary notion, that a book is judged by certain canons and receives recognition as inspired (the passive sense), should not be confused with the divine determination of canonicity. Only inspiration determines the authority of a book to be canonical or normative.

### THE DISCOVERY OF CANONICITY

The people of God have played a crucial role in the process of canonization through the centuries, albeit not a determinative one. Upon the believing community lays the task of discriminating and deciding which books were from God. In order to fulfill this role they had to look for certain earmarks of divine authority. How would one recognize an inspired book if he saw it? What are the characteristics which distinguish a divine declaration from a purely human one? Several criteria were involved in this recognition process.

#### THE PRINCIPLES FOR DISCOVERING CANONICITY

False books and false writings were not scarce (see chaps. 8 and 10). Their ever-present threat made it necessary for the people of God to carefully review their sacred collection. Even books accepted by other believers or in earlier days were subsequently brought into question by the church. Operating in the whole process are discernible some five basic criteria: (1) Is the book *authoritative*—does it claim to be of God? (2) Is it *prophetic*—was it written by a servant of God? (3) Is it *authentic*—does it tell the truth about God, man, etc.? (4) Is the book *dynamic*—does it possess the life-transforming power of God? (5) Is this book *received* or accepted by the people of God for whom it was originally written—is it recognized as being from God?

*The authority of a book.* As indicated earlier (chaps. 3 and 4), each book in the Bible bears the claim of divine authority. Often the explicit "thus says the Lord" is present. Sometimes the tone and exhortations reveal its divine origin. Always there is divine pronouncement. In the more didactic (teaching) literature there is divine pronouncement about *what believers should do.* In the historical books the exhortations are more implied and the authoritative pronouncements are more about *what God has done* in the history of His people (which is "His story"). If a book lacked the authority of God, it was not considered canonical and was rejected from the canon.

Let us illustrate this principle of authority as it relates to the canon. The books of the prophets were easily *recognized* by this principle of authority. The repeated, "And the Lord said unto me," or "The word of the Lord came unto me," is abundant evidence of their claim to divine authority. Some books lacked the claim to be divine and were thereby *rejected* as noncanonical. Perhaps this was the case with the Book of Jasher and the Book of the Wars of the Lord. Still other books were *questioned* and challenged as to their divine authority but finally accepted into the canon, such as Esther. Not until it was obvious to all that the protection and therefore the pronouncements of God on His people were unquestionably present in Esther was this book accorded a permanent place in the Jewish canon. Indeed, the very fact some canonical books were called into question provides assurance that the believers were discriminating. Unless they were convinced of the divine authority of the book it was rejected.

*The prophetic authorship of a Book.* Inspired books come only through Spirit-moved men known as prophets (2 Pe 1:20-21). The Word of God is given to His people only through His prophets. Every biblical author had a prophetic gift or function, even if he was not a prophet by occupation (Heb 1:1).

Paul argued in Galatians that his book should be *accepted* because he was an apostle, "not from men nor through man, but through Jesus Christ and God the Father" (Gal 1:1). His book was to be accepted because it was apostolic—it was from a God-appointed spokesman or prophet. Books were to be *rejected* if they did not come from prophets of God, as is evident from Paul's warnings not to accept a book from someone falsely claiming to be an apostle (2 Th 2:2) and from the warning in 2 Corinthians about false prophets (11:13). John's warnings about false messiahs and trying the spirits would fall into the same category (1 Jn 2:18-19; and 4:1-3). It was because of this prophetic principle that 2 Peter was disputed by some in the early church. Until the fathers were convinced that it was not a forgery but that it really came from Peter the apostle as it claimed (1:1), it was not accorded a permanent place in the Christian canon.

*The authenticity of a book.* Another hallmark of inspiration is authenticity. Any book with factual or doctrinal errors (judged by previous revelations) could not be inspired of God. God cannot lie; His word must be true and consistent.

In view of this principle, the Bereans accepted Paul's teachings and searched the Scriptures to see whether or not what Paul taught them was really in accord with God's revelation in the Old Testament (Ac 17:11). Simple agreement with previous revelation would not ipso facto make a teaching inspired. But contradiction of a previous revelation would clearly indicate that a teaching was not inspired.

Much of the Apocrypha was rejected because of the principle of authenticity. Their historical anomalies and theological heresies made it impossible to accept them as from God despite their authoritative format. They could not be from God and contain error at the same time.

Some canonical books were *questioned* on the basis of this same principle. Could the letter of James be inspired if it contradicted Paul's teaching on justification by faith and not by works? Until their essential compatibility was seen, James was questioned by some. Others questioned Jude because of its citation of inauthentic Pseudepigraphal books (vv. 9, 14). Once it was understood that Jude's quotations granted no more authority to those books than Paul's quotes from the non-Christian poets (see also Ac 17:28 and Titus 1:12), then there remained no reason to reject Jude.

*The dynamic nature of a book.* A fourth test for canonicity, at times less explicit than some of the others, was the life-transforming ability of the writing: "The word of God is alive and powerful" (Heb 4:12). As a result it can be used "for teaching, for correction, and for training in righteousness" (2 Ti 3:16-17).

The apostle Paul revealed that the dynamic ability of inspired writings was involved in the *acceptance* of all Scripture as 2 Timothy 3:16-17 indicates. He said to Timothy, "The holy scriptures . . . are able to make thee wise unto salvation" (v. 15, KJV). Elsewhere, Peter speaks of the edifying and evangelizing power of the Word (1 Pe 1:23; 2:2). Other messages and books were *rejected* because they held out false hope (1 Ki 22:6-8) or rang a false alarm (2 Th 2:2). Thus, they were not conducive to building up the believer in the truth of Christ. Jesus said, "You will know the truth, and the truth will make you free" (Jn 8:32). False teaching never liberates; only the truth has emancipating power.

Some biblical books, such as Song of Solomon and Ecclesiastes, were questioned because they were thought by some to lack this dynamic edifying power. Once they were convinced that the Song was not sensual but deeply spiritual and that Ecclesiastes was not skeptical and pessimistic but positive and edifying (e.g., 12:9-10), then there remained little doubt as to their canonicity.

*The acceptance of a book.* The final trademark of an authoritative writing is its recognition by the people of God to whom it was initially given. God's Word given through His prophet and with His truth must be recognized by His people. Later generations of believers sought to verify this fact. For if the book was received, collected, and used as God's work by those to whom it was originally given, then its canonicity was established. Communication and transportation being what it was in ancient times, it sometimes took much time and effort on the part of later church Fathers to determine this recognition. For this reason the full and final recognition by the whole church of the sixty-six books of the canon took many, many years (see chap. 9).

The books of Moses were immediately *accepted* by the people of God. They were collected, quoted, preserved, and even imposed on future generations (see chap. 3). Paul's epistles were immediately received by the churches to whom they were addressed (1 Th 2:13) and even by other apostles (2 Pe 3:16). Some writings were immediately *rejected* by the people of God as lacking divine authority (2 Th 2:2). False prophets (Mt 7:21-23) and lying spirits were to be tested and rejected (1 Jn 4:1-3), as indicated in many instances within the Bible itself (cf. Jer 5:2; 14:14). This principle of acceptance led some to *question* for a time certain biblical books such as 2 and 3 John. Their private nature and limited circulation being what it was, it is understandable that there would be some reluctance to accept them until they were assured that the books were received by the first-century people of God as from the apostle John.

It is almost needless to add that not everyone gave even initial recognition to a prophet's message. God vindicated His prophets against those who rejected them (e.g., 1 Ki 22:1-38) and, when challenged, He designated who His people were. When the authority of Moses was challenged by Korah and others, the earth opened and swallowed them alive (Num 16). The role of the people of God was decisive in the recognition of the Word of God. God determined the authority of the books of the canon, but the people of God were called upon to discover which books were authoritative and which were not. To assist them in this discovery were these five tests of canonicity.

### THE PROCEDURE FOR DISCOVERING CANONICITY

We should not imagine a committee of church Fathers with a large pile of books and these five guiding principles before them when we speak of the process of canonization. No ecumenical committee was commissioned to canonize the Bible. The process was far more natural and dynamic. The actual historical development of the Old and New Testament canons will be discussed later (in chaps. 7 and 9). What is to be noted here is how the five rules for canonicity were used in the process of discovering which books were inspired of God and therefore canonical.

*Some principles are only implicit in the process.* Although all five characteristics are present in each inspired writing, not all of the rules of recognition are apparent in the decision on each canonical book. It was not always immediately obvious to the early people of God that some historical books were "dynamic" or "authoritative." More obvious to them was the fact that certain books were "prophetic," and "accepted." One can easily see how the implied "thus says the Lord" played a most significant role in the discovery of the canonical books which reveal God's overall redemptive plan. Nevertheless, the reverse is sometimes true; namely, the power and authority of the book are more apparent than its authorship (e.g., Hebrews). In any event, all five characteristics were involved in discovering each canonical book, although some were used only implicitly.

*Some principles operate negatively in the process.* Some of the rules for recognition operate more negatively than others. For instance, the principle of authenticity would more readily eliminate noncanonical books than indicate which books are canonical. There are no false teachings which are canonical, but there are many true writings which are not inspired. Likewise many books which edify or have a dynamic are not canonic, even though no canonical book is without significance in the saving plan of God.

Similarly, a book may claim to be authoritative without being inspired, as many of the apocryphal writings indicate, but no book can be canonical unless it really is authoritative. In other words, if the book lacks authority it cannot be from God. But the simple fact that a book claims authority does not make it ipso facto inspired. The principle of acceptance has a primarily negative function. Even the fact that a book is received by some of the people of God is not a proof of inspiration. In later generations some Christians, not thoroughly informed about the acceptance or rejection by the people of God to whom it was originally addressed, gave local and temporal recognition to books which are not canonical (e.g., some apocryphal books; see chaps. 8 and 10). Simply because a book was received somewhere by some believers is far from proof of its inspiration. The initial reception by the people of God who were in the best position to test the prophetic authority of the book is crucial. It took some time for all segments of subsequent generations to be fully informed about the original circumstances. Thus, their acceptance is important but supportive in nature.

*The most essential principle supersedes all others.* Beneath the whole process of recognition lay one fundamental principle—the prophetic nature of the book. If a book were written by an accredited prophet of God, claiming to give an authoritative pronouncement from God, then there was no need to ask the other questions. Of course the people of God recognized the book as powerful and true when it was given to them by a prophet of God. When there were no directly available confirmations of the prophet's call (as there often were, cf. Ex 4:1-9), then the authenticity, dynamic ability, and reception of a book by the original believing community would be essential to its later recognition. On the other hand, simply establishing the book as prophetic was sufficient in itself to confirm the canonicity of the book.

The question as to whether inauthenticity would disconfirm a prophetic book is purely hypothetical. No book given by God can be false. If a book claiming to be prophetic seems to have indisputable falsehood, then the prophetic credentials must be re-examined. God cannot lie. In this way the other four principles serve as a check on the prophetic character of the books of the canon.

# 7

# THE DEVELOPMENT OF THE OLD TESTAMENT CANON

THE HISTORY of the canonization of the Bible is a most fascinating story. It is a book written and collected over almost two millennia without each contributing author being aware of how his "chapter" would fit into the overall plan. Each prophetic contribution was offered to the people of God simply on the basis that God had spoken to them through the prophet. Just how that message was to fit into an overall story was unknown to the prophet and even to the believers who first recognized it. Only the reflective consciousness of later Christians was able to perceive that the hand of God which moved each individual writer was also moving through them to produce an overall redemptive story of which God alone was the author. Neither the prophets who composed the books nor the people of God who collected them were consciously constructing the overall unity in which each book was to play a part.

## SOME PRELIMINARY DISTINCTIONS

God inspired the books, the original people of God recognized and collected them, and later believers categorized the canonical books according to the overall unity they perceived in them. This in brief is the story of the canonization of the Bible. Let us explicate some of the more important distinctions implied in this process.

### THE THREE BASIC STEPS IN THE PROCESS OF CANONIZATION

There are three basic steps in the overall process of canonization: inspiration by God, recognition by men of God and collection by the people of God. A brief look at each of them will indicate that the first step in the canonization of the Bible (inspiration) was God's; the next two (recognition and preservation) were committed by Him to His people.

*Inspiration by God.* God took the first step in canonization when He inspired the writings. Thus, the most fundamental reason why there are thirty-nine books in the Old Testament is that only that many books were inspired by God. It is evident that the people of God could not recognize the divine authority of a book if it did not possess any.

*Recognition by men of God.* Once God authorized a writing, men of God recognized it. This recognition was given immediately by the community to which it was addressed. Once the book was copied and circulated with credentials to the whole Christian community, it was recognized by the church universal as canonical. The writings of Moses were received in his day (Ex 24:3), as were those of Joshua (Jos 24:26), Samuel (1 Sa 10:25) and Jeremiah (Dan 9:2). This recognition is further confirmed by New Testament believers as well as by Jesus Himself (see chap. 3).

*Collection and preservation by the people of God.* The Word of God was treasured by His people. The writings of Moses were preserved by the ark (Deu 31:26). Samuel's words were put "in a book and laid . . . before the Lord" (1 Sa 10:25). The Law of Moses was preserved in the temple in Josiah's day (2 Ki 23:24). Daniel had a collection of "the books" in which were found "the law of Moses" and "the prophets" (Dan 9:2, 6, 13). Ezra possessed copies of the law of Moses and the prophets (Neh 9:14, 26-30). New Testament believers possessed the whole of the Old Testament "scripture[s]" (2 Ti 3:16), both law and prophets (Mt 5:17).

THE DIFFERENCE BETWEEN CANONICAL AND OTHER RELIGIOUS LITERATURE

Not all Jewish religious literature was considered canonical by the believing community. There was certainly religious significance to some of the earlier books such as the Book of Jasher

(Jos 10:13), the Book of the Wars of the Lord (Num 21:14) and others (see 1 Ki 11:41). The books of the Jewish Apocrypha, written after the close of the Old Testament period (c. 400 B.C.), have a definite religious significance but were never considered canonical by official Judaism (see chap. 8). The crucial difference between canonical and noncanonical literature is that the former is normative (authoritative) and the latter is not. Inspired books have divine binding authority on the believer; the latter may have some value for devotion and edification, but they are not to be used to define or delimit any doctrine. Canonical books provide the truth criteria by which all noncanonical books are to be judged. No article of faith may be based on any noncanonical work, regardless of its religious value. The divinely inspired and authoritative books are the sole *basis* for doctrine. Whatever complementary support canonical truth derives from other books, it in no way lends canonical value to those books. The support is purely historical and has no authoritative theological value. The truth of inspired Scripture alone is the canon or foundation of the truths of faith.

THE DIFFERENCE BETWEEN CANONIZATION AND CATEGORIZATION OF BIBLICAL BOOKS

The failure to distinguish between the *sections* into which the Hebrew Old Testament has been divided (law, prophets, and writings) and the *stages* or periods in which the collection developed has caused a great deal of confusion. For years the standard critical theory has held that the Hebrew Scriptures were canonized by sections, following the alleged dates of their composition, into law (*c.* 400 B.C.), prophets (*c.* 200 B.C.), and writings (*c.* A.D. 100). This theory is built on the mistaken notion that the threefold *categorization* of the Old Testament represents its stages of *canonization*. As we shall see shortly, there is no direct connection between these categories and events. The books of the Jewish Scriptures have been rearranged since their composition. Some of them, from the writings especially, were clearly written and accepted by the Jewish community centuries before the date ascribed to them by critical theorists.

### PROGRESSIVE COLLECTION OF OLD TESTAMENT BOOKS

The first and most basic fact about the process of Old Testament canonization is that it is not threefold but at most twofold. The earliest and most repeated descriptions of the canon refer to it as "Moses and the prophets," the "prophets," or simply "the books." Nowhere in Scripture or in the extrabiblical literature into the early Christian period is there any proof of a so-called third canonical stage comprised of writings which were written and collected after the time of the law and prophets. As far as canonicity is concerned, the so-called writings were always a part of the canonical section commonly called the prophets.

#### THE EVIDENCE OF A TWOFOLD CANON

*A threefold classification.* Even before New Testament times, however, there was a growing tradition which made a third section of the Old Testament books. In the Prologue to the apocryphal book, Sirach ( c. 132 B.C.) speaks of "the law and the prophets and the other books of our fathers" read by his grandfather ( c. 200 B.C.). Around the time of Christ the Jewish philosopher Philo made a threefold distinction in the Old Testament speaking of the "[1] laws and [2] oracles delivered through the mouth of prophets, and [3] psalms and anything else which fosters and perfects knowledge and piety" ( *De Vita Contemplativa* 3. 25). Jesus Himself alluded to a threefold division when He spoke of "the law of Moses and the prophets and the psalms" ( Lk 24:44). A little later in the first century, Josephus, the Jewish historian, referred to the twenty-two books of Hebrew Scripture, "five belonging to Moses . . . the prophets . . . in thirteen books. The remaining four books [apparently Job, Psalms, Proverbs, and Ecclesiastes] containing hymns of God, and the precepts for the conduct of human life" ( *Against Apion* I. 8). By the fifth century A.D. the Jewish Talmud ( *Baba Bathra* ) listed eleven books in a third section called the Writings ( *Kethubhim* ). The Hebrew Bible lists them the same way to date ( see chap. 1).

Several very important conclusions may be drawn from this data. First, the facts do not show that the present classification of writings, containing eleven of the twenty-two books, is earlier than the fifth century A.D. Second, the earliest reference which enumerates the books in a third division is Josephus who lists them as four. This is strong evidence against the claim of the critics that Daniel, Chronicles, and Ezra-Nehemiah were late books, listed among the writings which were not canonized until the first century A.D. Third, the number of the twenty-two books which were placed in the writings grew from four to eleven between the first and fifth centuries. None of these facts support the view that there was a group of books, inclusive of Daniel, Chronicles, and Ezra-Nehemiah, which were not brought into the Jewish canon until the first century A.D. There was to be sure an early tendency to arrange the Old Testament into a threefold classification (for reasons not fully known), and the number of books in this section grew over the years. But the number and rearrangement of these books had no essential connection with the basic twofold division and development of the Old Testament canon.

*The twofold canonization.* The earliest and most persistent references to the canon of the Old Testament indicate that it is one collection of prophetic books with two divisions, the law of Moses and the prophets who followed him. Let us trace the evidence historically.

Even before the time of the Exile (sixth century B.C.) there were hints of a separate classification of Moses from the prophets after him. This was by virtue of the fact that special accord was given to Moses as the great lawgiver and because of the establishment of a community of prophets after Moses (1 Sa 19:20). By the time of the Exile, Daniel had referred to "the books" as containing both "the law of Moses" and "the prophets" (Dan 9:2, 6, 11). The postexilic prophet Zechariah (sixth century B.C.) mentions "the law and the words which the Lord of hosts had sent by his Spirit through the former prophets" (Zech 7:12). Nehemiah makes the same distinction (Neh 9:14, 29-30).

During the intertestamental period, this same twofold distinction continues. God spoke out of "the law, and the prophets" (2 Maccabees 15:9). The *Manual of Discipline* of the Qumran community consistently refers to the Old Testament as the law and the prophets (1. 3; 8. 15; 9. 11). Finally, in the New Testament the twofold distinction of law and the prophets is made at least a dozen times.

Several significant facts emerge from a study of the New Testament references to "the law and the prophets." First, it is a phrase inclusive of all the books in the Hebrew canon. It will be remembered (see chap. 3) that some eighteen of the twenty-two books of the Hebrew Old Testament are cited authoritatively in the New Testament (all except Judges, Chronicles, Esther, and Song of Solomon). Although there are no clear citations of these four books there are allusions to them. When Jesus said, "*All* the law and the Prophets prophesied until John" (Lk 16:16, 29, 31), He included every inspired writing prior to New Testament times in that phrase. Matthew 22:40 carries the same implication: "On these two [love] commandments depend *all* the law and the prophets." Jesus used the same phrase when stressing the comprehensive Messianic truths of the Old Testament: "beginning with Moses and all the prophets, he interpreted to them in *all the scriptures* the things concerning himself" (Lk 24:27). Luke informs us that "the law and the prophets" were read in the synagogue on the sabbath (Ac 13:15). When attempting to convince the Jews of his complete orthodoxy, the apostle Paul said that he believed "everything laid down in the law or written in the prophets" (Ac 24:14; cf. 26:22). The reference to the Old Testament as the law and the prophets in the Sermon on the Mount is crucial (Mt 5:17; cf. Rom 1:2). Jesus declared, "Think not that I am come to destroy the law and the prophets; I have come not to abolish them but to fulfill them. For truly, I say to you, till heaven and earth pass away, not an iota, not a dot, will pass from the law until *all* is accomplished" (Mt 5:17-18). Such a forceful pronouncement could scarcely refer to less than the totality of the Jewish Scriptures.

From these facts, we conclude that the standard description of the whole canon of Old Testament Scripture is built on a distinction between Moses and the prophets after him. This was begun in preexilic times and carried through consistently to the time of Christ. Since the New Testament specifically cites virtually all of the twenty-two books of the Hebrew canon recognized by first-century Jews, we also conclude that the limits or extent of that canon have been defined for us. This Hebrew canon contains all twenty-four of the books later (fifth century A.D.) listed in a threefold categorization: law, prophets, and writings. Thus, whatever the origin of the tendency to divide the nineteen "prophets" into two sections of eight "prophets and eleven writings, it is definitely not the basis for a progressive three-stage development of the canon not completed until the writings were accepted in the first century A.D.

THE DEVELOPMENT OF THE OLD TESTAMENT CANON

There is not enough data to form a complete history of the Old Testament canon. Sufficient material is available, however, to provide an overall sketch and to illustrate some crucial links. The rest must be projected as a result of the exercise of reasonable judgment. The first significant factor in the development of the Old Testament canon was the immediate and progressive collection of prophetic books. These books were preserved as divinely authoritative writings.

*The evidence of a progressive collection of prophetic books.* From the very beginning the inspired writings were collected by the people of God and revered as sacred and divinely authoritative. Moses' laws were stored by the ark in the tabernacle of God (Deu 31:24-26) and later in the temple (2 Ki 22:8). Joshua added his words "in the book of the law of God . . . and set it up . . . in the sanctuary of the LORD" (Jos 24:26). Samuel informed the Israelites of the duties of their king "and he wrote them in a book and laid it up before the LORD" (1 Sa 10:25).

Samuel headed up a school of the prophets whose disciples were called "sons of the prophets" (1 Sa 19:20). According to Ezekiel there was an official register of prophets and their writings in the temple (Eze 13:9, ASV). Daniel refers to "the books" which contained the "law of Moses" and "the prophets" (9:2, 6, 11). The writers of the books of Kings and Chronicles were aware of many books by prophets which covered the whole of preexilic history (see under "The evidence of a prophetic continuity").

This general evidence of a growing collection of prophetic books is confirmed by specific usage of the earlier prophets by later ones. The books of Moses are cited throughout the Old

Testament from Joshua (1:7) to Malachi (4:4), including most of the major books between (1 Ki 2:3; 2 Ki 14:6; 2 Ch 14:4; Jer 8:8; Dan 9:11; Ezra 6:18 and Neh 13:1). Both Joshua and events in his book are referred to in Judges (1:1, 20-21; 2:8). The books of Kings cite the life of David as it was told in the books of Samuel (see 1 Ki 3:14; 5:7; 8:16; 9:5). Chronicles review Israel's history recorded from Genesis through Kings including the genealogical link mentioned only in Ruth (1 Ch 2:12-13). Nehemiah 9 reviews Israel's history as it is recorded from Genesis to Ezra. A psalm of David, Psalm 18, is recorded in 2 Samuel 22. Reference is made to Solomon's Proverbs and Songs in 1 Kings 4:32. Daniel cites Jeremiah 25 (Dan 9:2). The prophet Jonah recites parts from many Psalms (Jon 2). Ezekiel mentions both Job and Daniel (Eze 14:14, 20). Not every prior book is cited by a later one, however; but enough are cited to demonstrate that there was a growing collection of divinely authoritative books available to and quoted by subsequent prophets.

*The evidence of a prophetic continuity.* In addition to the continuous collection of prophetic writings presented in the Old Testament there appears to be a continuity among the writings themselves. Each of the leaders in the prophetic community seems to have linked his history to that of his predecessors to produce an unbroken chain of books.

Since the last chapter of Deuteronomy does not present itself as prophecy it would seem that Moses did not write about his own funeral. It is more likely that Joshua, his God-appointed successor, recorded the death of Moses (Deu 34). The first verse of Joshua links itself to Deuteronomy saying, "After the death of Moses the servant of the Lord, the Lord spoke to Joshua the son of Nun." Joshua added to the Mosaic law and put it in the tabernacle (Jos 24:26). Judges picked up at the end of Joshua saying, "After the death of Joshua the sons of Israel inquired of the Lord," but the record was not completed until Samuel's time. This is repeatedly shown by the statement, "*In those days* there was no king in Israel" (Judg 17:6; 18:1; 19:1; 21:25).

At this point the prophetic continuity was established in a school directed by Samuel (1 Sa 19:20). From its ranks came a

series of prophetic books which cover the entire history of the
kings of Israel and Judah, as the following sample illustrates:

1. The history of David was written by Samuel (cf. 1 Sa),
Nathan, and Gad (1 Ch 29:29),

2. The history of Solomon was recorded by the prophets Nathan,
Ahijah, and Iddo (2 Ch 9:29),

3. The acts of Rehoboam were written by Shemaiah and Iddo
(2 Ch 12:15),

4. The history of Abijah was added by the prophet Iddo (2 Ch
13:22),

5. The story of Jehoshaphat's reign was recorded by Jehu the
prophet (2 Ch 20:34),

6. The reign of Hezekiah was written by Isaiah (2 Ch 32:32),

7. The life of Manasseh was recorded by unnamed prophets
(2 Ch 33:19),

8. The other kings also have their histories recorded by prophets
(2 Ch 35:27).

Anyone familiar with the biblical books which cover the period
from David to the Exile will see that the prophetic books listed
above are not identical with the Samuels, Kings, and Chronicles.
Each time a cue is given in the repeated phrase, "and the *rest* of
the acts" of king so-and-so are written "in the book" of prophet
such-and-such. The biblical books appear to be prophetic abridge-
ments edited out of the more complete histories recorded by the
prophetic succession beginning with Samuel.

It is interesting to note that Jeremiah, who wrote just prior to
and during the Jewish Exile, is not mentioned as having written
one of these histories. Yet Jeremiah was a writing prophet, as his
books (Jeremiah and Lamentations) indicate, and as he explicitly claims on numerous occasions (cf. Jer 30:2; 36:1, 2; 45:1-2;
51:60, 63). In fact the scribe Baruch tells us that Jeremiah had
secretarial help. Speaking of Jeremiah, he confessed, "He dictated
all these words to me, while I wrote them with ink on a scroll"
(Jer 36:18; see also 45:1). Further, the last chapter of the Kings
parallels the material of Jeremiah 52, 39, 40 and 41. This is still
another indication that Jeremiah was responsible for both books.
Later in the Exile, Daniel claims to have had access to the books
of Moses and the prophets. From them he not only names Jere-

miah but quotes his prediction of the seventy-year captivity from chapter 25 (cf. Dan 9:2, 6, 11). On the basis of these facts, it is reasonable to suppose that the abridgment of the prophetic writings which took the form of the biblical books of the Kings was the work of Jeremiah. Thus, the continuity of the preexilic prophets from Moses, Joshua, and Samuel would be completed with the works of Jeremiah.

During the Exile, Daniel and Ezekiel continued the prophetic ministry. Ezekiel vouched to an official register of prophets in the temple records. He declared that false prophets "shall not be in the council of my people, neither shall they be written in the register of the house of Israel" (Eze 13:9, ASV margin). Ezekiel referred to Daniel by name as a noted servant of God (Eze 14:14, 20). Since Daniel possessed a copy of the books of Moses and the prophets, including Jeremiah's book, we may reasonably assume that the Jewish community in the Babylonian Exile possessed Genesis through Daniel.

After the Exile, Ezra the priest returned from Babylon with the books of Moses and the prophets (Ezra 6:18; Neh 9:14, 26-30). In the Chronicles he undoubtedly carried his own priestly account of the history of Judah and the temple (see Neh 12:23). Chronicles is connected with Ezra-Nehemiah by the repetition of the last verse of one as the first verse of the other.

With Nehemiah the chronology of prophetic continuity is complete. Each prophet from Moses through Nehemiah contributed to the growing collection which was preserved by the official prophetic community stemming from Samuel. As with the prophetic continuity, the canon of prophetic writings is complete with Nehemiah. All twenty-two (twenty-four) books of the Hebrew Scriptures are written by the prophets, preserved by the prophetic community, and recognized by the people of God. So far there is no evidence to demonstrate that other books, called "the writings," were written and canonized after this time (c. 400 B.C.).

*The evidence that the Old Testament canon was completed with the prophets.* To this point we have indicated that the complete Hebrew Testament was collected in two main sections: the five books of Moses and the seventeen (or nineteen) prophets who followed him. We have also shown that there was a continuity in those of prophetic writings, with each prophet making authoritative use of the former prophets and adding his contribution to the growing collection of sacred writings. By the time of Nehemiah (c. 400 B.C.) this prophetic succession had produced and collected the twenty-two books of the Hebrew canon. We must now substantiate this last point and show that no third section of the canon was written and recognized after this time. Briefly, the evidence is as follows:

1. The so-called Council of Jamnia (c. A.D. 90), at which time this third section of writings is alleged to have been canonized, has not been explored. There was no council held with authority for Judaism. It was only a gathering of scholars. This being the case, there was no authorized body present to make or recognize the canon. Hence, no canonization took place at Jamnia.

2. The book of Daniel, said by the higher critics to belong in the writings section because it was supposed to be a late (second century B.C.) and nonprophetic book, was clearly listed among the books of the prophets by Josephus. Of the twenty-two books, said Josephus, only four books, probably Job, Psalms, Proverbs and Ecclesiastes, were in the third section. Daniel, being one of the other books, must have been listed with the prophets by Josephus. Both the discovery of an early fragment of Daniel among the Dead Sea Scrolls (see chap. 12) and the reference by Jesus to Daniel the prophet confirm this position.

3. The New Testament cites almost every book of the Hebrew canon, including those called writings. Nevertheless, it clearly lists them all under the twofold classification of law and prophets (cf. Mt 5:17; Mk 13:11 and Lk 24:27).

4. The book of Psalms, listed in the third section by Josephus, was clearly part of the prophets. Jesus used the phrase, "the law of Moses and the prophets and the psalms" as a parallel to the phrase "Moses and all the prophets" (Lk 24:27, 44). Jesus spoke to the Jews and quoted a psalm as what is "written in your *law*" (Jn 10:34-35), and then He identified it as the Scripture and the Word of God. All this clearly indicates that the Psalms were part of the canonical Jewish Scriptures known as "the Law and the Prophets." Indeed, the New Testament authoritatively quotes the

Psalms as Scripture more than any other book in the Old Testament. This too verifies that they were held to be canonical before A.D. 100.

5. According to both Josephus (*Against Apion.* I. 8) and the Talmud, the succession of prophets ended in Nehemiah's day with Malachi. The Talmud records, "After the latter prophets Haggai, Zechariah, and Malachi, the Holy Spirit departed from Israel." In addition, the New Testament never quotes any book as authoritative after the time of Malachi.

Our investigation shows that as far as the evidence is concerned, the canon of the Old Testament was completed about 400 B.C. There were two main sections: the law and the prophets. Virtually all twenty-two (twenty-four) books in both sections are cited as Scripture by the New Testament. There is no scriptural nor historical support for the theory that a third division, known as "the writings," awaited canonization at a later date. Instead, the inspired books were brought into the canon as law and prophets. This *canonization* was a twofold process. Whatever the factors are which led to subsequent or parallel threefold *categorization* of these Old Testament books, this much seems clear—the complete canon of the Old Testament is consistently referred to as the law and the prophets.

# 8

# THE EXTENT OF THE
# OLD TESTAMENT CANON

THE INITIAL ACCEPTANCE of the twenty-two books (same as our thirty-nine) of the Hebrew Scriptúres did not settle the issue once and for all. Later scholars who were not always fully aware of the facts of the original acceptance raised questions about the canonicity of certain books. The discussion gave rise to a technical terminology. The biblical books which were accepted by all were called "homologoumena" (lit., to speak as one). Those biblical books which were on occasion questioned by some were labeled "antilegomena" (to speak against). Those nonbiblical works rejected by all were entitled "pseudepigrapha" (false writings). A fourth category, comprised of nonbiblical books which were (are) accepted by some but rejected by others, includes the disputed books of the "apocrypha" (hidden, or doubtful). Our discussion will follow this fourfold classification.

## THE BOOKS ACCEPTED BY ALL—HOMOLOGOUMENA

The canonicity of some books was never seriously challenged by any of the great rabbis within the Jewish community. Once these books were accepted by God's people as being from the hand of the prophet of God, they continued to be recognized as divinely authoritative by subsequent generations. Thirty-four of the thirty-nine books of the Old Testament may be classed as homologoumena. This includes every book except Song of Solomon, Ecclesiastes, Esther, Ezekiel, and Proverbs. Since none of these books has been seriously disputed, our attention may be turned to the other books.

86

### THE BOOKS REJECTED BY ALL—PSEUDEPIGRAPHA

A large number of spurious religious writings which circulated in the ancient Jewish community are known as the pseudepigrapha. Not everything in these pseudepigraphal writings is false. In fact, most of them arose from within the context of a religious 'fantasy or tradition which has its source in some truth. Frequently the origin of these writings was spiritual speculation on something not explicitly covered in canonical Scripture. The speculative traditions about the patriarch Enoch no doubt lay at the root of the Book of Enoch. Likewise, curiosity about the death and glorification of Moses is undoubtedly behind the Assumption of Moses. Such speculation, however, does not mean that there are no truths in these books. On the contrary, the New Testament refers to truths embodied in both of these books (see Jude 14, 15), and even makes allusion to the Penitence of Jannes and Jambres (2 Ti 3:8). Nonetheless these books are not cited authoritatively as Scripture. Like the quotations of Paul from the non-Christian poets Aratus (Ac 17:28), Menander (1 Co 15:33), and Epimenides (Titus 1:12), it is only a truth contained in the book which is verified by its citation and not the authority of the book itself. Truth is truth no matter where it is found, whether it is uttered by a heathen poet, a pagan prophet (Num 24:17), a dumb animal (Num 22:28), or even a demon (Ac 16:17).

You will observe that no formula such as "it is written" or "the Scriptures say" is used in referring to these pseudepigraphal works. Perhaps the most dangerous thing about these false writings is the fact that the elements of truth are presented in words of divine authority in a context of religious fancy which usually contains some theological heresy. It is important to remember that it is only the truth quoted, and not the book as such, that is given divine authority in the New Testament.

### THE NATURE OF THE PSEUDEPIGRAPHA

The Old Testament pseudepigrapha contain the extremes of Jewish religious fancy expressed between 200 B.C. and A.D. 200. Some books are theologically harmless (e.g., Psalm 151), while others contain historical errors and outright heresy. The genuineness of these books is particularly challenged, since it is claimed that they were written by biblical authors. The pseudepigrapha reflect the literary style of a period long after the close of the prophetic writings, and most of the books imitate the apocalyptic format of Ezekiel, Daniel, and Zechariah—speaking of dreams, visions, and revelations. Unlike these prophets, however, the religious fancy of pseudepigrapha often becomes magical. Overall, the pseudepigrapha depicts a bright Messianic future of rewards for those who engage in lives of suffering and self-denial. Beneath the surface there is often an innocent albeit misguided religious motive. But the false claim to divine authority, the highly fanciful character of the events and the questionable (even heretical) teachings have led the Jewish fathers to consider them spurious. As a result they have correctly received the label "pseudepigrapha."

THE NUMBER OF THE PSEUDEPIGRAPHA

The standard collection of the pseudepigrapha contains seventeen books. Add to this Psalm 151 which is found in the Septuagint Version of the Old Testament, and the principal list is as follows:

| Legendary | 1. The Book of Jubilee |
| | 2. The Letter of Aristeas |
| | 3. The Book of Adam and Eve |
| | 4. The Martyrdom of Isaiah |
| Apocalyptic | 1. 1 Enoch |
| | 2. The Testament of the Twelve Patriarchs |
| | 3. The Sibylline Oracle |
| | 4. The Assumption of Moses |
| | 5. 2 Enoch, or the Book of the Secrets of Enoch |
| | 6. 2 Baruch, or The Syriac Apocalypse of Baruch* |
| | 7. 3 Baruch, or The Greek Apocalypse of Baruch |
| Didactical | 1. 3 Maccabees |
| | 2. 4 Maccabees |
| | 3. Pirke Aboth |
| | 4. The Story of Ahikar |

| Poetical | 1. The Psalms of Solomon |
| | 2. Psalm 151 |
| Historical | 1. The Fragment of a Zadokite Work |

*1 Baruch is listed in the Apocrapha (see p. 93).

This list is by no means complete. Other books are known, including some interesting ones brought to light with the Dead Sea Scroll discoveries. Among those are the Genesis Apocryphon and the War of the Sons of Light Against the Sons of Darkness, etc. (see chap. 12).

## THE BOOKS DISPUTED BY SOME—THE ANTILEGOMENA

### THE NATURE OF THE ANTILEGOMENA

Of more interest to our study are the books which were originally and ultimately received as canonical but which were subjected to rabbinical debate in the process. The previous chapter revealed how all of the thirty-nine books of the Old Testament were initially accepted by the people of God from His prophets. During the centuries which followed, a different school of thought developed within Judaism which debated, among other things, the canonicity of certain books which had previously been received into the Old Testament. Ultimately these books were retained in the canon, as their original status prevailed. Nevertheless, because these books were at one time or another spoken against by some rabbi, they are called the Antilegomena.

### THE NUMBER OF THE ANTILEGOMENA

The canonicity of five Old Testament books was questioned at one time or another by some teacher within Judaism: Song of Solomon, Ecclesiastes, Esther, Ezekiel, and Proverbs. Each was questioned for a different reason, but in the end the divine authority of each was vindicated.

*Song of Solomon.* There were some within the school of Shammai which thought this canticle to be *sensual.* In an apparent attempt to cover over the controversy and defend the canonicity of the Song, Rabbi Akiba wrote,

God forbid!—No man in Israel ever disputed about the Song of
Songs That it does not render the hands unclean [i.e., is not
canonical], for all the ages are not worthy the day on which the
Song of Songs was given to Israel; for all the Writings are holy,
but the Song of Songs is the Holy of Holies.[1]

As others have observed, the very fact of such a statement indicates that someone had doubted the purity of the book. Whatever
doubts were centered in the alleged sensual character of the Song
of Solomon were misdirected. It is more likely that the purity
and nobility of marriage is part of the essential purpose of the
book. Whatever the questions about the various interpretations,
there should be no doubt about its inspiration, once it is viewed in
a proper spiritual perspective.

*Ecclesiastes.* The objection sometimes leveled against this book
is that it seems *skeptical.* Some have even called it the "Song of
Skepticism." Rabbi Akiba admitted that "if aught was in dispute
the dispute was about Ecclesiastes alone [and not about the
Song]."[2] There is little question about the occasional skeptical
*sound* of the book: "Vanity of vanities! All is vanity . . . there is
nothing new under the sun . . . For in much wisdom is vexation,
and he who increases knowledge increases sorrow" (Ec 1:1, 9,
18). What is overlooked when the charge of skepticism is made
is both the context of these statements and the general conclusion
of the book. A man seeking ultimate satisfaction "under the sun"
will certainly feel the same frustrations that Solomon felt, for
eternal happiness is not found in this temporal world. Moreover,
the conclusion and general teaching of the entire book is far from
skeptical. When "all has been heard," the reader is admonished,
"Fear God, and keep his commandments; for this is the whole duty
of man" (Ec 12:13). In Ecclesiastes, as in the Song, the basic
problem is one of interpretation and not of inspiration or canonization.

*Esther.* Because of the conspicuous absence of the name of God
in this book, some have thought it to be unspiritual. They ask,
how can a book be the Word of God when it does not even bear
His name? In addition, the story of the book seems to be purely

1. Herbert Danby, *The Mishnah,* (Oxford: Oxford U., 1933), p. 782.
2. Ibid.

secular in nature. As a result, several attempts have been made to explain the phenomenon of God's apparent absence in the book of Esther. Some have suggested that the Persian Jews, not being in the theocratic line, did not have the name of the covenant God associated with them. Others have argued that the omission of the name of God is intentional to protect the book from the possibility of a pagan plagiarism by the substitution of the name of a false god. Still others see the name of Jehovah or Yahweh (YHWH) in an acrostic at four crucial points in the story in such a way as to eliminate chance. Whatever the explanation, this much is obvious, the absence of the name of God is overshadowed by the presence of God in the preservation of His people. Esther and her companions were deeply devout: a religious fast was held, and Esther exercised great faith (Est 4:16). The fact that God granted His people deliverance in the book serves as the basis for the Jewish Feast of Purim (Est 9:26-28). This alone is sufficient indication of the authority ascribed to the book within Judaism.

*Ezekiel.* There were those within the rabbinical school who thought the book of Ezekiel was anti-Mosaic in its teaching. The school of Shammai, for example, felt that the book was not in harmony with the Mosaic law and that the first ten chapters exhibited a tendency toward Gnosticism. If there were actual contradictions then the book, of course, could not be canonical. However, no specific examples of contradictions with the Torah were provided. Here again it seems to be a question of interpretation rather than inspiration.

*Proverbs.* The dispute over Proverbs centered about the fact that some of the teachings within the book seemed incompatible with other proverbs. Speaking of this alleged internal inconsistency, the Talmud says, "The book of Proverbs also they sought to hide, because its words contradicted one to another" (Tractate "Shabbath," 30b). One supposed contradiction is found in chapter twenty-six, where the reader is exhorted both "to answer a fool according to his folly" and not to do so (Pr 26:4-5). But, as other rabbis have observed, the meaning here is that there are occasions when a fool should be answered according to his folly and other times when he should not. Since the statements are in successive verse, a legitimate form of Hebrew poetry, the composers obviously saw no contradiction. The qualifying phrase which indicates whether one should or should not answer a fool clearly reveals that the situations calling for different answers are not the same. No contradiction exists in Proverbs 26, none has been demonstrated elsewhere in Proverbs, and hence nothing stands in the way of its canonicity.

## The Books Accepted by Some—Apocrypha

The most crucial area of disagreement on the Old Testament canon among Christians is the debate over the so-called Apocrypha. In brief these books are accepted by Roman Catholics as canonical and rejected in Protestantism and Judaism. In point of fact, the meanings of the word *apocrypha* reflect the problem manifest in the two views on its canonicity. In classical Greek, the word *apocrypha* meant "hidden" or "hard to understand." Later it took on the connotation of *esoteric*, or something understood only by the initiated and not an outsider. By the times of Irenaeus and Jerome (third and fourth centuries) the term *apocrypha* came to be applied to the noncanonical books of the Old Testament, including what was previously classified as pseudepigrapha. Since the Reformation era, the word has been used to denote the noncanonical Jewish religious literature coming from the intertestamental period. The issue before us is to determine whether the books were hidden in order to be preserved, because their message was deep and spiritual, or because they were spurious and of doubtful authenticity.

### THE NATURE AND NUMBER OF THE OLD TESTAMENT APOCRYPHA

There are fifteen books in the Apocrypha (fourteen if the Letter of Jeremiah is combined with Baruch, as it is in Roman Catholic Douay versions). With the exception of 2 Esdras, these books bridge the gap between Malachi and Matthew and specifically cover the two or three centuries before Christ. Their dates and classification are as follows:

| TABLE OF BOOKS OF APOCRYPHA | | |
|---|---|---|
| Type of Book | Revised Standard Version | Douay |
| Didactic | 1. The Wisdom of Solomon (c. 30 B.C.) | Book of Wisdom |
| | 2. Ecclesiasticus (Sirach) (132 B.C.) | Ecclesiasticus |
| Religious | 3. Tobit (c. 200 B.C.) | Tobias |
| Romance | 4. Judith (c. 150 B.C.) | Judith |
| Historic | 5. 1 Esdras (c. 150-100 B.C.) | 3 Esdras* |
| | 6. 1 Maccabees (c. 110 B.C.) | 1 Machabees |
| | 7. 2 Maccabees (c. 110-70 B.C.) | 2 Machabees |
| Prophetic | 8. Baruch (c. 150-50 B.C.) | Baruch chaps. 1-5 |
| | 9. Letter of Jeremiah (c. 300-100 B.C.) | Baruch chap. 6 |
| | 10. 2 Esdras (c. A.D. 100) | 4 Esdras* |
| Legendary | 11. Additions to Esther (140-130 B.C.) | Esther 10:4—16:24† |
| | 12. Prayer of Azariah (second or first century B.C.) (Song of Three Young Men) | Daniel 3:24-90† |
| | 13. Susanna (second or first century B.C.) | Daniel 13† |
| | 14. Bel and the Dragon (c. 100 B.C.) | Daniel 14† |
| | 15. Prayer of Manasseh (second or first century B.C.) | Prayer of Manasseh* |

*Books not accepted as canonical at the Council of Trent, 1546.
†Books not listed in Douay table of contents because they are appended to other books.

THE ARGUMENTS FOR ACCEPTING THE OLD TESTAMENT APOCRYPHA

The Old Testament Apocrypha have received varying degrees of acceptance by Christians. Most Protestants and Jews accept them as having religious and even historical value but not canonical authority. Roman Catholics since the Council of Trent have held these books to be canonical. More recently Roman Catholics have defended a sort of deuterocanonicity, but the Apocrypha is still used to support extrabiblical doctrines and was proclaimed divinely inspired at Trent. Other groups, such as Anglicans and the various Orthodox churches, have views of varying respect for the Apocrypha. The following is a summary of the arguments generally advanced for accepting these books as having some kind of canonical status.

1. *New Testament allusions.* The New Testament reflects the thought of and records some events from the Apocrypha. Hebrews, for instance, speaks of women receiving their dead by resurrection (Heb 11:35), and makes reference to 2 Maccabees 7 and 12. The so-called wider Apocrypha or Pseudepigrapha are also cited by the New Testament (Jude 14-15; 2 Ti 3:8).

2. *New Testament usages of the Septuagint.* The Greek translation of the Hebrew Old Testament made at Alexandria is known as the Septuagint (LXX). It is the version most often cited by New Testament writers, for it was in many respects the Bible of the apostles and early Christians. The LXX contained the Apocrypha. The presence of these books in the LXX supports the broader Alexandrian canon of the Old Testament as opposed to the narrower Palestinian canon which omits them.

3. *The earliest complete manuscripts of the Bible.* The earliest Greek manuscripts of the Bible contain the Apocrypha interspersed among the Old Testament books. Manuscripts *Aleph* (א), A, and B (see chap. 12) all include these books, revealing that they were part of the early Christian Bible.

4. *Early Christian art.* Some of the earliest records of Christian art reflect usage of the Apocrypha. Catacomb scenes sometimes draw on the history of the faithful recorded in the intertestamental period.

5. *The early church Fathers.* Some of the very early church Fathers, particularly in the West, accepted and used the Apocrypha in their teaching and preaching. Even in the East, however, Clement of Alexandria recognized 2 Esdras as fully canonical. Origen added Maccabees as well as the Letter of Jeremiah to

his canonical list. Irenaeus quoted from the Book of Wisdom, and other Fathers cited other apocryphal books.

6. *The influence of St. Augustine.* St. Augustine (c. 354-430) brought the wider Western tradition about the Apocrypha to its culmination by giving to them canonical status. He influenced the church councils at Hippo (A.D. 393) and Carthage (A.D. 397) which listed the Apocrypha as canonical. From this time the western Church used the Apocrypha in public worship.

7. *The Council of Trent.* In 1546 the post-Reformation Roman Catholic Council of Trent proclaimed the Apocrypha as canonical, declaring,

> The Synod . . . receives and venerates . . . all of the books both of the Old and of the New Testament [including Apocrypha]— seeing that one God is the Author of both . . . as having been dictated, either by Christ's own word of mouth or by the Holy Ghost . . . if anyone receives not as sacred and canonical the said books entire with all their parts, as they have been used to be read in the Catholic Church . . . let him be anathema.[3]

Since the Council of Trent, the books of the Apocrypha have had binding and canonical authority in the Roman Catholic Church.

8. *Non-Catholic usage.* Protestant Bibles even since the Reformation have often contained the Apocrypha. Indeed, in Anglican churches the Apocrypha is read regularly along with the other books of the Old and New Testaments in public worship. The Apocrypha is also used by churches in the Eastern Orthodox tradition.

9. *The Dead Sea community.* Books of the Apocrypha were found among the scrolls of the Dead Sea community at Qumran. Some of these books were written in Hebrew, indicating their use among Palestinian Jews even before the time of Christ.

In summary argument, this position argues that the widespread employment of the Apocrypha by Christians from the earliest centuries is evidence of its acceptance by the people of God. This long tradition was culminated by an official recognition of these books as inspired and canonical by the Council of Trent (1546).

3. Philip Schaff, ed., *The Creeds of Christendom*, 6th ed. rev. (New York: Harper, 1919), 2:81.

Even non-Catholics to date give something of a quasicanonical status to the Apocrypha, as indicated by the place they give them in their Bibles and in the churches.

REASONS FOR REJECTING THE CANONICITY OF THE APOCRYPHA

The opponents of the Apocrypha have offered many reasons for excluding it from the canon. These arguments will be reviewed in the same order as those presented by the advocates of the larger canon.

1. *New Testament authority.* The New Testament never cites an apocryphal book as inspired. Allusions to these books lend no more authority to them than do the New Testament references to the pagan poets. Further, since the New Testament quotes from virtually every canonical book of the Old Testament and verifies the contents and limits of the Old Testament (omitting the Apocrypha—see chap. 7), it seems clear that the New Testament definitely excludes the Apocrypha from the Hebrew canon. Josephus, the Jewish historian, expressly rejects the Apocrypha by listing only twenty-two canonical books.

2. *The Septuagint translation.* Palestine was the home of the Jewish canon, not Alexandria, Egypt. The great Greek learning center in Egypt was no authority in determining which books belonged in the Jewish Old Testament. Alexandria was the place of translation, not of canonization. The fact that the Septuagint contains the Apocrypha only proves that the Alexandrian Jews translated the other Jewish religious literature from the intertestamental period along with the canonical books. Philo, the Alexandrian Jew, clearly rejected the canonicity of the Apocrypha at the time of Christ as does official Judaism at other places and times. In fact, the extant copies of the LXX date from the fourth century A.D. and do not prove what books were in LXX of earlier times.

3. *The early Christian Bible.* The early Greek manuscripts of the Bible date from the fourth century. They follow the LXX tradition which contains the Apocrypha. As was noted above, this is a Greek *translation,* not a Hebrew *canon.* Jesus and the New Testament writers quoted most often from the LXX but never once from any book of the Apocrypha. At best, the presence of

the Apocrypha in Christian Bibles of the fourth century shows only that these books were accepted to some degree by Christians at that time. It does not indicate that either the Jews or earlier Christians accepted these books as canonical, to say nothing of the universal church, which has not held them to be canonical.

5. *Early Christian art.* Artistic representations are not grounds for determining the canonicity of the Apocrypha. Catacomb scenes from the Apocrypha indicate only that believers of that period were aware of the events of the intertestamental period and considered them part of their religious heritage. Early Christian art does nothing to settle the question of the canonicity of the Apocrypha.

6. *The canon of St. Augustine.* The testimony of Augustine is neither definitive nor unequivocal. First, Augustine at times implies that the Apocrypha had only a deuterocanonicity (*City of God* 18. 36) instead of a primary canonicity. Further, the Councils of Hippo and Carthage were small local councils influenced by Augustine and the tradition of the Greek Septuagint translation. No qualified Hebrew scholars were present at either of these councils. The most qualified Hebrew scholar of the time, St. Jerome, argued strongly against Augustine in his rejecting the canonicity of the Apocrypha. Jerome refused even to translate the Apocrypha into Latin or to include it in his Latin Vulgate versions. It was not until after Jerome's day and literally over his dead body, that the Apocrypha was brought into the Latin Vulgate (see chap. 18).

7. *The Council of Trent.* The action of the Council of Trent was both polemical and prejudicial. In debates with Luther, the Roman Catholics had quoted the Maccabees in support of prayer for the dead (see 2 Mac 12:45-46). Luther and Protestants following him challenged the canonicity of that book, citing the New Testament, the early church Fathers, and Jewish teachers for support. The Council of Trent responded to Luther by canonizing the Apocrypha. Not only is the action of Trent obviously polemical, but it was also prejudicial, since not all of the fourteen (fifteen) books of the Apocrypha were accepted by Trent. One and 2 Esdras (Roman Catholic, 3 and 4 Esdras; the Douay version names the canonical books of Ezra and Nehemiah as 1 and 2

Esdras respectively) and the Prayer of Manasseh were rejected. The rejection of 2 Esdras is particularly suspect, for it contains a strong verse against praying for the dead (2 Esdras 7:105). In fact, some medieval scribe had cut this section out of the Latin manuscripts of 2 Esdras, and it was known by Arabic manuscripts until found again in Latin by Robert L. Bently in 1874 at a library in Amiens, France.

The decision at Trent did not reflect either a universal or indisputable consent within the Catholic church of the Reformation. During that very time Cardinal Cajetan, who opposed Luther at Augsburg in 1518, published a *Commentary on All the Authentic Historical Books of the Old Testament* (1532) which omitted the Apocrypha. Even before this, Cardinal Ximenes distinguished between the Apocrypha and the Old Testament canon in his *Coplutensian Polyglot* (1514-1517). With this data in view, Protestants generally reject the decision of Trent as unfounded.

8. *Non-Catholic usage.* The use of the Apocrypha among Orthodox, Anglican, and Protestant churches has been uneven. Some have used it in public worship. Many Bibles contain translations of the Apocrypha, although it is placed in a separate section, usually between the Old and New Testaments. However non-Catholics have employed the Apocrypha, they have never given to it the same canonical authority of the rest of the Bible. Instead, its use has been more devotional than canonical among non-Catholics.

9. *The Dead Sea Scrolls.* Many noncanonical books were discovered at Qumran, including commentaries and manuals. It was a library and as such it contained numerous books not believed by the community to be inspired. Since no commentaries on or authoritative quotes from the Apocrypha have been discovered at Qumran, there is no evidence to demonstrate that they held the Apocrypha to be inspired. We may assume that they did not regard the Apocrypha as canonical. Even if evidence to the contrary is found, the fact that the group was a sect which had broken off from official Judaism would mean that it was not expected to be orthodox in all its beliefs. As far as we can tell, however, they were orthodox in their view of the canonicity of the Old Testament; that is, they did not accept the canonicity of the Apocrypha.

## Summary and Conclusion

The extent of the Old Testament canon up to the time of Nehemiah comprised twenty-two (or twenty-four) books in Hebrew and relisted as thirty-nine in Christian Bibles, and was determined by the fourth century B.C. The minor disputes since that time have not changed the contents of the canon. It was the books written after this time, known as the Apocrypha, which because of the influence of the Greek translation at Alexandria, gained a wide circulation among Christians. Since some of the early Fathers, particularly in the West, made use of these books in their writings, the church (largely under the influence of Augustine) gave them a broader and ecclesiastical use. Until the time of the Reformation, however, these books were not considered canonical. Their canonization by the Council of Trent stands unsupported by history. Even that verdict was polemical and prejudiced, as shown earlier.

That these books, whatever devotional or ecclesiastical value they may possess, are not canonical is substantiated by the following facts:

1. The Jewish community has never accepted them as canonical.

2. They were not accepted by Jesus nor the New Testament writers.

3. Most great Fathers of the early church rejected their canonicity.

4. No church council held them to be canonical until the late fourth century.

5. Jerome, the great biblical scholar and translator of the Vulgate, strongly rejected the Apocrypha.

6. Many Roman Catholic scholars, even through the Reformation Period, rejected the canonicity of the Apocrypha.

7. Neither Eastern Orthodox, Anglican, nor Protestant churches to this date have recognized the Apocrypha as inspired and canonical in the full sense of the word. In view of this date it behooves Christians today not to use the Apocrypha as the Word of God, nor use it as an authoritative support for any point of doctrine.

Indeed, when examined by the criteria for canonicity set forth in chapter 6, the Apocrypha is found wanting:

1. The Apocrypha does not claim to be prophetic.

2. It does not come with the authority of God.
3. The Apocrypha contains historical errors (see Tobit 1:3-5 and 14:11) and such theological heresies as praying for the dead (2 Mac 12:45 [46]; 4).
4. The value of its contents for edification is mostly repetitious of the material already found in the canonical books.
5. There is a conspicuous absence of prophecy such as is found in the canonical books.
6. Nothing is added to our knowledge of Messianic truth by the Apocrypha.
7. The reception by the people of God to whom they were originally presented was negative.

The Jewish community has never changed this stand. Some Christians have been less definitive, but whatever value is placed upon them, it is evident that the church as a whole has never accepted the Apocrypha as canonical Scripture.

# 9

# THE DEVELOPMENT OF THE NEW TESTAMENT CANON

THE HISTORY of the New Testament canon differs from that of the Old in several respects. In the first place, since Christianity was an international religion from the beginning, there was no tightly knit prophetic community which received all inspired books and collected them in one place. Local and somewhat complete collections were made from the very beginning, but there is no evidence of a central and official clearinghouse for inspired writings. Hence, the process by which all of the apostolic writings became universally accepted took many centuries. Fortunately, because of the availability of source materials there is more data available on the New Testament canon than the Old.

Another difference between the history of the Old and New Testament canons is that once discussions resulted in the recognition of the twenty-seven canonical books of the New Testament canon, there have been no moves within Christendom to add to it or take away from it. The extent of the New Testament canon has met with general agreement within the church universal.

### THE STIMULI FOR AN OFFICIAL COLLECTION OF BOOKS

Several forces at work in the early Christian world led to an official recognition of the twenty-seven canonical books of the New Testament. Three of these forces are of special significance: the ecclesiastical, the theological, and the political.

#### THE ECCLESIASTICAL STIMULUS FOR A CANONICAL LIST

The early church had both internal and external needs for an official recognition of canonical books. From within there was the need to know which books should be read in the churches according to the practice indicated for the New Testament church by the apostles (1 Th 5:27). From outside the church was the need to know which books should be translated into the foreign languages of the converted peoples. Without a recognized list of books it would be difficult for the early church to perform either of these tasks. The combination of these forces put increasing pressure on the church Fathers to make an official list of the canonical books.

### THE THEOLOGICAL STIMULUS FOR A CANONICAL LIST

Another factor within early Christianity called for an ecclesiastical pronouncement on the canon. Since all Scripture was profitable for doctrine (2 Ti 3:16-17), it became increasingly necessary to define the limits of the apostolic doctrinal deposit. The need to know which books were to be used to teach doctrine with divine authority was made even more pressing as a result of the multitude of apocryphal and heretical books claiming divine authority. When the heretic Marcion published a sharply abridged list of canonical books (c. 140), including only the gospel of Luke and ten of Paul's epistles (omitting 1 and 2 Timothy and Titus), the need for a complete canonical list became acute. Caught in the tension between those who would add to the canon and others who would take from it, the burden fell on the early church Fathers to define precisely the limits of the canon.

### THE POLITICAL STIMULUS FOR A CANONICAL LIST

The forces for canonization culminated in the political pressures brought to bear on the early Christian church. The Diocletian persecutions (c. 302-305) provided a strong motive for the church to settle on a definitive list of canonical books. According to the Christian historian Eusebius, an imperial edict of Diocletian in 303 ordered "the destruction by fire of the Scriptures." Ironically enough, within twenty-five years the Emperor Constantine had become a convert to Christianity and ordered Eusebius to prepare and distribute fifty copies of the Bible. The persecution had occasioned a serious look at just which canonical books should be preserved, and the call for Bibles by Constantine also made an official list of canonical books necessary.

## THE PROGRESSIVE COLLECTION AND RECOGNITION OF CANONICAL BOOKS

There is evidence to indicate that the very first believers collected and preserved the inspired books of the New Testament. These books were circulated among the early churches and doubtlessly copied as well. But since no official listing was promulgated, universal recognition was delayed several centuries until the pressures had brought about the need for such a list.

### NEW TESTAMENT EVIDENCE FOR A GROWING CANON

The New Testament was written during the last half of the first century. Most of the books were written to local churches (e.g., the bulk of Paul's epistles) and some were addressed to individuals (e.g., Philemon, 2 and 3 John). Others were aimed at a broader audience, in eastern Asia (1 Peter), western Asia (Revelation) and even Europe (Romans). Some of the letters probably originated in Jerusalem (James) while others arose as far west as Rome (1 Peter). With such a geographical diversity of origin and destination it is understandable that not all the churches would immediately possess copies of all the inspired New Testament books. Add to this the problems of communication and transportation and it is easy to see that it would take some time before there was anything like a general recognition of all twenty-seven books of the New Testament canon. These difficulties notwithstanding, the early churches immediately began to make collections of whatever apostolic literature they could verify.

*Selecting authentic books.* From the very beginning there were inauthentic and nonapostolic writings in circulation. Because of some of these accounts of the life of Christ, Luke, the companion of Paul, undertook his gospel, saying, "inasmuch as many have undertaken to compile a narrative of the things which have been accomplished among us . . . it seemed good to me also . . . to write an orderly account for you, most excellent Theophilus, that you may know the truth concerning the things of which you have been informed" (Lk 1:1-4). The implication in Luke's pro-

logue is that in his day (c. A.D. 60) there were already some inaccurate accounts of Christ's life in circulation.

We know for sure that the Thessalonian Christians were warned
about any false epistles sent to them under the name of the
apostle Paul. "We beg you, brethren," he wrote, "not to be quickly
shaken in mind or excited . . . by . . . a letter purporting to be
from us, to the effect that the day of the Lord has come" (2 Th
2:2). In order to verify the authenticity of his epistle he closed
saying, "I, Paul, write this greeting with my own hand. This is
the mark in every letter of mine; it is the way I write" (2 Th 3:17).
In addition, the letter would be sent by personal envoy from the
apostle.

The apostle John further informs us that Jesus did many other
signs "which are not written in this book" (Jn 20:30), for if every
one were written, "I suppose the world itself could not contain the
books that would be written" (Jn 21:25). From the multitude of
His deeds which were not written by the apostles, there arose
many beliefs about the life of Christ which demanded apostolic
verification. While the original eyewitnesses of the life and resurrection of Christ were alive (Ac 1:21-22), everything could be
subjected to the authority of the oral teaching or tradition of the
apostles (see 1 Th 2:13; 1 Co 11:2). Some have suggested that
these eyewitness traditions of the apostles formed the *kerygma*
(literally, proclamation) which served as a sort of canon within
the canon. Whether the *kerygma* was the criterion or not, it is
clear that even the apostolic church was called upon to be selec-
tive in determining the authenticity of the many stories and
sayings about Christ. In his gospel John put to rest a false belief
circulating in the first-century church which held that he would
never die (Jn 21:23-24). The same apostle also issued a strong
warning to believers when he wrote, "Beloved, do not believe
every spirit, but test the spirits to see whether they are of God;
for many false prophets have gone out into the world" (1 Jn 4:1).

In brief, there is every indication that within the first-century
church, there was a selecting process at work. Every alleged word
about Christ, whether oral or written, was subjected to authoritative apostolic teaching. If word or work could not be verified by
those who were eyewitnesses (see Lk 1:2; Ac 1:21-22), it was

rejected. The apostles who could say, "That which we have seen and heard we proclaim also to you" (1 Jn 1:3) were the final court of appeal. As another apostle wrote, "We did not follow cleverly devised myths when we made known unto you the power and coming of our Lord Jesus Christ, but we were eyewitnesses of His majesty" (2 Pe 1:16). This primary source of apostolic authority was the canon by which the first church selected the writings through which they devoted themselves to the apostles' teaching and fellowship (Ac 2:42). Thus the living "canon" of eyewitnesses became the criterion by which the earliest canonical writings were recognized, and God Himself bore witness to the apostles (Heb 2:3-4).

*Reading authoritative books.* Another indication that the process of New Testament canonization began immediately in the first-century church was the practice of official public reading of apostolic books. Paul commanded the Thessalonians, "I adjure you by the Lord that this letter be read to all the brethren" (1 Th 5:27). Likewise, Timothy was told to present Paul's message to the churches along with the Old Testament Scriptures. "Till I come," he wrote, "attend to the public reading of the Scripture, to preaching, to teaching" (1 Ti 4:13; see also v. 11). The public reading of authoritative words from God was a practice of long standing. Moses and Joshua did it (Ex 24:7; Jos 8:34). Josiah had the Bible read to the people of his day (2 Ki 23:2) as did Ezra and the Levites when, "they read from the book, from the law of God; clearly; and they gave the sense, so that the people understood the reading" (Neh 8:8). The reading of apostolic letters to the churches is a continuation of this long prophetic tradition.

There is a significant passage on the reading of the apostolic letters in the churches. Paul wrote to the Colossians, "And when this letter has been read among you, have it read also in the church of Laodiceans" (Col 4:16). John promised a blessing for him who reads aloud this book (Rev 1:3), which he sent to seven different churches. This clearly indicates that the apostolic letters were intended to have a broader application than merely one local congregation. They were binding on all the churches, and as the churches were receiving and reading those authoritative writings they were thereby laying the foundation of a growing collection of received writings. In brief, they were involved in an incipient process of canonization. This original acceptance of a book as one authoritatively read in the churches would be crucial to later recognition of the book as canonical.

*The circulation and collection of books.* There was already in New Testament times something of a round-robin, circulated canon of inspired Scripture. At first no church possessed all the apostolic letters, but their collection grew as copies could be made and authenticated by apostolic signature or emissary. Undoubtedly the first copies of Scripture emerged from this procedure of circulating epistles. As the churches grew, the demand for copies became greater, so that more congregations could keep them for their regular readings and study along with the Old Testament Scriptures.

The Colossian passage previously cited informs us that circulation was an apostolic practice. There are also other indications of this practice. John was commanded of God, "Write what you see in a book and send it to the seven churches [of Asia Minor]" (Rev 1:11). Since it was one book and they were many churches, the book had to be circulated among them. The same is true of many of the general epistles. James is addressed to the twelve tribes in the dispersion (Ja 1:1). Peter wrote a letter to "the exiles of the dispersion in Pontus, Galatia, Cappadocia, Asia and Bithynia" (1 Pe 1:1). Some have felt that Paul's Ephesian epistle was general since the term *Ephesians* is not in the earliest manuscripts. The letter is simply addressed "to the saints who are also faithful in Christ Jesus" (Eph 1:1).

All these circulating letters reveal the beginning of a canonization process. First, the letters were obviously intended for the churches in general. Then, each church would be obliged to make copies of the letters so they would possess them for further reference and study. The commands to read and study the Scriptures in the New Testament (which include some apostolic letters) do not indicate a mere once-for-all reading. Christians were urged to continually read the Scriptures (1 Ti 4:11, 13). The only way this could be accomplished among the ever-growing number of churches was to make copies so that each church or group of churches could have its own collection of authoritative writings.

But one may wonder if there is any evidence within the New Testament that such collections were developing. Yes there is. Peter apparently possessed a collection of Paul's letters and placed them alongside the "other scriptures" (2 Pe 3:15-16). We may assume that Peter had a collection of copies of Paul's works, since there is no good reason that Peter would have possessed the original copies of Paul's epistles. After all, they were not written to Peter, but to the churches scattered throughout the world. This is indicative that other collections must have arisen to fulfill the needs of the growing churches. The fact that one writer quotes from another also indicates that letters with divine authority were collected. Jude quotes from Peter (Jude 17; see also 2 Pe 3:2), and Paul cites Luke's gospel as Scripture (1 Ti 5:18; cf., Lk 10:7). Luke assumes that Theophilus had a first book or account (Ac 1:1).

Thus, the process of canonization was at work from the very beginning. The first churches were exhorted to select only the authentic apostolic writings. When a book was verified as authentic either by signature or by apostolic envoy, it was officially read to the church and then circulated among other churches. Collections of these apostolic writings began to take form in apostolic times. By the end of the first century all twenty-seven New Testament books were written and received by the churches. The canon was complete and all the books were recognized by believers somewhere. Because of the multiplicity of false writings and the lack of immediate access to the conditions related to the initial acceptance of a book, the debate about the canon continued for several centuries, until the church universal finally recognized the canonicity of the twenty-seven books of the New Testament.

### THE CONFIRMATION OF THE OFFICIAL COLLECTION OF BOOKS

The confirmation of the canonicity of the New Testament is evidenced in several ways. Immediately after the times of the apostles, in the writings of the earliest Fathers, there is a recognition of the inspiration of all of the twenty-seven books. Supporting their witness are the early translations, canonical lists, and pronouncements of church councils. All together they provide a continuity of recognition from the very inception of the canon in the time of the apostles until the final confirmation of the universal church at the end of the fourth century.

THE WITNESS OF THE CHURCH FATHERS TO THE CANON

Just over a generation following the end of the apostolic age, every book of the New Testament had been cited as authoritative by some church Father. In fact, within about two hundred years after the first century, nearly every verse of the New Testament was cited in one or more of the over thirty-six thousand citations by the Fathers (see chap. 13). Since the patristic witness to New Testament Scripture has already been reviewed (see chap. 4), it will not be repeated here. The following chart shows exactly which Father cited what book as Scripture in the early centuries. The reader should be cautioned however that the lack of reference to a book by a Father does not necessarily imply its rejection. The argument from silence is in these cases, as it is in general, a weak one. The absence of a citation may merely indicate the lack of occasion to make one in the extant writings of the Father. To illustrate this point, the reader might ask himself when he last quoted Philemon or 3 John. Not every book of the New Testament is quoted by every Father, but every book is quoted as canonical by some Father. In the final analysis, this is sufficient to indicate that the book was recognized as apostolic from the very beginning.

THE WITNESS OF THE EARLY LISTS, AND TRANSLATIONS TO THE CANON

Other confirmations of the canon of the first century are found in the translations and canonical lists of the second and third centuries. Translations could not be made unless there was first a recognition of the books to be included in the translation.

*The Old Syriac translation.* A translation of the New Testament was circulated in Syria by the end of the fourth century which represented a text dating from the second century. It included all the twenty-seven New Testament books except 2 Peter, 2 and 3 John, Jude, and Revelation. The noted biblical scholar B. F. Westcott observed, "Its general agreement with our own [canon]

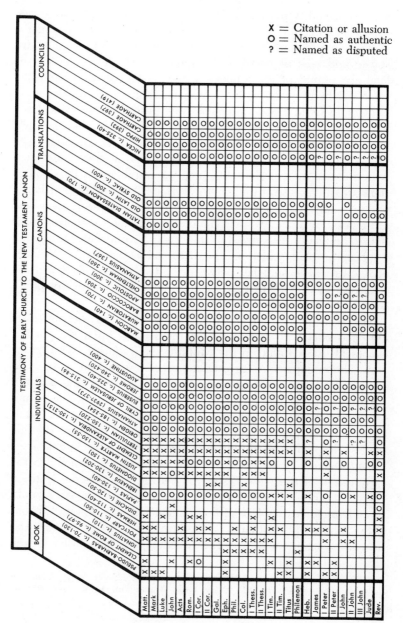

X = Citation or allusion
O = Named as authentic
? = Named as disputed

is striking and important; and its omissions admit of easy explanation."[1] The omitted books were originally destined for the Western world, and the Syriac church was in the East. The distance and lack of verifying communications slowed down the final acceptance of these books in the Eastern Bible, which had come out before that evidence was available to them.

*The Old Latin translation.* The New Testament was translated into Latin prior to 200 and served as the Bible for the early Western church, just as the Syriac version did for the East. The Old Latin version contained every book of the New Testament with the exception of Hebrews, James, 1 and 2 Peter. These omissions are the reverse of these in the Syriac Bible. Hebrews, 1 Peter, and probably James were written to churches at the Eastern end of the Mediterranean world. Hence, it took time for their credentials to be finally recognized in the West. Second Peter presented a special problem which will be discussed in chapter 10. What is of interest is the fact that between the two earliest Bibles in the Christian church there is a recognition of the canonicity of all twenty-seven New Testament books.

*The Muratorian Canon* (A.D. *170*). Aside from the obviously abridged canon of the heretic Marcion (A.D. 140), the earliest canonical list is found in the Muratorian Fragment. The list of New Testament books corresponds exactly with that of the Old Latin translation, omitting only Hebrews, James, 1 and 2 Peter. Westcott argues that there was probably a break in the manuscript which may have at one time included these books.[2] It is rather unusual that Hebrews and 1 Peter should be omitted while the less frequently cited Philemon and 3 John are included.

*Codex Barococcio (206).* Another supporting testimony to the early canon of the New Testament comes from a codex entitled "The Sixty Books." Upon careful examination these sixty books actually include sixty-four of the familiar sixty-six canonical books of the Bible. Only Esther is omitted from the Old Testament, and Revelation from the New. The canonicity of Revelation is well

---

1. Brooke Foss Westcott, *A General Survey of the History of the Canon of the New Testament,* 7th ed. (New York: Macmillan, 1896), pp. 249-50.
2. Ibid., p. 223.

attested elsewhere, being supported by Justin Martyr, Irenaeus, Clement of Alexandria, Tertullian, and the Muratorian list.

*Eusebius of Caesarea (c. 340).* The situation of the New Testament canon in the West at the beginning of the fourth century was well summarized by the historian Eusebius in his *Ecclesiastical History* (3. 25). He listed as fully accepted all of the twenty-seven New Testament books except James, Jude, 2 Peter, and 2 and 3 John. These he listed as disputed by some, while he rejected Revelation altogether. Thus all but Revelation had gained acceptance, although several of the general epistles were not without dispute.

*Athanasius of Alexandria (c. 373).* Whatever doubts existed in the West about some of the general epistles and Revelation were dispelled in the fifty years following Eusebius' work. Athanasius, the Father of Orthodoxy, clearly lists all twenty-seven books of the New Testament as canonical (*Letters* 3. 267.5). Within a generation both Jerome and Augustine had confirmed the same list of books, and these twenty-seven books remained the accepted canon of the New Testament (see Augustine, *On Christian Doctrine* 2. 8. 13).

*The councils of Hippo (393) and Carthage (397).* The supporting witness to the canon of the New Testament was not limited to individual voices. Two local councils ratified the twenty-seven canonical books of the New Testament. The variation on the Old Testament canon accepted by these councils has already been discussed in chapter 8. There is also a list from the Synod at Laodicea (343-381) which includes all except Revelation; but eleven scholars have questioned the genuineness of this list.

Since the fifth century the church has accepted these twenty-seven books as the New Testament canon. Although subsequently there have been disputes about the Old Testament, the Christian church in all of its main branches continues to this day to recognize only these twenty-seven books of the New Testament as apostolic.

To summarize, the process of collecting authentic apostolic literature began within New Testament times. In the second century, there was verification of this literature by quotation of the divine authority of each of the twenty-seven books of the New Testament. In the third century, doubts and debates over certain books culminated in the fourth century with the decisions of influential Fathers and councils. Through the centuries since that time, the Christian church has maintained the canonicity of these twenty-seven books.

# 10

# THE EXTENT OF THE
# NEW TESTAMENT CANON

PRECISELY WHICH BOOKS of the New Testament canon were in dispute in the early church? On what basis did they gain their final acceptance? What were some of the New Testament apocryphal books which hovered on the borders of the canon? These questions will provide the basis for our discussion in the present chapter.

## THE BOOKS ACCEPTED BY ALL—HOMOLOGOUMENA

Like the Old Testament, the vast majority of New Testament books were accepted by the church from the very beginning and never disputed. These are called homologoumena, because all the Fathers spoke in favor of their canonicity. The homologoumena appear in virtually all of the major translations and canons of the early church. Generally speaking, twenty of the twenty-seven books of the New Testament are homologoumena. This includes all but Hebrews, James, 2 Peter, 2 John, 3 John, Jude, and Revelation. Three more books, Philemon, 1 Peter, and 1 John, are sometimes lacking in recognition, but it is better to refer to these books as omitted rather than disputed. Since the books of the homologoumena were accepted by all, we will direct our attention to the other groups of books.

## THE BOOKS REJECTED BY ALL—PSEUDEPIGRAPHA

During the second and third centuries numerous spurious and heretical works appeared which have been called pseudepigrapha, or false writings. Eusebius called these books "totally absurd and impious."

THE NATURE OF THE PSEUDEPIGRAPHA

Virtually no Father, canon, or council pronounced any of those books canonical. So far as Christians are concerned, these books are mainly of historical interest. Their contents are heretical teachings of Gnostic, Docetic, and ascetic errors. The Gnostics were a philosophical sect claiming special knowledge into the divine mysteries. They held that matter is evil and denied the Incarnation of Christ. Docetists held to the deity of Christ but denied His humanity, saying He only appeared to be human. The ascetic Monophysites taught that Christ had only one nature, which was a fusion of the divine and human.

At best, these books were revered by some cult or were referred to by some orthodox Fathers. The mainstream of Christianity followed Eusebius and never considered them anything but spurious and impious. Like the Old Testament pseudepigrapha, these books manifested a wild religious fancy. They evidence an incurable curiosity to discover things not revealed in the canonical books (for example, about the childhood of Jesus) and display an unhealthy tendency to support doctrinal idiosyncrasies by means of pious frauds. There is perhaps a kernel of truth behind some of what is presented, but the pseudepigrapha must be carefully "demythologized" in order to discover that truth.

THE NUMBER OF THE PSEUDEPIGRAPHA

The exact number of these books is difficult to determine. By the ninth century, Photius listed some 280 of them. Since then more have been brought to light. Some of the more important pseudepigrapha and the traditions traceable to them are listed below:

GOSPELS.

1. *The Gospel of Thomas* (first century) is a Gnostic view of the alleged miracles of the childhood of Jesus.

2. *The Gospel of the Ebionites* (second century) is a Gnostic Christian perpetuation of Old Testament practices.

3. *The Gospel of Peter* (second century) is a Docetic and Gnostic forgery.

4. *Protevangelium of James* (second century) is a narration by Mary of King Herod's massacre of the babies.

5. *The Gospel of the Egyptians* (second century) is an ascetic teaching against marriage, meat, and wine.

6. *Arabic Gospel of Childhood* (?) records childhood miracles of Jesus in Egypt and the visit of Zoroastrian Magi.

7. *The Gospel of Nicodemus* (second or fifth century) contains the *Acts of Pilate* and the *Descent of Jesus*.

8. *The Gospel of Joseph the Carpenter* (fourth century) is the writing of a Monophysite cult which glorified Joseph.

9. *The History of Joseph the Carpenter* (fifth century) is a Monophysite version of Joseph's life.

10. *The Passing of Mary* (fourth century) relates the bodily assumption of Mary and shows advanced stages of Mary worship.

11. *The Gospel of Nativity of Mary* (sixth century) promotes Mary worship and forms the basis of the *Golden Legend*, a popular thirteenth-century book of lives of the saints.

12. *The Gospel of Pseudo-Matthew* (fifth century) contains a narrative about the visit to Egypt by Jesus and some of His later boyhood miracles.

13-21. *The Gospel of the Twelve, of Barnabas, of Bartholomew, of the Hebrews* (see Apocrypha), *of Marcion, of Andrew, of Mathias, of Peter, of Philip.*


Acts.

1. *The Acts of Peter* (second century) contains the legend that Peter was crucified upside down.

2. *The Acts of John* (second century) shows influence from Gnostic and Docetic teachings.

3. *The Acts of Andrew* (?) is a Gnostic story of the imprisonment and death of Andrew.

4. *The Acts of Thomas* (?) presents the mission and martyrdom of Thomas in India.

5. *The Acts of Paul* describes Paul as small, large-nosed, bald-headed, and bowlegged.

6-8. *The Acts of Mattias, of Philip, of Thaddaeus.*

EPISTLES.

1. *The Letter Attributed to Our Lord* is an alleged record of the response of Jesus to a request for healing by the king of Mesopotamia. It says He would send someone after His resurrection.

2. *The Lost Epistle to the Corinthians* (second, third century) is a forgery based on 1 Corinthians 5:9 found in a fifth-century Armenian Bible.

3. *The (6) Letters of Paul to Seneca* (fourth century) is a forgery recommending Christianity to Seneca's students.

4. *The Epistle of Paul to the Laodiceans* is a forgery based on Colossians 4:16. (We have also listed this letter under Apocrypha, p. 123.)

APOCALYPSES.

1. *The Apocalypse of Peter* (also listed under Apocrypha)
2. *The Apocalypse of Paul*
3. *The Apocalypse of Thomas*
4. *The Apocalypse of Stephen*
5. *Second Apocalypse of James*
6. *The Apocalypse of Messos*
7. *The Apocalypse of Dositheos*

These last three are third century Coptic Gnostic works found in 1946 at Nag-Hammadi, Egypt.*

SOME OTHER WORKS

1. *Secret Book of John*
2. *Traditions of Matthias*
3. *Dialogue of the Saviour*

All three of these are also from Nag-Hammadi and were unknown before 1946.

Since the great teachers and councils of the church were virtually unanimous in rejecting these books because of their inauthenticity or heresies, they are properly called pseudepigrapha. Whatever fragments of truth they preserve are obscured both by their religious fancy and heretical tendencies. The books are not only

*For an introduction to the apocalypses, see volume 1 of *New Testament Apocrypha*, ed. Edgar Hennecke and Wilhelm Schmeemelcher (Philadelphia: Westminster, 1963).

uncanonical but are not of much value for religious or devotional purposes. Their main value is historical, revealing the beliefs of their composers.

## THE BOOKS DISPUTED BY SOME—ANTILEGOMENA

According to the historian Eusebius, there were seven books whose genuineness was disputed by some church fathers and which had not yet gained universal recognition by the early fourth century. The books questioned were Hebrews, James, 2 Peter, 2 John, 3 John, Jude, and Revelation.

### THE NATURE OF THE ANTILEGOMENA

The fact that these books had not gained universal recognition by the beginning of the fourth century does not mean that they did not have an initial recognition by the apostolic and subapostolic communities. On the contrary, these books are cited as inspired by a number of the earliest sources (see chaps. 3 and 9). Nor does the fact that they were once disputed by some in the church indicate that their present place in the canon is any less firm than other books. On the contrary, the basic problem of acceptance for most of these books was not the inspiration of the book but the lack of communication between East and West with regard to their divine authority. Once the facts were known by the Fathers, the final acceptance of all twenty-seven books of the New Testament was not long coming.

#### THE NUMBER OF THE ANTILEGOMENA

Each book was disputed for its own particular reasons. A brief survey of why each book was disputed and how it was finally recognized is in order at this juncture.

*Hebrews.* Basically the anonymity of the author raised questions about Hebrews. Since the author does not identify himself and disclaims being one of the apostles (Heb 2:3), the book remained suspect among those in the West who were not aware of the authority and original acceptance of the book in the East. In addition, the fact that the heretical Montanists appealed to Hebrews to support some of their erroneous views slowed its acceptance in orthodox circles. By the fourth century, however, through the influence of Jerome and Augustine, the epistle to the Hebrews found a permanent place in the canon.

The anonymity of Hebrews kept open the question of the apostolic authority of the epistle. In time, the Western church came to accept Hebrews as Pauline and, therefore, that issue was resolved. Once the West was convinced of the apostolicity of the book, there remained no obstacle to its full and final acceptance into the canon. The contents of the book are clearly authentic as is its claim to divine authority (cf. 1:1; 2:3-4; 13:22).

*James.* The veracity of the book of James was challenged as well as its authorship. As with the book of Hebrews, the author does not claim to be an apostle. The original readers and those after them could verify whether this was the James of the apostolic circle, the brother of Jesus (cf. Ac 15, Gal 1). But the Western church did not have access to this original information. There was also the problem of the teaching on justification and works as presented in James. The supposed conflict with Paul's teaching of justification by faith plagued the book of James. Even Martin Luther called James a "right strawy epistle" and placed it at the end of his New Testament. But, as the result of the efforts of Origen, Eusebius (who personally favored James), Jerome, and Augustine, the veracity and apostolicity of the book came to be recognized in the Western church. From that time to the present, James has occupied a canonical position in Christendom. Its acceptance, of course, hinged on the understanding of its essential compatibility with the Pauline teachings on justification.

*Second Peter.* No other epistle in the New Testament had occasioned greater doubts as to its genuineness than 2 Peter. Jerome seemed to understand the problem and asserted that the hesitancy to accept it as a genuine work of the apostle Peter was due to a dissimilarity of style with 1 Peter. There are some notable differences in style between these two epistles, but the historic and linguistic problems notwithstanding, there are at present more than ample reasons to accept 2 Peter into the canon.

William F. Albright, noting the similarities to Qumran literature, dates the book before A.D. 80. This would mean that it is not a second-century fraud but a work emanating from the apostolic period. The recently discovered Bodmer manuscript

(P72) contains a copy of 2 Peter from the third century in Egypt. This discovery also reveals that 2 Peter was in use and highly respected by the Coptic Christians at that early date. Second Peter is cited by both Clement of Rome and *Pseudo-Barnabas* in the first and second centuries respectively. Then there are the testimonies of Origen, Eusebius, Jerome, and Augustine in the third through fifth centuries. In fact, there is more verification for 2 Peter than for such classics of the ancient world as the works of Herodotus and Thucydides. Finally, there is positive internal evidence for the authentication of 2 Peter. There are marked Petrine characteristics and doctrinal interests. The differences in style can be explained easily because of the use of a scribe in 1 Peter and the lack of one in 2 Peter (see 1 Pe 5:12).

*Second and 3 John.* The two shortest epistles of John were also questioned as to their genuineness. The writer identifies himself only as "the elder," and because of their anonymity and limited circulation, these epistles did not enjoy a wide acceptance, albeit they were more widely accepted than 2 Peter. Both Polycarp and Irenaeus acknowledged 2 John as authentic. The Muratorian canon and the Old Latin version contained them as well. Their similarity in style and message to 1 John, which was widely accepted, made it obvious that they were from John the apostle (cf. 1 Jn 1:1-4). Who else was so familiar to the early Asian believers that he could write authoritatively under the affectionate title of "the elder"? The term *elder* was used as a designation by other apostles (see 1 Pe 5:1), as it denoted their office (see Ac 1:20) and apostleship designated their gift (cf. Eph 4:11).

*Jude.* The authenticity of this book was questioned by some. Most of the dispute centered around the references to the pseudepigraphal Book of Enoch (Jude 14-15) and a possible reference to the Assumption of Moses (Jude 9). Origen hints at this problem in his day (*Commentary on Matthew* 18:30) and Jerome specifically declares this to be the problem (Jerome, *Lives of Illustrious Men,* chapter 4). Nevertheless, Jude was substantially recognized by the early fathers. Irenaeus, Clement of Alexandria, and Tertullian all accepted the authenticity of the book, as did the Muratorian canon. The explanation of the pseudepigraphal quotes which commends itself most is that they are not essentially differ-

ent from those citations made by Paul of the non-Christian poets
(see Ac 17:28; 1 Co 15:33; Titus 1:12). In neither case are the
books cited as authoritative, nor does the quote vouch for everything in the book—it merely cites a truth contained in the book.
The recently discovered Bodmer papyrus (P 72) confirms the use
of Jude, along with 2 Peter, in the Coptic church of the third
century.

*Revelation.* This book was labeled Antilegomena in the early
fourth century because some had challenged its authenticity. The
doctrine of chiliasm (millennialism) from Revelation 20 was a
focal point of the controversy. The debate over Revelation lasted
longer than that about any other New Testament book. It extended into the late fourth century. Strangely enough, Revelation
was one of the first books to be recognized among the writings of
the early Fathers. It was accepted by the writers of the *Didache*
and the *Shepherd,* by Papias, and by Irenaeus, as well as by the
Muratorian canon. But, when the Montanists attached their heretical teachings to the Revelation in the third century, the final acceptance of the book was considerably delayed. Dionysius, the
Bishop of Alexandria, raised his influential voice against Revelation in the mid third century. His influence waned when Athanasius, Jerome, and Augustine came to its defense. Once it became
evident that the book of Revelation was being misused by the
cults, although it originated with the apostle John (Rev 1:4; see
22:8-9), rather than with them, its final place in the canon was
secure.

In summary then, the Antilegomena books were spoken against
by some Fathers. This was usually because of a lack of communication or because of misinterpretations which had attached themselves to those books. Once the truth was known by all, they were
fully and finally accepted into the canon, just as they had been
recognized by Christians at the very beginning.

## THE BOOKS ACCEPTED BY SOME—APOCRYPHA

The distinction between the New Testament Apocrypha and
pseudepigrapha is not definitive. For the most part, the later books
were not received by any of the orthodox Fathers or churches

as canonical, whereas the apocryphal books were held in high esteem by at least one church father.

## THE NATURE OF THE NEW TESTAMENT APOCRYPHA

The New Testament Apocrypha had only at best what Alexander Souter called a "temporal and local canonicity."[1] They were accepted by a limited group of Christians for a limited time but never gained very wide or permanent recognition. The fact that these books possessed more value than the pseudepigrapha undoubtedly accounts for the higher esteem given them by Christians. There are several reasons why they are an important part of the homiletical and devotional libraries from the early church: (1) they revealed the teachings of the second-century church; (2) they provide documentation for the acceptance of the twenty-seven canonical books of the New Testament; and (3) they provide other valuable historical information about the early Christian church concerning its doctrine and liturgy.

## THE NUMBER OF THE NEW TESTAMENT APOCRYPHA

The enumeration of the New Testament Apocrypha is difficult because it depends upon the distinction made between Apocrypha and pseudepigrapha. If the criteria include acceptance by at least one of the orthodox fathers or lists of the first five centuries,** then discussion.

*The Epistle of Pseudo-Barnabas (c. 70-79).* This widely circulated first-century letter is found in the Codex Sinaiticus manuscript (Aleph) and is mentioned in the table of contents of Codex Bezae (D) as late as 550. It was quoted as Scripture by both Clement of Alexandria and Origen. Its style is similar to Hebrews, but its contents are more allegorical. Some have questioned whether it is really a first-century document. But as Westcott has said, "While the antiquity of the Epistle is firmly established, its Apostolicity is more than questionable."[2] The writer of the epistle

1. Alexander Souter, *The Text and Canon of the New Testament* (London: Duckworth, 1913), pp. 178-81.
** "Orthodox" indicates being in accordance with the teachings of the creeds and councils of the first five centuries, such as the Apostle's Creed, Nicean Creed, etc.
2. Brooke Foss Westcott, *A General Survey of the History of the Canon of the New Testament*, p. 41.

is a layman who does not claim divine authority (chap. 1), and who obviously is not the Barnabas named among the apostles of the New Testament (Ac 14:14).

*The Epistle to the Corinthians (c. 96)*. According to Dionysius of Corinth, this letter by Clement of Rome was read publicly at Corinth and elsewhere. It is also found in Codex Alexandrian (A) around 450, and Eusebius informs us that this letter had been read in many churches (*Ecclesiastical History* 3. 16). The author was probably the Clement mentioned in Philippians 4:3, but the book does not claim divine inspiration. There is a rather fanciful use made of Old Testament statements, and the apocryphal Book of Wisdom is quoted as Scripture in chapter 27. The tone of the letter is evangelical but its spirit is decidedly subapostolic. There has never been a wide acceptance of this book, and the Christian church has never recognized it as canonical.

*Ancient Homily*. The so-called *Second Epistle of Clement* (c. 120-140) was once wrongly attributed to Clement of Rome. It was known and used in the second century. In Codex Alexandrinus (A) it is placed at the end of the New Testament along with *1 Clement* and *Psalms of Solomon*. There is no evidence that this book was ever considered fully canonical. If it ever was, it certainly was not received on a large scale. The New Testament canon has excluded it to date.

*Shepherd of Hermas (c. 115-140)*. This was the most popular noncanonical book in the early church. It is found in Codex Sinaiticus (Aleph) in the table of contents of Bezae (D), in some Latin Bibles and was quoted as inspired by Irenaeus and Origen. Eusebius relates that it was read publicly in the churches and used for instruction classes in the faith. The *Shepherd* is a great Christian allegory and, like Bunyan's *Pilgrims Progress* later, it ranked second only to the canonical books in circulation in the early church. Like the *Wisdom of Sirach* (*Ecclesiastes*) of the Old Testament Apocrypha, the *Shepherd* has ethical and devotional value but was never recognized by the church as canonical. The note in the Muratorian Fragment summarizes the status of the *Shepherd* in the early church, "It ought to be read; but it cannot be publicly read in the church to the people, either among the

Prophets, since their number is complete, or among the Apostles, to the end of time."[3]

*The Didache Teaching of the Twelve (c. 100-120).* This early work was also held in high regard in the early church. Clement of Alexandria quoted it as Scripture, and Athanasius said it was used in catechetical instruction. Eusebius however, listed it among the "rejected writings," as did the major Fathers after him and the church in general. Nonetheless, the book has great historical importance as a link between the apostles and the early Fathers, with its many references to the gospels, Paul's epistles and even the Revelation. However, it was not recognized as canonical in any of the official translations and lists of the early church.

*The Apocalypse of Peter (c. 150).* This is one of the oldest of the noncanonical New Testament apocalypses and was widely circulated in the early church. It is mentioned in the Muratorian Fragment, in the table of contents of Bezae (D), and is quoted by Clement of Alexandria. Its vivid imagery of the spiritual worlds had a wide influence on medieval thought from which Dante's *Inferno* was derived. The Muratorian Fragment had questions about its authenticity, claiming that some would not permit it to be read in the churches. The church universal has never recognized it as canonical.

*The Acts of Paul and Thecla (170).* This was quoted by Origen and is in the table of contents of Codex Bezae (D). Stripped of its mythical elements, it is the story of Thecla, an Iconian lady who supposedly was converted under Paul in Acts 14:1-7. Many scholars feel that the book embodies a genuine tradition, but most are inclined to agree with Adolf von Harnack that the book contains "a great deal of fiction and very little truth." The book has never really gained anything like canonical recognition.

*Epistle to the Laodiceans (fourth century?).* This forgery was known to Jerome, but it appears in many Bibles from the sixth to the fifteenth centuries. As J. B. Lightfoot noted, "The Epistle is a

3. Henry Bettenson, *Documents of the Christian Church* (Oxford: Oxford U., 1947), p. 41.
4. J. B. Lightfoot, *Saint Paul's Epistles to the Colossians and to Philemon* (Grand Rapids: Zondervan, 1965), p. 285.

centro of Pauline phrases strung together without any definite
connection or any clear object."[1] It has no doctrinal peculiarities
and is as innocent as any forgery can be. Combined with the fact
that a book by this name appears in Colossians 4:16, these factors
no doubt account for its very late appearance in Christian circles.
Although the Council of Nicea II (787) warned against it, calling
it a "forged epistle," it reappeared in the Reformation era in German and English Bibles. Nevertheless, it has never gained canonical recognition.

A book by this name is mentioned in the Muratorian Fragment,
but some have thought this to be a reference to Ephesians or
Philemon which Paul called the "epistle from Laodicea." This
confusion has lent to the persistent reappearance of this noncanonical book, but the epistle is definitely not canonical.

*The Gospel According to the Hebrews (65-100).* This is probably the earliest extant noncanonical gospel and has survived only
in fragments found in quotations from various Fathers. According
to Jerome, some called it the true gospel, but this is questionable
since it bears little resemblance to the canonical Matthew, for it is
in many respects more pseudepigraphal than apocryphal in nature.
Its usage by the Fathers was probably largely homiletical, and it
never gained anything like canonical status.

*Epistle of Polycarp to the Philippians (c. 108).* Polycarp, the
disciple of John the apostle and the teacher of Irenaeus, is an
important link with the first-century apostles. Polycarp laid no
claim to inspiration, but said that he only taught the things he
had learned from the apostles. There is very little originality in
this epistle, as both the content and style is borrowed from the
New Testament, and particularly from Paul's epistle to the Philippians. Even though Polycarp's work is not canonical, it is a most
valuable source of information about many other New Testament
books which he cites as canonical.

*The Seven Epistles of Ignatius (c. 110).* These letters reveal
a definite familiarity with the teachings of the New Testament,
especially the Pauline epistles. The style of the letters, however,
is more Johannine. Irenaeus quotes from the epistle to the
Ephesians, and Origen quotes from both the epistle to the Romans
and the epistle to the Ephesians. Ignatius, whom tradition claims

was a disciple of John, does not claim to speak with divine authority. To the Ephesians, for instance, he writes, "I do not issue orders to you, as if I were some great person. . . . I speak to you as fellow-disciples with me" (chap. 3). The letters are no doubt genuine but not apostolic and therefore not canonic. Such has been the consent of the Christian church through the years. The genuine writings from the subapostolic period are most helpful from a historical point of view, for they reveal the state of the church and the recognition of canonical books of the New Testament.

We may summarize by saying that the vast majority of the New Testament books were never disputed from the beginning. Of the books originally recognized as inspired but later questioned, all of them came to full and final acceptance by the universal church. Some other books which enjoyed wide usage and were included in local lists for a time were valuable for devotional and homiletical use but never gained canonical recognition by the church. Only the twenty-seven books of the New Testament are known to be genuinely apostolic. Only these twenty-seven have found a permanent place in the New Testament canon.

# 11

# LANGUAGES AND MATERIALS OF THE BIBLE

To THIS POINT our study has centered around the first two links in the chain from God to us. The first, inspiration, involved the giving and recording of God's revelation to man by the prophets. The second, canonization, involved the recognition and collection of the prophetic records by the people of God. In order to share these records with new believers and with future generations, it was necessary to copy, translate, recopy, and retranslate them. This procedure is the third link in the chain of communication, and it is known as the transmission of the Bible.

Since the Bible has undergone nearly two thousand years of transmission, it is reasonable to ask if the twentieth-century English Bible is an accurate reproduction of the Hebrew and Greek texts. In short, how much has the Bible suffered in the process of transmission? In order to address this issue, it will be necessary to look into the science of textual criticism (see chaps. 14 and 15), which includes the languages and materials of the Bible as well as the manuscript evidence itself (see chaps. 12 and 13).

### THE IMPORTANCE OF WRITTEN LANGUAGES

#### ALTERNATIVE MEANS OF COMMUNICATION

Several alternatives were open to God in His choice of a means of communicating His truth to men (Heb 1:1). He could have used any one or more of the media employed on various occasions in biblical times. For example, God used angels throughout the Bible (see Gen 18-19; Rev 22:8-21). The lot and the Urim and Thummim were also employed to determine God's will (Ex

126

28:30; Pr 16:33), as were the voices of conscience (Ro 2:15) and creation (Ps 19:1-6). In addition, God used audible voices (1 Sa 3) and direct miracles (Judg 6:36-40).

All these media suffered from some shortcoming. The sending of an angel to deliver each message of God to every man in every situation, or the use of audible voices and direct miracles would be both cumbersome and repetitive. The use of the lot or the simple yes-or-no answer of the Urim and Thummim were too limited in scope when compared with the detailed descriptions available in other media of communication. On occasion, some means were too subjective and open to distortion or cultural corruption, as in the case of visions, dreams, and the voices of conscience or creation. This situation is especially true when compared to the more objective means of communication available in written language.

LANGUAGE IN GENERAL

It would be incorrect to say that any or all of these media were not good, for they were in fact the various means by which God spoke to the prophets. Nevertheless, there was "a more excellent way" to communicate to the men of all ages through the prophets. God chose to make permanent and immortalize His message to men by means of a written record. This way was more precise, more permanent, more objective, and more easily disseminated than any other media He utilized.

*Precision.* One of the advantages of written language over other media is its precision. For a thought to be apprehended and expressed in writing, it must have been clearly understood by its author. In addition, the reader can understand more precisely the thought transmitted through written expression. Since mankind's most treasured knowledge to date is preserved in the form of written records and books, it is understandable that God should choose to convey His truth to man in the same manner.

*Permanence.* Another advantage of written language is the matter of its permanence. It provides a means whereby a thought or expression can be preserved rather than lost through lapse of memory or vacillation of thought into other realms. In addition, a written record stimulates the reader's memory and stirs his

imagination to include a host of personal implications latent in
the words or symbols of the record. Words are not so wooden as
to prevent personal enrichment for the reader.

*Objectivity.* The transmission of a communication in written
form also tends to make it more objective. A written expression
carries with it a note of finality not inherent in other modes of
communication. This finality transcends the subjectivity of each
individual reader, thus complementing the precision and permanence of the message disseminated. In addition, it militates
against misinterpretation and mistransmission of the message.

*Dissemination.* Still another advantage of written language
over some other media of communication is its ability to be prop-
agated, or disseminated. No matter how carefully an oral communication is related, there is always a greater chance for corruption and alteration than with recorded words. In short, oral
tradition has tended to corrupt rather than to preserve a message.
In the propagation of His revelation to mankind, especially for
future generations, God chose a more accurate means of transmitting His Word.

BIBLICAL LANGUAGES IN PARTICULAR

The languages used in recording God's revelation in the Bible
come from the Semitic and Indo-European families of languages.
The Semitic family provided the basic languages of the Old
Testament in Hebrew and Aramaic (Syriac). In addition to them,
Latin and Greek represent the Indo-European family. Indirectly,
the Phoenicians played a role in the transmission of the Bible by
providing the basic vehicle which made written language less
cumbersome than it had been previously, namely the alphabet.

*Old Testament Languages.* Aramaic was the language of the
Syrians and was used throughout the Old Testament period. During the sixth century B.C. it became the basic language of the entire
Near East. Its widespread use is reflected in the place names and
text portions of Ezra 4:7—6:18; 7:12-26; and Daniel 2:4—7:28.

Hebrew is the primary language of the Old Testament, and it
is particularly suited for its task of relating the biography of
God's people and His dealings with them. It is suited for this task
because Hebrew is a *pictorial* language. It speaks with vivid, bold

metaphors which challenge and dramatize the narrative of events. In addition, Hebrew is a *personal* language. It addresses itself to the heart and emotions rather than to the mind and reason alone. It is a language through which the message is felt rather than merely thought.

*New Testament Languages.* The Semitic languages were also used in the New Testament. In fact, Jesus and the disciples used it as their native tongue, since Aramaic had become the spoken language of Palestine by that time. During His agony on the cross Jesus cried out in Aramaic, " '*Eli, Eli, lama sabachthani?*', that is to say, 'My God, my God, why hast thou forsaken me?' " (Mt 27:46). Hebrew made its influence felt through more idiomatic expressions than statements as such. One such Hebrew idiom is, "and it came to pass." Another example of Hebrew influence may be seen in the use of a second noun to describe a quality rather than an adjective. Some examples would include the expressions, "work of faith, labor of love, patience of hope," (1 Th 1:3).

In addition to the Semitic languages in the New Testament are the Indo-European: Latin and Greek. The former was influential mainly in its loanwords, such as "centurion," "tribute," and "legion," as well as the inscription on the cross which was written in Latin, Hebrew, and Greek.

The basic language of the New Testament, however, was Greek. Until the late nineteenth century, New Testament Greek was believed to be a special "Holy Ghost" language, but since that time it has come to be identified as one of the five stages in the development of Greek itself. This *Koine* Greek was the most widely known language throughout the world of the first century. Its alphabet was derived from the Phoenicians; its cultural values and vocabulary encompassed a vast geographical expanse, and it became the official language of the empires into which Alexander the Great's conquests were divided. Its providential appearance, along with other cultural, political, social, and religious developments during the first centuries B.C. is implied in Paul's statement, "When the fulness of time had come, God sent forth his Son" (Gal 4:4).

New Testament Greek was appropriately adapted to the end of

interpreting the revelation of Christ in theological language. It was especially suited for this task because Greek was an *intellectual* language. It was more a language of the mind than of the heart, a fact to which the great Greek philosophers give ample evidence. Greek possessed a technical precision of expression not to be found in Hebrew. In addition, Greek was a nearly *universal* language. The Old Testament truth about God was initially revealed to one nation, Israel, in its own language, Hebrew. The fuller revelation given by Christ in the New Testament was not so restricted. Instead, the message of Christ was to "be preached in his name to all nations" (Lk 24:47).

### THE DEVELOPMENT OF WRITTEN LANGUAGES

#### ADVANCES IN WRITING

Although the Old Testament does not say anything about the development of writing itself, three stages in that development may be discerned. These stages include *pictograms,* or crude representations which antedated the actual development of writing. These pictures represented such objects as a man, an ox, a lion, or an eagle. As time passed, however, pictograms lost their dominant position as the means of written communication. They were replaced by *ideograms,* which were pictures representing ideas rather than objects. Such objects as a sun representing heat, an old man representing old age, an eagle representing power, an ox representing strength, or a lion depicting royalty gradually replaced pictograms. Still another extension of pictograms were *phonograms,* representations of sound rather than ideas or objects. A sun might be used to depict a son, or a bear might be used to convey the notion of the verb *bear.* As a result, still another step was taken toward written languages. After a long period, the Phoenicians developed their major innovation in the history of writing when they reduced their language to more specific elements—the *alphabet.*

#### THE AGE OF WRITING

Although evidence of writing in antiquity is far from abundant, enough exists to indicate that it was the hallmark of cultural achievement. Writing seems to have been developed during the fourth millennium B.C. In the second millennium B.C., several experiments led to the development of the alphabet and written documents by the Phoenicians. All this was completed before the time of Moses, who wrote not earlier than about 1450 B.C.

As early as c. 3500 B.C. cuneiform tablets were used by the Sumerians to record events in their history in Mesopotamia. The Sumerian flood narrative is an example of such writing, although it was recorded c. 2100 B.C. In Egypt (c. 3100 B.C.) there were additional documents written in hieroglyphic (pictographic) script. Among these early Egyptian writings were *The Teachings of Kagemni* and *The Teaching of Ptha-Hetep*, dating from c. 2700 B.C. From c. 2500 B.C. pictographic signs were used at Byblos (Gebal) and Syria. At Knossos and Atchana, great commercial centers, additional written records appear which antedated the works of Moses. Other items for the mid-to-late-second millennium B.C. add still more evidence that writing had become well developed before the time of Moses. In short, Moses and the other biblical writers wrote during man's age of literacy.

## WRITING MATERIALS AND INSTRUMENTS

### WRITING MATERIALS

The writers of Scripture employed the same materials as were used throughout the ancient world. *Clay tablets*, for example, were not only used in ancient Sumer as early as c. 3500 B.C., they were also utilized by Jeremiah (17:13) and Ezekiel (4:1). *Stone* was used to make inscriptions in Mesopotamia, Egypt and Palestine for such records as the Code of Hammurabi, the Rosetta Stone and the Moabite Stone. It was also employed at the Dog River in Lebanon and at Behistun in Persia (Iran) as well as by biblical writers (see Ex 24:12; 32:15-16; Deu 27:2-3; Jos 8:31-32).

*Papyrus* was utilized in ancient Gebal (Byblos) and Egypt about 2100 B.C. Formed into a scroll by pressing and gluing, these papyrus sheets were used by the apostle John in writing the Revelation (5:1) as well as his epistles (2 Jn 12). *Vellum, parchment,* and *leather* describe the various grades of writing material made from animal skins. Vellum was unknown before 200 B.C., so

Jeremiah (36:23) must have had leather in mind. Parchments are indicated by Paul in 2 Timothy 4:13. Other materials for writing include *metal* (Ex 28:36; Job 19:24; Mt 22:19-20), *wax* (Is 8:1; 30:8; Hab 2:2; Lk 1:63), *precious stones* (Ex 39:6-14), and *potsherds* (ostraca), as indicated in Job 2:8. *Linen* was used in Egypt, Greece, and Italy, although there is no indication of its employment in the Bible record.

WRITING INSTRUMENTS

Several basic instruments were employed in the production of written records on the materials previously mentioned. Among these instruments were the *stylus*, a three-sided instrument with a beveled head for writing. It was especially used to make incursions into clay and wax tablets, although it was sometimes called a pen by biblical writers (see Jer 17:1). A *chisel* was employed to make inscriptions in stone, as in Joshua 8:31-32. Job referred to a chisel as an "iron pen" (19:24) with which words could be engraved into rock. The *pen* was utilized in writing on papyrus, leather, vellum, and parchment (3 Jn 13).

Other instruments were needed by the scribe in order to carry out his writing task. Jeremiah spoke of a *penknife* used to destroy a scroll (Jer 36:23). Its use indicates that the scroll was probably made of a material stronger than papyrus, which could be torn. The penknife was also used when a writer wished to sharpen his pen after it had begun to wear down. *Ink* was the necessary concomitant of the pen, and the *inkhorn* was employed to contain the ink for writing on papyrus, leather, parchment, and vellum. Thus, all the materials and instruments available to writers throughout the ancient world were available for use by the biblical writers.

THE PREPARATION AND PRESERVATION OF MANUSCRIPTS

The authentic writings produced under the direction and authorization of a prophet or apostle, called *autographa* (autographs), are no longer in existence. As a result, they must be reconstructed from early manuscripts and versions of the Bible text. The manuscripts provide tangible and important evidence about the transmission of the Bible from God to us.

### THE PREPARATION OF MANUSCRIPT COPIES

*The Old Testament.* Although Hebrew writing began before the time of Moses, it is impossible to determine just when it was introduced. No manuscripts exist that were written before the Babylonian Captivity (586 B.C.), but there was a great flood of Scripture copies dating from the Talmudic era (c. 300 B.C.—A.D. 500). During this period two general classes of manuscript copies emerged: the *synagogue rolls* and the *private copies.*

The synagogue rolls were regarded as "sacred copies" of the Old Testament text because of the strict rules employed in their transmission. As a result, these copies were used in public meeting places and at the annual feasts. Separate rolls contained the Torah (Law) on one roll, portions of the Nebhiim (Prophets) on another, the Kethubhim (Writings) on two others, and the Megilloth ("Five Rolls") on five separate rolls. The Megilloth were undoubtedly produced on separate rolls in order to facilitate their being read at the annual feasts.

The private copies were regarded as common copies of the Old Testament text and were not used in public meetings. These rolls were prepared with great care, although they were not governed by the strict rules employed in making the synagogue roll copies. The desires of the purchaser determined the quality of the particular copy. Seldom did an individual have a collection of scrolls which contained the entire Old Testament.

*The New Testament.* The autographs of the New Testament have long since disappeared, but there is much evidence to warrant the assumption that these documents were written on rolls and books made of papyrus. Paul indicated that the Old Testament had been copied into books and parchments (2 Ti 4:13), but the New Testament was probably written on papyrus rolls between A.D. 50 and 100. By the early second century, papyrus codices were introduced, but they too were perishable. With the introduction of persecutions within the Roman Empire, the Scriptures became jeopardized and were not systematically copied until the time of Constantine. With the Letter of Constantine to Eusebius of Caesarea, systematic copying of the New Testament began in the West. From that time, vellum and parchment were also employed in making manuscript copies of the New Testament. Not until the Reformation era were printed copies of the Bible available.

Since no printing process was available at the time of manuscript copying, the age and preservation of manuscripts must be determined by other means than finding the date of publication printed on the opening pages. The means employed in determining a manuscript's age include the *materials* used, its *letter size* and form, its punctuation, text divisions, and some miscellaneous factors.

*Materials* are an important clue. For present purposes, only those materials usable in making rolls or books are considered. The earliest of these were skins, although they made heavy, bulky rolls of the Old Testament. Papyrus rolls were used in the New Testament period because they were inexpensive when compared with vellum and parchment. Papyrus codices were introduced to gather individual rolls together by the beginning of the second century A.D. Vellum and parchment were employed for the Old Testament during New Testament times (2 Ti 4:13), and for the New Testament following the end of the persecutions in the fourth century. Redressed parchment was employed in copying manuscripts after the original writings had become faded.

Sometimes parchments were erased and rewritten, as in the case of the Codex Ephraemi Rescriptus (C). These manuscripts are also called *palimpsest* (Gk., rubbed out again) or *rescriptus* (Lat., rewritten). Paper was invented in China in the second century A.D., introduced into Eastern Turkestan as early as the fourth century, manufactured in Arabia in the eighth, introduced into Europe in the tenth, manufactured there in the twelfth, and commonly used by the thirteenth century. Other developments in the manufacture of paper appeared which also help to determine manuscript age from its materials.

*Letter size* and *form* also provides evidence for determining the date of a given manuscript. The earliest form of letters in Hebrew resembled the prong shape of Phoenician script. This style prevailed until the time of Nehemiah (c. 444 B.C.). After that time the Aramaic script was employed, since it became the vernacular language of Israel during the fifth century B.C. After 200 B.C. the Old Testament was copied in the square letters of Aramaic script. The discovery of the Dead Sea Scrolls at Qumran in 1947 cast further light on the study of Hebrew paleography. These manuscripts revealed three different types of text as well as differences in matters of spelling, grammatical forms, and, to some extent, wording from the Masoretic text. By the time of the Masoretes, Jewish scribes who standardized the Hebrew text of the Old Testament (c. A.D. 500-1000), the principles of the late Talmudic period became rather stereotyped.

Greek manuscripts during the New Testament period were generally written in two styles: literary and nonliterary. The New Testament was undoubtedly written in the nonliterary style. During the first three centuries, the New Testament was probably circulated outside the regular channels of ordinary book trade because of the political status of Christianity. During the first three formative centuries of the church and its canon of New Testament Scriptures, various oral and written traditions followed the whims of individual interpreters and prevailing fashions among scribes. Not until the fourth century were serious attempts made at recension of the manuscripts.

The style of letters used in these revisions and early manuscripts is called *uncial* (capital). The letters were written separately, and there were no breaks between words or sentences. Until the tenth century this slow process of copying a manuscript was employed. By that time the demand for manuscripts was so great that a faster writing style was developed. This *cursive* style employed smaller, connected letters with breaks between words and sentences. The name *minuscule* was applied to these manuscripts, which became the dominant form during the golden age of manuscript copying, the eleventh through fifteenth centuries.

*Punctuation* adds further light to the age of a manuscript. At the outset words were run together and very little punctuation was used. During the sixth century scribes began to make more liberal use of punctuation. By the eighth they had come to utilize not only the spaces, but periods, commas, colons, breath, and accent marks, and they added interrogatives later. This slow process was completed by the tenth century, in time to be employed with cursive writing in the golden age of manuscript copying.

*Text Divisions* were begun in the Old Testament autographs in some instances, such as the Book of Lamentations and Psalm 119. Additional sections were added to the Pentateuch prior to the Babylonian Captivity, called *sedarim* (plural). During the Babylonian Captivity the Torah was divided into fifty-four sections called *parashiyyoth* (plural), which were later subdivided even further. The Maccabean sections were made during the second century B.C. These were divisions in the prophets, called *haphtaroth* (plural), corresponding to the *sedarim* of the law. During the Reformation era the Hebrew Old Testament began to follow the Protestant chapter divisions for the most part. Some chapter divisions, however, had been placed in the margins as early as 1330. The Masoretes added vowel points to the Hebrew text, but it was not until A.D. 900 that the versification of the Old Testament began to become standardized. In 1571, Arius Montanus published the first Hebrew Old Testament which had verse markings in the margin as well as chapter divisions.

Prior to the Council at Nicea (A.D. 325) the New Testament was divided into sections. These sections, called *kephalaia* (Greek), differed from modern chapter divisions. Another system was utilized in the Codex Vaticanus (B) during the fourth century, and still another was employed by Eusebius of Caesarea. These divisions were longer than modern verses, but shorter than modern chapters. Not until the thirteenth century were these divisions modified, and then only gradually. The work of modification was done by Stephen Langton, a professor at the University of Paris and later Archbishop of Canterbury, although others may give the credit to Cardinal Hugo of St. Cher (d. 1263). The Wycliffe Bible (1382) followed this pattern. Since it provided the basis for subsequent versions and translations, the system became standardized. Modern verses had not yet appeared, although they were employed in the Greek New Testament published by Robert Stephanus in 1551 and introduced into the English Bible in 1557. In 1555 they were placed into a Latin Vulgate edition published by Stephanus. The first English Bible to employ both the modern chapter and verse divisions was the Geneva Bible (1560).

*Miscellaneous factors* involved in the dating of a manuscript include the size and shape of letters, the ornamentation of a manuscript, spelling, ink color, and the texture and coloration of parchment. The ornamentation of manuscripts became more and more elaborate in the uncial manuscripts during the fourth to late ninth centuries. From that time onward the ornamentation declined as uncials were less carefully copied. These factors were paralleled in the minuscules from that time until the introduction of printed editions and translations of the Bible in the sixteenth century. At the outset, only black ink was used in writing a manuscript. Later green, red, and other colors were employed. Just as the spoken language changes through the centuries, so do these physical components. Then, the changing quality and texture of materials can be coupled with the aging process in determining the age of a manuscript.

RESULTS

A cursory survey of the evidence available concerning the age and preservation of manuscripts presents us with some important information about the relative value of a given manuscript in the transmission of the Bible.

*Old Testament manuscripts* generally come from two broad periods of production. The Talmudic period ( 300 B.C.-A.D. 500 ) produced manuscripts which were used in the synagogues and for private study. By comparison with the later Masoretic period ( 500-1000 ), these earlier manuscript copies were few in number but they were carefully transmitted "offical" copies. During the Masoretic period the Old Testament manuscript copying underwent a complete review of established rules, and a systematic renovation of transmission techniques resulted.

*New Testament manuscripts* may be classified into four general periods of transmission:

1. During the first three centuries the integrity of the New Testament Scriptures comes from a combined testimony of sources because of the illegal status of Christianity. Not many complete manuscripts from this period can be found, but the ones extant are significant.

2. From the fourth and fifth centuries, following the legalization

138 From God to Us

of Christianity, a multiplication of New Testament manuscripts
appeared. These manuscripts were on vellum and parchment
instead of the papyrus used earlier.

3. From the sixth century onward manuscripts were copied by
monks, who collected and cared for them in monasteries. This was
a period of rather uncritical reproduction, increased production
and a generally decreased quality of text.

4. After the introduction of minuscule manuscripts in the tenth
century, manuscript copies were multiplied rapidly and the decline in quality of textual transmission continued.

# 12

## THE MAJOR MANUSCRIPTS
## OF THE BIBLE

THE CLASSICAL WRITINGS of Greece and Rome illustrate the character of biblical manuscript preservation quite strikingly. In contrast to the total number of over 5,000 New Testament manuscripts known today, other religious and historicial books of the ancient world pale in significance. Only 643 copies of Homer's *Iliad* have survived in manuscript form. Titus Livy's *History of Rome* has only 20 manuscripts, and Caesar's *Gallic Wars* is known from a mere 9 or 10 manuscripts. *The Peloponnesian War* of Thucydides remains in only 8 manuscripts and the *Works* of Tacitus are to be found in only 2 manuscripts. A survey of the manuscript evidence of the Old Testament, although not as vast as the New Testament manuscripts available, will indicate the nature and amount of documentary evidence for the original text of the Hebrew Bible.

### MANUSCRIPTS OF THE OLD TESTAMENT

Compared with the New Testament there are relatively few early manuscripts of the Old Testament text. This was especially true before the discovery in 1947 of the Dead Sea Scrolls. This situation provides a convenient arrangement for our consideration of the *Masoretic Text* and the *Dead Sea Scrolls* traditions.

#### THE MASORETIC TEXT

Until recently, very few Old Testament manuscripts in Hebrew were known. Before the discovery of the Cairo Geneza manuscripts in 1890, only 731 Hebrew manuscripts were published.

In fact, the current edition of the Hebrew Bible, Kittel's *Biblia Hebraica*, is based on only four major Hebrew manuscripts, and primarily on just one of those (the *Leningrad Codex*). The major texts in this tradition were copied during the Masoretic period, as the following sample indicates. The *Cairo Codex*, or *Codex Cairensis* (C) (A.D. 895) is perhaps the oldest known Masoretic manuscript of the prophets, and it contains both the former and the latter prophets. The *Leningrad Codex of the Prophets*, or *Babylonian Codex of the Latter Prophets* (MX B 3), also known as the *[St.] Petersburg Codex* (A.D. 916), contains only the latter prophets (Isaiah, Jeremiah, Ezekiel, and the Twelve), and was written with a Babylonian punctuation. The *Aleppo Codex* (A.D. 930) of the entire Old Testament is no longer complete. It is to be the primary authority of the Hebrew Bible to be published in Jerusalem, and it was corrected and punctuated by Aaron ben Asher in A.D. 930. The *British Museum Codex* (Oriental 445) dates from A.D. 950 and is an incomplete manuscript of the Pentateuch. It presently contains only Genesis 39:20 through Deuteronomy 1:33. The *Leningrad Codex* (B 19 A or L) (A.D. 1008) is the largest and only complete manuscript of the entire Old Testament. It was written on vellum, three columns of twenty-one lines each per sheet. The vowel points and accents follow the Babylonian custom, being placed above the line. The *Reuchlin Codex* (MS *Ad.* 21161) of the prophets (A.D. 1105) contains a recension text which attests to the fidelity of Leningrad. The *Cairo Geneza* fragments (A.D. 500-800), discovered in 1890 at Cairo, are scattered throughout various libraries. Ernst Wurthwein says there are some 10,000 biblical manuscripts and fragments from this storehouse.

The relatively scarce number of early Old Testament manuscripts, with the exception of the Cairo Geneza, may be attributed to several factors. First and most obviously, the very antiquity of these manuscripts combined with their destructibility virtually assure that they will not survive. A second factor working against their survival is the fact that the Israelites were subject to the ravages of deportation during the Babylonian Captivity and to foreign domination following their return to Palestine. In its history, from 1800 B.C. to A.D. 1948, Jerusalem was conquered forty-seven times. This also explains why those Masoretic texts discovered have been found outside Palestine proper. A third factor involved in the scarcity of Old Testament manuscripts centers around the sacred scribal laws demanding the burial of worn or flawed manuscripts. According to Talmudic tradition, any manuscript that contained a mistake or error, and all those that were aged beyond use, were systematically and religiously destroyed. Such practice undoubtedly decreased the number of discoverable manuscripts appreciably. Finally, during the fifth and sixth centuries A.D., when the Masoretes (Jewish scribes) standardized the Hebrew text, it is believed that they systematically and completely destroyed all the manuscripts which did not agree with their vocalization (adding of vowel letters) and standardization of the Scripture text. Archaeological evidence, the absence of surviving early manuscripts, tends to support this judgment. As a result, the printed Masoretic text of the Old Testament as it appears today is based on relatively few manuscripts, none of which antedates the tenth century A.D.

Although there are relatively few early Masoretic manuscripts, the quality of the extant manuscripts is very good. This too is to be attributed to several factors. In the first place, there are very few variants in the available texts because they are all descendants of one text type which was established about A.D. 100. Unlike the New Testament, which bases its textual fidelity on the multiplicity of manuscript copies, the Old Testament text owes its accuracy to the ability and reliability of the scribes who transmitted it. With respect to the Jewish Scriptures, however, scribal accuracy alone does not guarantee the product. Rather, their almost superstitious reverence for the Bible is paramount. According to the Talmud only certain kinds of skins could be used, the size of columns was regulated and the ritual a scribe followed in copying a manuscript followed religious rules. If a manuscript was found to contain even one mistake, it was discarded and destroyed. This scribal formalism was responsible, at least in part, for the extreme care exercised in copying the Scriptures.

Another line of evidence for the integrity of the Masoretic text is found in the comparison of duplicate passages of the Old Testament Masoretic text itself. Psalm 14, for example, occurs again in

Psalm 53, much of Isaiah 36-39 is also found in 2 Kings 18-20, Isaiah 2:2-4 parallels Micah 4:1-3, and large portions of the Chronicles are to be found in Samuel and Kings. An examination of these and other passages shows not only substantial textual agreement but, in some cases, almost a word-for-word identity. As a result, it may be concluded that the Old Testament texts have not undergone radical revisions even if the parallel passages stem from identical sources.

Still another substantial proof for the accuracy of the Masoretic text comes from archaeology. Robert Dick Wilson and William F. Albright, for example, have made numerous discoveries which confirm the historical accuracy of the biblical documents, even to obsolete names of foreign kings. Wilson's work, *A Scientific Investigation of the Old Testament*, and Albright's *From the Stone Age to Christianity* may be consulted in support of this view.

Perhaps the best line of evidence to support the integrity of the Masoretic text comes from the Greek translation of the Old Testament known as the Septuagint (LXX). This work was performed during the third and second centuries B.C. in Alexandria, Egypt. For the most part it was almost a book-by-book, chapter-by-chapter reproduction of the Masoretic text, containing common stylistic and idiomatic differences. Furthermore, the Septuagint was the Bible of Jesus and the apostles, and most New Testament quotations are taken from it directly. On the whole, the Septuagint closely parallels the Masoretic text and tends to confirm the fidelity of the tenth century A.D. Hebrew text. If no other evidence were available, the case for the fidelity of the Masoretic text could rest with confidence upon the foregoing lines of evidence alone.

THE DEAD SEA SCROLLS

This great manuscript discovery came about in March, 1947, when a young Arab boy (Muhammad adh-Dhib) was pursuing a lost goat in the caves seven and one-half miles south of Jericho and a mile west of the Dead Sea. In one of the caves he discovered some jars containing several leather scrolls. Between that time and February 1956, eleven caves containing scrolls and fragments were excavated near Qumran. In these caves the Essenes, a Jewish religious sect dating from about the time of Christ, had housed their library. Altogether the thousands of manuscript fragments constituted the remains of some six hundred manuscripts.

Of particular interest to us are those manuscripts which bear on the text of the Old Testament. Cave 1 was discovered by the Arab boy, and it contained seven more or less complete scrolls and some fragments, including the earliest known complete book of the Bible (Isaiah A), a manual of discipline, a commentary on Habakkuk, a Genesis apocryphon, an incomplete text of Isaiah (Isaiah B), the War Scroll, and about thirty thanksgiving hymns. Additional manuscripts were found in Cave 2, although it had been discovered by Bedouins who pilfered it. Fragments of about a hundred manuscripts were found here, but nothing was discovered so spectacular as what was found in other caves. In Cave 3 two halves of a copper scroll were discovered which provided directions to sixty or more sites containing hidden treasures mostly in and around the Jerusalem area.

Cave 4 (Partridge Cave) had also been ransacked by Bedouins before it was excavated in September 1952. Nevertheless, it proved to be the most productive of all caves, for literally thousands of fragments were recovered either by purchase from the Bedouins or as a result of archaeological sifting of the dust on the floor of the cave. The fragment of Samuel found here is thought to be the oldest known piece of biblical Hebrew, dating from the fourth century b.c. Cave 5 revealed some biblical and apocryphal books in an advanced stage of deterioration. Cave 6 produced mostly papyrus fragments rather than leather. Caves 7-10 provided data of interest to the professional archaeologist, but nothing of relevance to the present study. Cave 11 was the last to be excavated, in early 1956. It produced a well-preserved copy of some of the psalms, including the apocryphal Psalm 151 which was hitherto known only in Greek texts. In addition, it contained a very fine scroll of a portion of Leviticus and an Aramaic Targum (paraphrase) of Job.

Prompted by these original finds, the Bedouins pursued their search and discovered caves to the southwest of Bethlehem. Here at Murabba'at they discovered some self-dated manuscripts and documents from the Second Jewish Revolt (a.d. 132-135). These manuscripts helped to establish the antiquity of the Dead Sea

Scrolls, and they produced another scroll of the Minor Prophets (Joel through Haggai) which closely supports the Masoretic text. In addition, the oldest known Semitic papyrus, a palimpsest, inscribed the second time in the ancient Hebrew script of the seventh and eighth centuries B.C. was discovered here.

Several lines of evidence tend to support the dates of the Dead Sea Scrolls. First is the Carbon 14 process, which dates them at 1,917 years with a two-hundred-year variant (10 percent). This places the Dead Sea Scrolls somewhere between 168 B.C. and A.D 233. Paleography and orthography, writing forms and spelling, indicated a date for some of the manuscripts before 100 B.C. Archaeology provided collaborative evidence when the pottery found in the caves was analyzed to be from the Late Hellenistic (150-63 B.C.) and Early Roman (63 B.C.–A.D. 100) period. Finally, the Murabba'at discoveries corroborate the Qumran findings.

The nature and number of these Dead Sea discoveries produced the following general conclusions about the integrity of the Masoretic text. The scrolls give overwhelming confirmation to the fidelity of the Masoretic text. Millar Burrows, in his work *The Dead Sea Scrolls*, indicates that there is very little alteration in the text in something like a thousand years. R. Laird Harris, in *Inspiration and Canonicity of the Bible*, argues that there is less variation in these two traditions in a thousand years than there is in two of the families of New Testament manuscripts. Gleason Archer, in *A Survey of Old Testament Introduction*, supports the integrity of the Masoretic text by stating that it agrees with the Isaiah manuscript from Cave 1 in 95 percent of its contents, with the remaining 5 percent being comprised of obvious slips of the pen and variations in spelling which developed in the interim.

## MANUSCRIPTS OF THE NEW TESTAMENT

The integrity of the Old Testament text was established primarily by the fidelity of the transmission process which was later confirmed by the Dead Sea Scrolls. The fidelity of the New Testament text, however, rests in the multiplicity of the extant manuscripts. Whereas the Old Testament had only a few complete manuscripts, all of which were good, the New Testament has many more copies which are of generally poorer quality. A manuscript is a handwritten literary composition in contrast to a printed copy. As indicated in the previous chapter, the New Testament was written in a formal printed style known as uncials (or majuscules). After the sixth century this style went into decline as it was gradually displaced by minuscule manuscripts. These minuscules gained dominance in the period from the ninth to the fifteenth centuries.

Testimony to the fidelity of the New Testament text comes from three basic sources: Greek manuscripts, ancient translations, and patristic citations. The first of these sources is the most important and can itself be divided into three classes. These classes of manuscripts are commonly termed the papyruses, the uncials, and the minuscules because of their most distinguishing characteristics.

## THE PAPYRUSES

The manuscripts classified as papyruses date from the second and third centuries, when Christianity was illegal and its Scriptures were transcribed on the cheapest possible materials. There are some seventy-six of these papyrus manuscripts of the New Testament. Their witness to the text is invaluable since they range chronologically from the very threshold of the second century, a mere generation removed from the autographs, and contain most of the New Testament.

The more important representatives of the papyrus manuscripts are treated here. P52, the John Rylands Fragment (117-38), is the earliest known and attested fragment of the New Testament. It was written on both sides and contains portions of five verses from the gospel of John (18:31-33, 37-38). P45, 46, 47, the Chester Beatty Papyri (250), consists of three codices containing most of the New Testament. P45 is comprised of thirty leaves of a papyrus codex containing the gospels and Acts. P46 contains most of Paul's epistles, as well as Hebrews, although portions of Romans, I Thessalonians, and all of II Thessalonians are missing. P47 contains portions of Revelation. P66, 72, 75, the Bodmer Papyri (175-225), comprise the most important New Testament papyrus discoveries since the Chester Beatty Papyri. P66 dates from 200 and contains portions of the gospel of John. P72 is the earliest known copy of Jude, 1 Peter, and 2 Peter. Dating from the early third century, it contains several Apocryphal and canonical books. P75 contains Luke and John in clear and carefully printed uncials dated between 175 and 225. Consequently, it is the earliest known copy of Luke.

### THE UNCIAL MANUSCRIPTS

As a whole, the most important manuscripts of the New Testament are generally considered to be the great uncials written on vellum and parchment during the fourth-to-ninth centuries. There are about 297 of these uncial manuscripts. Some of the more important of these manuscripts will be described here. The most important manuscripts א (Aleph), B, A, and C were not available to the translators of the King James Bible. As a matter of fact, only D was available to these translators, and it was used only slightly by them. This fact alone was sufficient to call for a new translation of the Bible after these great uncials were discovered.

*Codex Vaticanus* (*B*) is perhaps the oldest uncial on either parchment or vellum (325-50), and one of the most important witnesses to the text of the New Testament. It was unknown to biblical scholars until after 1475, when it was catalogued in the Vatican Library. It was published in a complete photographic facsimile for the first time in 1889-90. It contains most of the Old Testament (LXX), the New Testament in Greek, and the Apocrypha with some omissions. Also missing from this codex is Genesis 1:1–46:28; 2 Kings 2:5-7, 10-13; Psalm 106:27–138:6; as well as Hebrews 9:14 to the end of the New Testament. Mark 16:9-20 and John 7:58–8:11 were purposely omitted from the text which was written in small and delicate uncials on fine vellum.

*Codex Sinaiticus* (א, *Aleph*) is the fourth-century Greek manuscript generally considered to be the most important witness to the text because of its antiquity, accuracy, and lack of omissions. The story of its discovery is one of the most fascinating and romantic in the history of the biblical text. The manuscript was found by the German Count Tischendorf in the monastery of St. Catherine at Mount Sinai. In 1844 he discovered forty-three leaves of vellum, containing portions of the Septuagint (1 Chronicles, Jeremiah, Nehemiah, and Esther) in a basket of scraps which were used by the monks to light their fires. He secured the manuscript and took it to Leipzig, Germany, where it remains as the Codex Frederico-Augustanus. On a second visit in 1853, Tischendorf found nothing new, but in 1859 he made a third visit, under the direction of Czar Alexander II. Just before he was to depart for home, the monastery steward showed to him an almost complete copy of the Scriptures and some other books. These were subsequently acquired for the Czar as a "conditional gift." Now known as Codex Sinaiticus (ℵ), this manuscript contains more than half the Old Testament (LXX) and all the New, with the exception of Mark 16:9-20 and John 7:58—8:11, all the Old Testament Apocrypha, the Epistle of Barnabas, and the Shepherd of Hermas. The material is good vellum, made from antelope skins. The manuscript underwent several scribal "corrections," known by the seglum ℵ (Aleph). At Caesarea in the sixth or seventh century a group of scribes introduced a large number of alterations known as ℵ$^{ca}$ or ℵ$^{cb}$. In 1933 the British government purchased the Codex Sinaiticus for £100,000. It was published in a volume entitled *Scribes and Correctors of Codex Sinaiticus* in 1938.

Codex Alexandrinus (A) is a well-preserved fifth-century manuscript which ranks immediately following B and Aleph as representative of the New Testament text. Although some have dated this codex in the late fourth century, it was probably the result of scribal work at Alexandria, Egypt, about 450. In 1078 this codex was presented to the Patriarch of Alexandria, for which it received its designation. In 1621 it was taken to Constantinople before being presented to Sir Thomas Roe, English ambassador to Turkey in 1624, for presentation to King James I. He died before the manuscript reached England, and it was presented to Charles I in 1627. This made it unavailable for use by the translators of the King James Bible in 1611, although the manuscript was known to be in existence at that time. In 1757, George II presented the codex to the National Library of the British Museum. It contains the entire Old Testament, except for several mutilated portions (Gen 14:14-17; 15:1-5, 16-19; 16:6-9; 1 Kingdoms [1 Sa] 12:18—14:9; Ps 49:19—79:100, and most of the New Testament, missing only Mt 1:1—25:6; Jn 6:50—8:52 and 2 Co 4:13—12:6. The codex does contain 1 and 2 Clement and the Psalms of Solomon, with some missing parts. The large square uncial letters are written on very thin vellum and are divided into sections marked by large letters. It is a text of varied quality.

*Ephraemi Rescriptus Codex* (*C*) probably originated in Alexandria, Egypt, around 345. It was brought to Italy about 1500 by John Lascaris and later sold to Pietro Strozzi. Catherine de Medici, an Italian who was the wife and mother of French kings, acquired it in 1533. Following her death, the manuscript was placed in the National Library at Paris, where it remains today. Most of the Old Testament is missing from this codex, except portions of Job, Proverbs, Ecclesiastes, Song of Solomon, and two Apocryphal books—the Wisdom of Solomon and Ecclesiasticus. The New Testament lacks 2 Thessalonians, 2 John, and parts of other books. The manuscript is a *palimpsest* (rubbed out, erased) *rescriptus* (rewritten) which originally contained the Old and New Testaments. These texts were erased to make space for sermons written by Ephraem, a fourth-century Syrian father. By chemical reactivation, Count Tischendorf was able to decipher the almost invisible writing on the parchment leaves of the codex. Located in the National Library at Paris, this manuscript shows evidence of two sets of corrections: the first, $C^2$ or $C^b$, was done in sixth-century Palestine and the second, $C^3$ or $C^c$, was added in ninth-century Constantinople.

*Codex Bezae* (*D*), also known as Codex Cantabrigiensis, was transcribed in 450 or 550. It is the oldest known bilingual manuscript of the New Testament, written in Greek and Latin in the general region of southern Gaul (France) or northern Italy. This was discovered in 1562 by Théodore de Bèze (Lat., Beza), the French theologian, at St. Irenaeus Monastery in Lyons, France. In 1581 Beza gave it to Cambridge University. This codex contains the four gospels, Acts, and 3 John 11-15, with variations from other manuscripts indicated. It has many omissions in its text, and only the Latin text of 3 John 11-15 remains.

*Codex Claromontanus* ($D^2$ or $D^{p2}$) is a sixth-century complement of Codex D dated 550. It contains much of the New Testament which is missing in D. $D^2$ seems to have originated in Italy or Sardinia and receives its name from a monastery at Clermont, France, where it was found by Beza. Following Beza's death, the codex was owned by several private individuals before it was purchased by King Louis XIV for the National Library in 1656. It was fully edited by Count Tischendorf in 1852. The codex contains all of Paul's epistles and Hebrews, although Romans 1:1-7, 27-30, and 1 Corinthians 14:13-22 are missing in Greek, and 1 Corinthians 14:8-18 and Hebrews 13:21-23 are missing in Latin. This bilingual manuscript was artistically written on thin, high-quality vellum. The Greek is good, but the Latin grammar is inferior in places.

*Codex Washingtonianus I* (W) dates from the fourth or early fifth century. It was purchased by Charles F. Freer of Detroit in 1906 from a dealer in Cairo, Egypt. Between 1910 and 1918 it was edited by Professor H. A. Sanders of the University of Michigan, and it is currently located in the Smithsonian Institute, Washington, D. C. The manuscript contains the four gospels, portions of Paul's epistles (except Romans), Hebrews, Deuteronomy, Joshua, and Psalms. Its arrangement of the gospels is Matthew, John, Luke, and Mark. Mark contains the long ending (Mk 16:9-20); however, an additional insertion is added following verse 14. This thick vellum codex is comprised of a curiously mixed text type.

The remaining uncial manuscripts add supportive evidence to the various textual traditions of those already presented. For all practical purposes, the major vellum and parchment manuscripts have been indicated and our attention may now turn to the minuscules.

### THE MINUSCULE MANUSCRIPTS

The dates of the minuscule manuscripts (ninth through fifteenth centuries) indicate that they are generally of inferior quality when compared to either the papyrus or uncial manuscripts. Their main importance rests on the accent they place on their textual families rather than their multitude. Their number totals over 4,643: 2,646 as manuscripts and 1,997 as lectionaries (early church-service books). Some of the more important minuscule manuscripts are identified below.

Minuscules in the Alexandrian family are represented by manuscript 33, the "queen of the cursives," which dates from the ninth or possibly the tenth century. It contains the entire New Testa-

ment except Revelation and is in the possession of the Bibliothèque
Nationale in Paris.

The Caesarean text type has survived in family 1 of the minuscules. This family contains manuscripts 1, 118, 131, and 209; and
they all date from the twelfth to the fourteenth centuries.

The Italian subfamily of the Caesarean text type is represented
by about a dozen manuscripts known as family 13. These manuscripts were copied between the eleventh and fifteenth centuries
and include manuscripts 13, 69, 124, 230, 346, 543, 788, 826, 828,
983, 1689, and 1709. Some of these manuscripts were formerly
thought to be of the Syrian text type.

Many of the remaining minuscule manuscripts may be placed
into one or another of the various text type families, but they
stand on their own merits rather than belonging to one of the
families of manuscripts mentioned above. In all, however, they
were copied from earlier uncial or minuscule manuscripts and add
little new evidence to the text of the New Testament. They do
provide a continual line of transmission of the biblical text,
whereas the manuscripts of other classical works have breaks of
nine hundred to a thousand years between the autographs and
their manuscript copies, as may be seen in the examples of
Caesar's *Gallic Wars* and the *Works* of Tacitus.

# 13

## ADDITIONAL WITNESSES TO THE BIBLE TEXT

THE TRANSMISSION of the biblical text can be traced rather clearly from the late second and early third centuries to modern times by means of the great manuscripts. The linking of these manuscripts to the first century, however, rests on a few papyrus fragments and some quotations from the apostolic fathers. In addition to these lines of evidence, there are materials from archaeological discoveries such as the nonbiblical papyruses, biblical and related papyruses, ostraca, and inscriptions.

### THE NONBIBLICAL PAPYRUSES

The epochal discovery of papyruses, ostraca, and inscriptions transformed some basic notions about the very nature of the New Testament itself. Until the work by Moulton and Milligan, *Vocabulary of the Greek New Testament, Illustrated from the Papyri and Other Non-Literary Sources* (1914), A. T. Robertson, *A Grammar of the Greek New Testament in Light of Historical Research* (1914) and Adolf Deissman, *Light From the Ancient East* (trans. 1923), the New Testament had been regarded as a mysteriously written book communicated to man in a supposedly Holy Ghost language. Their works combined with the efforts of others proved indisputably that the New Testament was a lucid example of first-century colloquial speech—Koine Greek. They discovered that the New Testament was not written in a "perfect language," as some of the Latin Fathers had assumed, but that in phonology, vocabulary, syntax, and style, the New Testament is really a record of late colloquial Greek.

In addition, they discovered among the nonbiblical papyruses that background which formed the cultural and religious backdrop of the first century. By looking into the cultural similarities between these papyruses and the New Testament they saw that there were competing cults which were also missionary religions. The ancient world became an open book which reflected the same patterns of life and interests as reflected in the Bible. The phraseology of the New Testament was like that of the broader setting; in fact, the language of popular religion, law, and emperor worship were similar to the New Testament.

That a common language was used in the New Testament and its setting does not imply that the two had the same meanings in their expressions. In other words, the same words used by the different religions could, at best, be expected to have parallel but not identical meanings with Christianity. There are some unavoidable conclusions, however, which the nonbiblical papyruses indicate. Among these are the facts that the New Testament was not written in a so-called Holy Ghost language. Instead, it was written in the common (Koine) trade language of the Roman world, the language of the masses and the marketplace. In addition, the "Pauline" and other styles of Greek syntax and vocabulary were all commonly used throughout the first century. These facts imply that if the Greek of the New Testament was the common language of the first century, then the New Testament must have been written in the first century.

### BIBLICAL PAPYRUSES, OSTRACA AND INSCRIPTIONS

#### BIBLICAL PAPYRUSES

In addition to the materials discussed in chapter 12, a few supplementary papyruses add further light on the New Testament text. A group of noncanonical Logia of Jesus (Sayings of Jesus) were discovered among the papyruses. A comparison of their contents with the canonical text indicates their apocryphal tone. There can be little doubt that these so-called sayings have local, and possibly heretical appeal, but they did give rise to collections of "sayings" which can be used to reflect the popular religious experience of the first and second centuries.

OSTRACA

Ostraca are broken pieces of pottery which were frequently used as a writing material by the poorer classes in antiquity. One example of the use of this means of transmitting the Bible text is to be found in a seventh-century copy of the gospels recorded on twenty pieces of ostraca. This represents what may be called a "poor man's Bible." Long overlooked by scholars, these pieces of potsherds (see Is 45:9, RV) have cast additional light on the biblical text. Allen P. Wikgren has listed some 1,624 specimens of these humble records of history in his work entitled *Greek Ostraca.*

INSCRIPTIONS

The wide distribution and variety of ancient inscriptions testify to the importance of the biblical text as well as to its very existence. There is an abundance of engravings on walls, pillars, coins, monuments, and other items which have preserved a witness to the New Testament text. This witness, however, is merely supportive and is not of importance in establishing the text of the New Testament.

LECTIONARIES

Still another witness to the text of the New Testament which has been generally undervalued are the numerous lectionaries (church-service books) containing selected readings from the Bible itself. These lectionaries served as manuals and were used in religious services throughout the year. Most of the lectionaries probably originated between the seventh and the twelfth centuries, although a dozen leaves and fragments have survived, dated between the fourth and sixth. Only five or six lectionaries have survived which were copied onto papyrus, and they utilized uncial script even after it had been superseded by the minuscule type script.

Although Caspar René Gregory listed about 1,545 Greek lectionaries in his *Canon and Text of the New Testament* (1912), approximately 2,000 have been utilized in the critical apparatus of the United Bible Societies edition of *The Greek New Testament*

(1966). The great majority of lectionaries consist of readings taken from the gospels. The remainder contain portions of Acts, either with or without the epistles. Although they were often elaborately adorned, and sometimes even included musical notations, it must be admitted that the lectionaries are only of secondary value at best in establishing the New Testament text. They do, however, play an important role in the understanding of specific passages of Scripture, such as John 7:53—8:11 and Mark 16:9-20.

### PATRISTIC REFERENCES TO THE BIBLE TEXT

In addition to the manuscripts and the miscellaneous items witnessing to the New Testament text, the student of textual criticism has available to him the patristic citations of the Scriptures which aid him in his quest of the true text. The Fathers who made these references and citations lived during the early centuries of the church. Their closeness to the apostles and their use of the text provide information about the precise area, date, and type of text used throughout the early church.

#### WHEN THE FATHERS LIVED

Since the Old Testament canon was closed and recognized prior to the time of Christ, the attitude of the early church Fathers (first to the fourth centuries) may be summarized in the words of B. F. Westcott:

> They continued to look upon the Old Testament as a full and lasting record of the revelation of God. In one remarkable particular they carried this belief yet further than it had been carried before. With them the individuality of the several writers falls into the background. They practically regarded the whole Book as one Divine utterance.[1]

When considering their use of the New Testament, the picture is more diverse and the role of the Fathers is much more significant, since the New Testament canon was not finally and completely recognized until the fourth century. As a result of this situation, it will be helpful to trace again briefly the history of the recogni-

1. Brooke Foss Westcott, *The Bible in the Church*, 2d ed. (New York: MacMillan, 1887), pp. 83-84.

tion of the canon in order to bring the position of the Fathers into sharper focus.

The last half of the first century saw the process of selecting, sorting (Lk 1:1-4; 1 Th 2:13), reading (1 Th 5:27), circulating (Col 4:16), collecting (2 Pe 3:15-16), and quoting (1 Ti 5:18) of apostolic literature. All twenty-seven books of the New Testament were written and copied, and began to be distributed among the churches before the close of the first century. In the first half of the second century the apostolic writings became more generally known and more widely circulated. By this time almost every book of the New Testament was explicitly cited as Scripture. The writings of the Fathers were also widely read and circulated in the churches, and their quoting of the New Testament as authoritative in their struggles against heretical groups, dialogues with unbelievers, and exhortations against vice tell much about the history, doctrine, and practices of the early church.

In the last half of the second century the New Testament books were widely recognized as Scripture, as were those of the Old Testament. This was a period of missionary activity, and the Scriptures were translated into other languages as the church spread beyond the confines of the Roman Empire. It was also during these years that commentaries began to appear, such as Papias' *Exposition of the Lord's Oracles*, Heracleon's *Commentary on the Gospels*, and Melito's *Commentary on the Apocalypse*. The *Diatessaron* of Tatian also came into being. The writings of the Fathers were profuse with citations from the New Testament as authoritative Scriptures, and all but five were listed as such in the Muratorian Fragment (c. 170).

During the third century the New Testament books were collected into a single catalog of "recognized books" and separated from other types of Christian literature. It was during this century that a great surge of intellectual activity within the church occurred, as Origen's *Hexapla* (six-column Bible) and other works attest. No longer were there merely two classes of Christian literature (Scripture and writing of the Fathers), as a body of apocryphal and pseudepigraphal literature emerged. The rise of these diverse kinds of literature gave impetus to the sorting and sifting tests for all religious literature in the church. These tests and others led ultimately to the recognition of the canonical New Testament and the erasure of doubts about the disputed books belonging to it.

By the time the fourth century dawned, the New Testament canon was fully settled and acknowledged. The writings of the Fathers present and indicate the general agreement of all Christians about the New Testament canon as indicated in the discussion in chapters 9 and 10.

WHAT THE FATHERS DID

While the testimony of the Fathers is quite early, actually older than the best codices, it is not always reliable. A Father may have quoted a variant reading from an existing manuscript which would perpetuate the error. In addition, the writing of a particular Father might itself have been subject to alteration or corruption during its transmission, just as the Greek text of the New Testament was. A third factor involved is the method itself of the particular Father's quotation. It may have been verbatim, a loose citation, a paraphrase, or perhaps even a mere allusion. Even if the quote were verbatim, it would be important to discern whether it was cited from memory or read from a written text. Even if the text were being read, it would be significant to determine whether he were a member of some heretical group. If a Father cited a given passage more than once, it would be necessary to compare those examples to determine whether they are identical or divergent. Finally, if an amanuensis were employed, it could be that he would take notes and search for the particular passage at a later time.

All of these difficulties notwithstanding, the evidence from the patristic writers is of such great importance that the labor of refining the ore from the dross is well worth the effort. Their importance may be summarized in a threefold manner: they show the history of the text of the New Testament, render the best evidence as to the canon of the New Testament, provide a means of dating the manuscripts of the New Testament, and assist in determining just when translations, versions, and revisions of the New Testament text occur.

WHO THE PRINCIPAL FATHERS WERE

During the period before the Council at Nicea (325) there were three broad classes of patristic writers: the apostolic Fathers (70-150), the Ante-Nicene Fathers (150-300) and the Nicene and Post-Nicene Fathers (300-430). Their writings give overwhelming support to the existence of the New Testament canon in two ways. First, they cited as authoritative every book of the New Testament. Secondly, they quoted with authority virtually every verse of the twenty-seven books of the New Testament.

CITATION OF NEW TESTAMENT BOOKS BY CHURCH FATHERS

The chart "Testimony of Early Church to the New Testament Canon" (chap. 10) should be reviewed at this point. By the end of the first century, some fourteen books of the New Testament were cited. By A.D. 110 there were nineteen books recognized by citation. And within another forty years (A.D. 150) some twenty-four New Testament books were acknowledged. Before the century ended, which is about one hundred years after the New Testament was written, twenty-six books had been cited. Only 3 John, perhaps because of its lack in size and significance, remained without corroboration. But within about a generation Origen had confirmed the existence of 3 John, as did both the Muratorian Canon and the Old Latin version by the same time. Most of the twenty-seven books are acknowledged many times by several Fathers within the first century after the books were written.

QUOTATIONS OF NEW TESTAMENT VERSES BY CHURCH FATHERS

Not only did the early Fathers cite all twenty-seven books of the New Testament, they also quoted virtually all of the verses in all of these twenty-seven books. Five Fathers alone from Irenaeus to Eusebius possess almost 36,000 quotations from the New Testament.[2] Sir David Dalrymple claimed to have found among the quotations of the second and third centuries "the entire New Testament, except eleven verses." We know of no other book

2. Norman L. Geisler and William E. Nix, *A General Introduction to the Bible* (Chicago: Moody, 1968), p. 357.

from the ancient world which exists en toto by way of thousands of individual and selected quotations of it. It is an amazing fact that the New Testament could be reconstructed simply from quotations made within two hundred years of its composition.

## WITNESS FROM EARLY APOCRYPHAL LITERATURE

Despite its heretical nature and religious fancy, the apocryphal literature from the second and third centuries A.D. provides a corroborative witness to the existence of the books of the New Testament canon. This it does in several ways. First, the names of the books with their alleged apostolic authors are a clear imitation of the real books of the apostles in the New Testament (see chap. 10). Second, there is often both literary and doctrinal dependence on the canonical books reflected in these false writings. Third, their style and literary type is imitative of the first century books. Fourth, some books (for example, the Epistle of the Laodiceans, supposedly fourth century) is similar in content to biblical books (specifically, Ephesians and Colossians). Fifth, some of the third-century Gnostic books from Nag-Hammadi, Egypt (discovered 1946), cite several New Testament books. The Gospel of Truth cites most of the New Testament, including Hebrews and Revelation. The Epistle of Reginus cites 1 and 2 Corinthians, Romans, Ephesians, Philippians, Colossians, and the Transfiguration narrative from the gospels, and uses Johannine language in places.

## SUMMARY AND CONCLUSION

In addition to the three thousand Greek manuscripts there are some two thousand lectionary manuscripts which support the text of the New Testament. Besides the nonbiblical literary support for the New Testament from the papyruses, there are numerous ostraca and inscriptions with biblical quotations. And from the early church Fathers' quotations alone, virtually the entire New Testament is preserved. In addition to all these witnesses, there are from the second and third centuries numbers of allusions and citations in apocryphal books which give direct testimony to the existence of most of the twenty-seven books of the New Testament. In totality, this is a highly significant corroborative witness to the biblical text.

# 14

# THE DEVELOPMENT OF TEXTUAL CRITICISM

ONCE ALL THE MANUSCRIPTS and other evidence bearing witness to the text of the Scriptures have been gathered, the student of textual criticism becomes the heir to a great tradition. He has at his disposal much of the material used to determine the true reading of the biblical text. This chapter is concerned with the historical development of the science of textual criticism.

## HIGHER AND LOWER CRITICISM DISTINGUISHED

Much confusion and controversy has arisen over the matter of "higher" (historical) and "lower" (textual) criticism of the Bible. Some of this controversy has resulted from a misunderstanding of the term *criticism* as it is applied to the Scriptures. In its grammatical sense the term refers merely to the exercise of judgment. When applied to the Bible it is used in the sense of exercising judgment about the Bible itself. But there are two basic types of criticism, and two basic attitudes toward each type. The titles ascribed to these two types of criticism have nothing at all to do with their importance, as the following discussion will illustrate.

### HIGHER (HISTORICAL) CRITICISM

When scholarly judgment is applied to the genuineness of the biblical text, it is classified as higher or historical criticism. The subject matter of this type of scholarly judgment concerns such matters as the date of the text, its literary style and structure, its historicity and its authorship. As a result, higher criticism is not actually an integral part of General Introduction to the Bible.

Instead, higher criticism is the very essence of Special Introduction. The results of higher critical studies by the heirs to the destructive theology of the late eighteenth century has been a kind of destructive criticism.

*The Old Testament.* The late date ascribed to Old Testament documents led some scholars to attribute its supernatural elements to legend or myth. This resulted in the denial of the historicity and genuineness of much of the Old Testament by skeptical scholars. In an attempt at mediation between Traditionalism and Skepticism, Julius Wellhausen and his followers developed the documentary theory, which proposed to date the Old Testament books in a less supernaturalistic manner. As a result they developed the JEDP Theory of the Old Testament.

This theory was based largely on the argument that Israel had no writing prior to the monarchy, and that an Elohist (E) Code and a Yahwist or Jehovahist (J) Code were based on two oral traditions about God ("E using the name Elohim and "J" using Jehovah [Yahweh]). To these were added the Deuteronomic (D) Code (documents ascribed to the time of Josiah) and the so-called Priestly (P) documents allied to postexilic Judaism. These views were not palatable to orthodox scholars and a wave of opposition arose. This opposition emerged only after a considerable period of time, and the scholarly world largely followed the theory of Wellhausen, W. Robertson Smith and Samuel R. Driver. When opposition finally raised its voice against this "destructive criticism," it was generally written off as an insignificant minority and ignored. Among the opposition were such proponents of "constructive criticism" as William Henry Green, A. H. Sayce, Franz Delitzsch, James Orr, Wilhelm Moller, Eduard Naville, and Robert Dick Wilson.

*The New Testament.* Application of similar principles to the New Testament writings appeared in the Tübingen school of theology following the lead of Heinrich Paulus, Wilhelm De Wette, and others. They developed principles to challenge the authorship, structure, style, and date of the New Testament books. The destructive criticism of modernism led to the form criticism in the gospels and to a denial of Paul's authorship of most of the Pauline epistles. It came to recognize as *genuinely* Pauline only the "Big Four" (Romans, Galatians, 1 and 2 Corinthians). Toward the end of the nineteenth century, capable orthodox scholars began to challenge the destructive criticism of the higher critical school. Among these orthodox scholars were George Salmon, Theodor von Zahn, and R. H. Lightfoot. Their work in higher criticism must surely be regarded as constructive criticism. Much of the recent work done in the field of higher criticism has revealed itself as rationalistic in theology, although it makes claim to be upholding orthodox Christian doctrine. This recent rationalism manifests itself most openly when it considers such matters as miracles, the virgin birth of Jesus, and His bodily resurrection.

LOWER (TEXTUAL) CRITICISM

When scholarly judgment is applied to the *authenticity* of the biblical text, it is classified as lower or textual criticism. Lower criticism is applied to the form or text of the Bible in an attempt to restore the original text. It should not be confused with higher criticism, since the textual (lower) critic studies the form of the words of a document rather than its value as a document. Many examples of lower criticism may be seen in the history of the transmission of the Bible text. Some of these examples were done by staunch supporters of orthodox Christianity, while others were done by its sharpest opponents. Those who are interested in obtaining the original reading of the text by application of certain criteria or standards of quality are textual critics. In general, their work is constructive and their basic attitude positive. Some of these individuals follow the example of B. F. Westcott, Sir Frederic G. Kenyon, Bruce M. Metzger, and others. Those who use these criteria to undermine the text are fault-finders and their work is basically negative and destructive.

Since many adherents of higher criticism have also spent considerable time and energy in the study of textual criticism, there has been a tendency to classify all textual critics as "modernists," destructive critics, or higher critics. In so doing, some Christians have virtually "thrown the baby out with the bath water." To avoid textual criticism merely because certain higher critics have used its method in their work is hardly a justifiable position to maintain. The issue of importance is not whether criticism is higher, but whether or not it is sound. That is a matter of evidence and argument, not one of a priori assumptions.

### HISTORICAL DEVELOPMENT OF TEXTUAL CRITICISM

The history of the text of the Bible in the church may be divided into several basic periods, especially with reference to the New Testament: (1) the period of reduplication (to 325), (2) the period of standardization of the text (325-1500), (3) the period of crystallization (1500-1648), and (4) the period of criticism and revision (1648-present). During the period of criticism and revision, a struggle has been waged between the proponents of the "received text," and those advocating the "critical text." In this struggle the critical text has come into the position of dominance. Although not many modern scholars seriously defend the superiority of the received text, it should be noted that there is no substantial difference between it and the critical text. What differences there are between these two textual traditions are merely technical rather than doctrinal, for the variants are doctrinally inconsequential. Nevertheless, the "critical" readings are often helpful in interpreting the Bible, and for all practical purposes both text traditions convey the *content* of the autographs even though they are separately garnished with their own minor scribal and technical differences.

#### THE PERIOD OF REDUPLICATION (to 325)

From as early as the third century B.C. scholars in Alexandria attempted to restore the texts of the Greek poets and writers of prose. It was at this center that the Septuagint (LXX) version of the Old Testament was produced about 280-150 B.C. Alexandria was also a center of Christianity during the early centuries of the church, a position it retained until the rise of Islam in the seventh century. It is understandable that this city would be a center of activity in attempts at restoring the Bible text prior to 325. Basically, however, there was no real textual criticism of New Testament books during these centuries. Instead, it was a period of reduplication of manuscripts rather than one of textual evaluation. In contrast to Alexandria, however, diligent textual work was performed on the Old Testament by rabbinical scholars in Palestine A.D. 70-100.

*Copies of the autographs* (to 150). During the second half of the first century the New Testament books were written under the direction of the Holy Spirit and were inerrant. Undoubtedly written on papyrus, these autograph copies have all subsequently been lost. Before they perished, however, they were providentially copied and circulated. These first copies were made as early as A.D. 95, very soon after the autographs had been written. These early copies were also written on papyrus rolls, and later they were recopied in papyrus codices, and parchment and vellum were employed later. Very few, if any, of these early copies are extant today.

While there were many early copies of the autographs, not all of them were of the same quality, for as soon as copies began to appear errors and misprints crept into the text. The quality of a copy depended upon the capabilities of the particular scribe. Highly accurate copies were quite expensive, for they were the work of professional scribes. Less capable scribes made poorer copies, although their very cost made them more widely distributed. Still other copies were of quite poor quality since they were done by nonprofessionals for use by individuals or groups.

*Copies of the copies* (150-325). As the apostolic period drew to a close, persecution became more widespread against the Christian church. The sporadic persecutions culminated in two imperial persecutions under Decius and Diocletian. In addition to their confrontation with intense persecution, suffering and even death, Christians frequently saw their sacred writings confiscated and destroyed. As a result of this destruction, the Scriptures were in danger of being lost to the church. Therefore, Christians often made copies of whatever manuscripts they had, however hastily it was deemed necessary. Since scribes were in danger of persecution if apprehended, the Scriptures were often copied "unprofessionally," or in an amateur manner by members of a given church. The possibility of errors creeping into the text became even more pronounced in this situation.

Meanwhile, during these very years, the church at Alexandria began to do pioneer work at the local level and compared and published texts in the period around 200-250. Their leadership was followed in other parts of the empire as well, and some basic work in textual criticism was done by the time of the persecution under Decius (249-251). Origen in Alexandria worked on his *Hexapla*, although it was never published in its entirety. In addition to this work in the Old Testament, he wrote commentaries on the New Testament and became something of a textual critic in that area as well. Other examples of early textual criticism include such works as the *Lucian Recension*, Julius Africanus' work on *Susanna*, and Theodore of Mopsuestia's *Song of Songs* in the area about Caesarea. These early textual critics did some elementary selection and editorial revision of the text materials, but their work did not stem the tide of casual, unsystematic, and largely unintentional creation of variant readings in the New Testament text.

THE PERIOD OF STANDARDIZATION (325-1500)

After the church was released from the threat of persecution following the Edict of Milan (313), the influence was soon felt on the copying of biblical manuscripts. This period was marked by the introduction of parchment and vellum codices, and paper books toward its close. During this period Greek uncials gave way to minuscules; i.e., printed works were replaced by those written in a modified cursive script. Throughout the period critical revisions of the texts were relatively rare, except for the efforts of such scholars as Jerome (c. 340-420) and Alcuin of York (735-804). Nevertheless, the particular period between 500 and 1000 witnessed the Masoretic work on the text of the Old Testament which resulted in the Masoretic text.

When the Emperor Constantine wrote to Eusebius of Caesarea instructing him to make fifty copies of the Christian Scriptures, a new direction in the history of the New Testament began. This was the period of standardization of the text, as the New Testament began to be carefully and faithfully copied from existing manuscripts. The text of a particular region was copied by copyists of that region. When Constantine moved the seat of the empire to the city named after him (Constantinople) it was only reasonable that that city would come to dominate the Greek-speaking world and that its scripture text would become the dominant text of the church. This was especially true in light of the emperor's patronage in producing careful copies of the New Testament text.

As a result of the precedent set by Constantine, great numbers of carefully copied manuscripts were produced throughout the Middle Ages, but official and carefully planned revision of the text was relatively rare. Since a standardized text was developed, there was little need for classification and critical evaluation of the earlier manuscripts of the New Testament. As a result, the text remained relatively unchanged throughout the entire period. Toward the end of the period a completely standardized text with unlimited more-or-less identical copies became possible with the introduction of cheap paper and the printing press. Paper copies of the Bible became more abundant after the twelfth century. About 1454 Johann Gutenberg developed movable type for the printing press, and the door was open for efforts at more careful textual criticism during the Reformation era.

THE PERIOD OF CRYSTALLIZATION ( 1500-1648 )

In the Reformation era the biblical text entered into a period of crystallization in printed rather than manuscript form. Attempts were made to publish printed texts of the Bible as accurately as possible. Frequently these were published in polyglot (multilingual) form, including such titles as the Complutensian Polyglot (1514-17), the Antwerp Polyglot (1569-72), the Paris Polyglot (1629-45) and the London Polyglot (1657-69). It was also during this period that a standard edition of the Masoretic text was published ( c. 1525) under the editorship of Jacob Ben Chayyim, a Hebrew Christian, based on manuscripts dating from the fourteenth century. The text is essentially a recension of the Masorete Ben Asher (fl. c. 920), and it became the basis for all subsequent copies of the Hebrew Bible, whether in manuscript or printed form. Work on the New Testament text was more varied and sweeping in its outreach as a result of Gutenberg's invention.

*Cardinal Francisco Ximenes de Cisneros* (1437-1517) of Spain planned the first printed Greek New Testament to come off the press in 1502. It was to be a part of the Complutensian Polyglot, consisting of the Hebrew, Aramaic, Greek, and Latin texts, and published in the university town of Alcala (*Complutum* in Latin), after which the polyglot received its name when printed there in 1514 and 1517. Although this was the first printed New Testament, it was not the first to be placed on the market. Pope Leo X did not give his sanction until March 1520. The Greek manuscripts underlying Ximenes' work have never been adequately determined; and there was some question about Ximenes' statements in the dedication about them.

*Desiderius Erasmus* (c. 1466-1536) of Rotterdam, the Dutch scholar and humanist, had the honor of editing the first Greek New Testament to be published. As early as 1514 Erasmus discussed such a work with the printer Johann Froben of Basel. Erasmus traveled to Basel in July 1515 in an attempt to find Greek manuscripts to set alongside his own Latin translation. Although the manuscripts he found needed editing, he proceeded with his task. Erasmus was hasty in his work; and his first edition, published in March, 1516, contained numerous errors, including hundreds of typographical and mechanical mistakes. Bruce M. Metzger has indicated in *The Text of the New Testament* that Erasmus' text, which was later to become the basis for the so-called Textus Receptus, was not based on early manuscripts, not reliably edited, and consequently not trustworthy.[1] Even the reception of Erasmus' edition of the Greek New Testament was quite mixed. Nevertheless, by 1519 a new edition was needed. This second edition became the basis for Luther's German translation, although only one additional manuscript was used in its preparation. Further editions appeared in 1522, 1527, and 1535. All these editions were based on the Byzantine type text, contained readings from very late manuscripts, and included such spurious readings as 1 John 5:7-8 as well as Erasmus' translation into Greek of the Latin text of some verses in Revelation.

*Robert Estienne (Etienne;* Lat., *Stephanus),* royal printer in Paris, published the Greek New Testament in 1546, 1549, 1550, and 1551. The third edition (1550) was the earliest edition to contain a critical apparatus, although it was a mere fifteen manuscripts. This edition was based on Erasmus' fourth edition and became

1. Bruce M. Metzger, *The Text of the New Testament* (New York: Oxford U., 1964), pp. 99-100.

the basis for the Textus Receptus. After its publication this third edition became the dominant text in England. In his fourth edition, Estienne indicated his conversion to Protestantism and demonstrated the modern verse divisions which he produced for the first time.

*Théodore de Bèze (Beza)* (1519-1605) was the successor to John Calvin at Geneva. He published nine editions of the New Testament after the death of his famous predecessor in 1564, as well as a posthumous tenth edition in 1611. The most outstanding edition published by Beza came in 1582, when he included a few readings from Codex Bezae (D) and Codex Claromontanus ($D^2$). His spare use of these manuscripts may be attributed to the fact that they differed too radically from the Erasmusan and Complutensian texts. As a result, Beza's Greek New Testament editions were in general agreement with the 1550 edition of Estienne. Their influence lies in the fact that they tended to popularize and stereotype the Textus Receptus. The King James translators made use of Beza's 1588/89 edition.

*Bonaventure and Abraham Elzevir* (1583-1652 and 1592-1652) produced the Received Text (Textus Receptus). While the text of Stephanus held sway over England, this text became the most popular on the Continent. The uncle and nephew were quite enterprising as publishers, and their Leiden company released seven editions of the New Testament between 1624 and 1787. The 1624 edition drew basically from Beza's 1565 edition, and their second edition (1633) is the source of the title given to their text, as the preface reads, *"Textum ergo habes, nunc ab omnibus receptum: in quo nihil immutatum aut corruptum damus."* Thus, a publisher's blurb became the catchword (textus receptus means "received text") to designate the Greek text which they had derived from the editions of Ximenes, Beza, and Stephanus. This text is almost identical to that of Stephanus, which was the basis for the King James translation. Nevertheless, the textual basis was actually very late, from only a handful of manuscripts, and several passages were inserted which have no textual support. Only new manuscript discoveries, classification, and comparison could remedy such a state of affairs.

THE PERIOD OF CRITICISM AND REVISION ( 1648-Present )

At the close of the Reformation era the Bible entered into a period of criticism and revision which actually involves three shorter ones. Each of these subperiods is characterized by an important phase of criticism and revision, namely, they were periods of preparation, progression, and purification. It is important to remember that each of these phases of criticism was constructive rather than destructive in nature.

*The Period of Preparation* (1648–1831) was characterized by the gathering of textual materials and their systematic collection. When Brian Walton (1600-1661) edited the London Polyglot, he included the variant readings of Estienne's 1550 edition. This Polyglot contained the New Testament in Greek, Latin, Syrian, Ethiopic, Arabic, and Persian (in the gospels). In the annotations the variant readings of the recently discovered Codex Alexandrinus (A) and a critical apparatus by Archbishop Ussher appeared. In 1675 John Fell (1625-1686) published an anonymous edition of the Greek New Testament at Oxford which contained evidence for the first time of the Gothic and Bohairic versions. Then, in 1707, John Mill (1645-1707) reprinted the 1550 Estienne text and added some thirty thousand variants from nearly one hundred manuscripts. This work was a monumental contribution to subsequent scholars as it provided them with a broad basis of established textual evidence.

Richard Bentley (1662-1742) was an outstanding classical scholar who issued a prospectus for a New Testament text which he never completed. Nevertheless, he challenged others to gather available textual materials and translations for intensive study. Among those scholars was Johann Albrecht Bengel (1687-1752), who established one of the basic canons of textual criticism: the difficult reading is to be preferred to the easy. One of Bentley's collators who had showed an early disposition for textual criticism was Johann Jakob Wettstein (1693-1754), who published the first apparatus identifying the uncial manuscripts by capital Roman letters and the minuscules by Arabic numerals. He also advocated the sound principle that manuscripts must be evaluated by their weight rather than by their numbers. The fruit of his forty-year efforts was published in 1751-1752 at Amsterdam.

A reprint of Wettstein's *Prolegomena* was made in 1764 by Johann Salomo Semler (1725-1791) who is known as the "father of German rationalism." He followed Bengel's pattern of classifying manuscripts by groups, but carried the process farther. Semler was the first scholar to apply the term *recension* to groups of New Testament witnesses. He identified three of these recensions: Alexandrian, Eastern, and Western. All later materials were regarded by Semler as mixtures of these.

The individual who actually carried Bengel's and Semler's principles to fruition was Johann Jakob Griesbach (1745-1812). He classified the New Testament manuscripts into three groups (Alexandrian, Western, and Byzantine), and laid the foundation for all subsequent work on the Greek New Testament. In his work Griesbach established fifteen canons of criticism. Shortly after he published the first edition of his New Testament (1775-1777), several other scholars published collations which greatly increased the availability of textual evidence from the church Fathers, early versions, and the Greek text.

Christian Friedrich Matthaei (1744-1811) published a valuable critical apparatus in his Greek and Latin New Testament, for he added new evidence from the Slavonic translations. Frary Karl Alter (1749-1804), a Jesuit scholar from Vienna, added evidence from the Slavic manuscripts from twenty additional Greek manuscripts and other manuscripts as well. In 1788-1801 a group of Danish scholars published four volumes of textual work under the direction of Andrew Birch (1758-1829). In these volumes the readings from Codex Vaticanus (B) appeared in print for the first time.

Meanwhile, two Roman Catholic scholars were intense in their textual work. Johann Leonhard Hug (1765-1846) and his pupil Johannes Martin Augustinus Scholz (1794-1852) developed the theory that a "common edition" (*koine ekdosis*) followed the degeneration of the New Testament text in the third century. Scholz added 616 new manuscripts to the growing body of available textual materials and stressed, for the first time, the importance of ascribing geographical provenance represented by several manuscripts. This last point was elaborated by B. H. Streeter in 1924 as part of his theory of "local texts." After some time, Scholz adopted Bengel's classification of manuscripts and published a

New Testament in 1830-1836 which indicated a regression toward the Textus Receptus, as he followed the Byzatine rather than the Alexandrian text. Only in 1845 did Scholz retract this view in favor of the Alexandrian readings.

*The Period of Progression* (1831-1881) brought the constructive critics to the fore in their grouping of textual materials. The first complete break with the Received Text was made by such men as Karl Lachmann (1793–1851), who published the first Greek New Testament resting wholly on a critical text and evaluation of variant readings; Lobegott Friedrich Constantin von Tischendorf (1815-1874), who sought out, discovered, and published manuscripts and critical texts; Samuel Prideaux Tregelles (1813-1875) who was instrumental in directing England away from the Received Text; and Henry Alford (1810-1871) who wrote numerous commentaries and otherwise demolished the unworthy and pedentic reverence for the Received Text.

Several other great scholars must be mentioned at this point, as they also played key roles in the development of textual criticism. Caspar Rene Gregory completed the last edition of Tischendorf's Greek Testament with a prolegomenon (1894). This work provided the chief source of textual materials upon which scholars still depend as well as the basis for the universally accepted catalogue of manuscripts. Two Cambridge scholars, Brooke Foss Westcott (1825-1901) and Fenton John Anthony Hort (1828-1892), rank with Tischendorf as making outstanding contributions to the study of the New Testament text. They published *The New Testament in the Original Greek* (1881-1882) in two volumes. The text of this work had been made available to the revision committee which produced the English Revised New Testament in 1881. Their views were not original but were based on the work of Lachmann, Tregelles, Griesbach, Tischendorf, and others. The use of their text for the English Revised Version and the thoroughness of the explanation of their views in their introduction added to the acceptance of their critical text.

Nevertheless, some scholarly advocates for the Received Text spared no efforts in arguing against the text of Westcott and Hort. Three of these were John W. Burgon (1813-1888), who vehemently denounced the critical text, F. H. A. Scrivener (1813-1891), who was somewhat milder in his criticism, and George Salmon (1819-1904), who decried the lack of weight ascribed to the "Western" readings by Wesctott and Hort.

The "genealogical theory" of Westcott and Hort divided the textual materials into four types: Syrian, Western, Neutral, and Alexandrian. The Syrian text type included the Syrian, Antiochian, and Byzantine texts, such as A, E, F, G, H, S, V, Z, and most of the minuscules. The Western text type for Westcott and Hort had its roots in the Syrian church but was carried farther west, as observed in *Delta* (Δ), Old Latin, Cyriac^c and the *Theta* (0) family so far as it was known. The Neutral text type was supposedly of Egyptian origin and included the codices B and *Aleph* (א). Their fourth text type was Alexandrian and comprised of a small number of witnesses in Egypt which were not of the Neutral type. This family contained C, L, family 33, the Sahidic, and the Bohairic texts. According to Westcott and Hort, there was a common ancestor (X) to both the Neutral and Alexandrian text types which was quite early and pure. The accompanying chart illustrates the relationships of each of these text-type families of the New Testament:

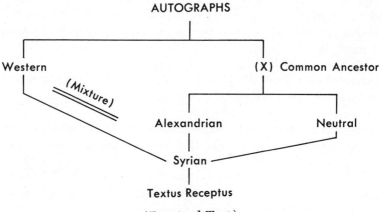

(Received Text)

*The Period of Purification* (1881—present) witnessed the reaction against the theory of Westcott and Hort which had all but dethroned the Received Text as well as the further growth of materials utilized in textual criticism. The chief opponents of the critical text were Burgon and Scrivener, while its major proponents included Bernhard Weiss (1827-1918), Alexander Souter (1873-1949), and others. The arguments against the critical text may be summarized as follows: (1) the traditional text used by the church for fifteen hundred years must be correct because of its duration; (2) the traditional text had hundreds of manuscripts in its favor, whereas the critical text had only a few early ones; and (3) the traditional text is better because it is older. Following the deaths of Burgeon and Scrivener, opposition to the critical text became less seriously considered by scholars.

Another critic of the Westcott-Hort position was Hermann Freiherr von Soden (1852-1914). He began his work on a different basis from Westcott and Hort, but confirmed many of their findings in his New Testament work. Although he had vast financial assistance for his work, von Soden's enterprise has been regarded as a magnificent failure. Nevertheless, he did agree with other opponents in indicating that Westcott and Hort had a nonacceptable notion about the Syrian recension as well as the Syrian text.

This situation resulted in a reinvestigation of the textual materials utilized by Westcott and Hort. The results of this scholarly and constructive criticism may be seen in the current status of the Westcott-Hort theory. The text types have been reclassified as a result of von Soden and other critics. The Syrian family has been renamed as Byzantine or Antiochian because of the possibility of being confused with the Old Syriac version. At present there is a general recognition of more intermixture between the Alexandrian and Neutral text types, and that both these text types are actually only slightly different variations of the same family. Hence, the Alexandrian designation now includes the Neutral text. In a reevaluation of the Western type text, scholars have determined that there are actually three subgroups—Codex D, Old Latin and Old Syriac—and they agree that the text is not generally reliable when its readings stand alone. Since the deaths of Westcott, Hort, and von Soden, a new text type has been discovered, the Caesarean. This family lies midway between the Alexandrian and Western texts, or possibly closer to the Western.

The most recent collations of these text materials are available in Eberhard Nestle's *Novum Testamentum Graece* and *The Greek New Testament* of the United Bible Societies, edited by K. Aland and others. They generally rank the manuscript evidence in the following descending order of importance: Alexandrian, Caesarean, Western, and Byzantine. Since the Received Text follows the Byzantine text basically, it is almost redundant to indicate that its authority is not highly regarded by scholars.

| | GOSPELS | ACTS | CATHOLIC EPISTLES | PAUL, HEBREWS | REVELATION |
|---|---|---|---|---|---|
| Alexandrian | P¹ P³ P⁴ P⁵ P⁷ P²² P³⁴ P²⁹ (P⁶⁶) P⁷⁵ ℵ B C L Q T (W-Luke 1– John 8:12) Z Δ Ξ Ψ 054 059 060 0162 220 33 164 215 376 579 718 850 892 1241 (1342 Mark) | P⁸ (P⁵⁰) ℵ A B C Ψ 048 076 096 6 33 81 104 326 1175 | P²⁰ P²³ P⁷² ℵ A B C P Ψ 048 056 0142 0156 33 81 104 323 326 424ᶜ 1175 1739 2298 | P¹⁰ P¹³ P¹⁵ P¹⁶ P²⁷ P³² P⁴⁰ P⁶⁵ ℵ A B C H I M P Psi 048 081 088 0220 6 33 81 104 326 424ᶜ 1175 1739 1908 | P¹⁸ P² P⁴⁷ ℵ A C P 0207 0169 61 59 94 241 254 1006 1175 1611 1841 1852 2040 2053 2344 2351 |
| | Boh (Sah) Ath Cyr-Alex (Or) | Boh (Sah) Ath Cyr-Alex Clem-Alex? (Or) | Boh (Sah) Ath Cyr-Alex Clem-Alex? (Or) | Boh (Sah) | |
| Caesarean | P³⁷ P⁴⁵ Θ (W-Mark 5 ff.) N O Σ Φ Fam 1 Fam 13 28 565 700 7071 1604 Geo Arm Pal-Syr Eus Cyr-Jer (Or) | P⁴⁵? I? I? Cyr-Jer? | (Text type not determined in the remainder of the New Testament) | | |
| Western | P²⁵ D (W-Mark 1–5?) 0171 It, especially k e Sin-Syr Cur-Syr Tert Ir Clem-Alex Cyp (Aug) | P³⁸ P⁴¹ P⁴⁸ D E 066 257 440 614 913 1108 1245 1518 1611 1739 2138 2298 It Hark-Syr mg | P³⁸ D E It Hark-Syr mg Ir Tert Cyp Aug Eph | D E F G 88 181 915 917 1836 1898 1912 It | F? It? |
| Byzantine | A E F G H K M S U V (W-Matt., Luke 8:12 ff.) Y Γ Δ Π Ω Most minuscules Goth Later versions Later Fathers | H L S P Most minuscules Goth Later versions Later Fathers | H K L S 42 398 Most other minuscules Goth Later versions Later Fathers | K L Most other minuscules Goth Later versions Later Fathers | 046 82 93 429 469 808 920 2048 Most other minuscules Goth Later versions Later Fathers |

# 15

# RESTORATION OF THE BIBLE TEXT

ALTHOUGH there are no known autographs of the Old and New Testaments, numerous manuscript copies and quotations are available which assist biblical scholars in their efforts to restore the original Bible text. In addition to the evidence we have discussed in the past few chapters, there is supportive evidence to the Bible text from its various translations, but these items will be the basic subject matter of the following chapters. For the present, our concern will be the matter of textual criticism in restoring the text itself rather than its translation into various languages.

## THE PROBLEM OF TEXTUAL CRITICISM

The problem of textual criticism centers about three basic issues: genuineness and authenticity, manuscript evidence, and variant readings in the text. Although each of these issues have been mentioned repeatedly in earlier discussions, a more detailed treatment of them is in order.

### GENUINENESS AND AUTHENTICITY

*Genuineness* is used in the matter of textual criticism as it relates to the truth of the origin of a document, that is, its authorship. As indicated in chapter 14, genuineness is primarily the subject of Special Introduction to the Bible, since it relates to such things as the authorship, date, and destiny of biblical books. General Introduction is concerned with such topics as inspiration, authority, canonicity, and authenticity of the books of the Bible. The question answered by genuineness is simply this: is this document really from its alleged source or author? Is it genuinely the work of the stated writer?

*Authenticity* refers to the truth about the facts and content of the documents of the Bible. It deals primarily with the integrity (trustworthiness) and the credibility (truthfulness) of the record. In short, a book may be genuine without being authentic, if the professed writer is the real one, even if the content is untrue. Then, again, a book may be authentic without being genuine, if the content is true but the professed writer is not the actual one. In General Introduction, then, the concern is with the integrity of the text based on its credibility and authority. It is assumed that a biblical book, which has divine authority, and hence credibility, and has been transmitted with integrity, will automatically have genuineness. If there were a lie in the book regarding its origin or authorship, how could its contents be believed?

MANUSCRIPT EVIDENCE

A summary review of the manuscript evidence pertaining to the biblical text will prove beneficial at this point. It will reveal the basic difference in approach to the textual criticism of each Testament.

*The Old Testament* has survived in few complete manuscripts, most of which date from the ninth century A.D. or later. There are, however, abundant reasons for believing that these copies are good. Several lines of evidence support this contention: (1) the few variants existing in these Masoretic manuscripts; (2) the almost literal agreement of most of the LXX with the Masoretic Hebrew text; (3) the scrupulous rules of the scribes who copied the manuscripts; (4) the similarity of parallel Old Testament passages; (5) archaeological confirmation of historical details of the text; (6) the agreement, by and large, of the Samaritan Pentateuch; (7) the thousands of Cairo Geneza manuscripts; and (8) the phenomenal confirmation of the Hebrew text by the Dead Sea Scroll discoveries.

*The New Testament* manuscripts are numerous but so are the variant readings. Consequently, the science of textual criticism is necessary to the restoration of the New Testament text. Over five thousand Greek manuscripts, dating from the second century onward, bear witness to the text. In contrast to the Old Testament which has few but good early manuscripts, the New Testament has many manuscripts which are of poorer quality, that is, they possess more variant readings.

## VARIANT READINGS IN THE TEXT

The multiplicity of manuscripts produces a corresponding number of variant readings, for the more manuscripts that were copied, the greater the possible number of errors made by copyists. Instead of being a hindrance to reconstructing the biblical text, this situation actually becomes extremely beneficial.

*Old Testament Variants* are relatively rare for several reasons: (1) because there is only one major manuscript tradition the total number of possible errors is less; (2) because copies were made by official scribes who labored under strict rules; (3) because the Masoretes systematically destroyed all copies with "mistakes" or variant readings. The discovery of the Dead Sea Scrolls has provided overwhelming confirmation of the fidelity of the Masoretic text, as may be observed in the conclusions of such Old Testament scholars as Millar Burrows, *The Dead Sea Scrolls*; R. Laird Harris, *Inspiration and Canonicity of the Bible*; Gleason L. Archer, Jr., *A Survey of Old Testament Introduction*; and F. F. Bruce, *Second Thoughts on the Dead Sea Scrolls*. The sum of their testimony is that there are so few variant readings between the Masoretic text and the Dead Sea Scrolls that the latter confirm the integrity of the former. Where there are differences, the Dead Sea Scrolls tend to support the readings found in the Septuagint (LXX).

Since the Masoretic text stemmed from a single source which was standardized by Hebrew scholars about A.D. 100, the discovery of manuscripts antedating this period cast new light on the history of the Old Testament text prior to that time. In addition to the three basic textual traditions of the Old Testament which had been recognized already (Masoretic, Samaritan, and Greek), the Dead Sea Scrolls revealed a Proto-Masoretic text type, a Proto-Septuagint text type, and a Proto-Samaritan text type. Attempts at drawing the lines of relationship between these textual families are in the embryonic stage, and the situation calls for dedicated scholarship. For the present, the Masoretic text is considered basic, since both the Samaritan (see chap. 16) and Septuagint (see chap. 17) texts are based on translations of the

Hebrew text. Nevertheless, the Dead Sea Scrolls have indicated that there are places where the Septuagint contains the preferred reading. The basic problem is to determine how great the difference is between the Hebrew and the Greek traditions.

*New Testament Variants* are much more abundant than their Old Testament counterparts because of the numerous manuscripts and because there were many private and unofficial copies made. Every time a new manuscript is discovered, the gross number of variants increases. This may be seen by comparing the approximately 30,000 variants estimated by John Mill in 1707, the nearly 150,000 counted by F. H. A. Scrivener in 1874, and the more than 200,000 known variants at the present time. There is an ambiguity in saying there are some 200,000 variants, since these represent only about 10,000 places in the New Testament. If a single word were misspelled in 3,000 different manuscripts, they are counted as 3,000 variants. Once the counting procedure is understood, and the mechanical (orthographic) variants have been eliminated, the remaining significant variants are surprisingly few in number.

In order to fully understand the significance of variant readings, and to determine which are correct (or original) readings, it is first necessary to examine just how these variants came into the text. Although these principles also apply to the Old Testament, they are here used with reference to the New Testament only.

In general, careful students of textual criticism have suggested two classes of errors: *unintentional* and *intentional*.

Unintentional changes of various kinds all arise from the imperfection of some human faculty. These have resulted in the vast number of transcriptional errors in the text.

Errors of the eye, for example, have resulted in several kinds of variant readings. Among these are wrong division of words which have resulted in the introduction of new words. Since early manuscripts did not separate words by spaces, such divisions would have a bearing on the resultant reading of the text. To use an English example, HEISNOWHERE could mean either HE IS NOW HERE or HE IS NOWHERE. Even more amusing is DIDYOUEVERSEEABUNDANCEONTHETABLE. Omissions of letters, words, and even whole lines of text occurred when an astigmatic eye jumped from one group of letters or words to a similar group. This particular error is caused by *homeoteleuton* (similar ending). When only one letter is missing the error is called *haplography* (single writing). *Repetitions* are the opposite of errors of omission. When the eye picked up the same letter or word twice, it was called *dittography*. It is from such an error in some minuscules that the following reading emerged: "Whom do you want me to release for you, Jesus Barabbas or Jesus?" (Mt 27:17, marg).

*Transposition* is the reversal of position of two letters or words, technically known as *metathesis*. In 2 Chronicles 3:4, the transposition of letters altered the measurements of the porch of Solomon's temple to 120 cubits instead of 20 cubits, as it correctly appears in the LXX. Other confusions of spelling, abbreviation, or scribal insertions account for the remainder of scribal errors. This is especially true of Hebrew letters which were used as numerals too. The confusion of such numbers in the Old Testament may be seen in the conflicts of parallel passages: see, for example, 40,000 in 1 Kings 4:26 as opposed to 4,000 in 2 Chronicles 9:25; the 42 years in 2 Chronicles 22:2 in contrast to the correct reading of 22 years in 2 Kings 8:26 also fits into this category.

Errors of the ear occurred only when manuscripts were copied by a scribe listening to a reader. This may explain why some manuscripts (after the fifth century A.D.) read *kamelos* (rope) instead of *kamēlos* (a camel) in Matthew 19:24, *kauthasomai* (he burns) instead of *kauchasomai* (he boasts) in 1 Corinthians 13:3, and other such alterations in the text of the New Testament.

Errors of memory are not so numerous, but occasionally a scribe forgot the precise word in a passage and substituted a synonym. He may have been influenced by a parallel passage or truth, as in the case of Ephesians 5:9, possibly confused with Galatians 5:22, as well as the addition to Hebrews 9:22 (AV) of ". . . there is no remission [of sins]."

Errors of judgment are generally ascribed to dim lighting and poor eyesight at the occasion of copying the manuscript. Sometimes marginal notations were incorporated into the text in such instances, or perhaps they were the product of a sleepy scribe at work. No doubt one of these causes is to be blamed for the variant readings in John 5:4, 2 Corinthians 8:4-5, etc. It is difficult at times to tell whether a variant is the result of faulty judgment or intentional doctrinal changes. No doubt I John 5:8, John 7:53-8:11, and Acts 8:37 fit into one of these categories.

Errors of writing are attributed to scribes who, due to imperfect style or accident, wrote indistinctly or imprecisely and set the stage for future sight or judgment errors. On some occasions, for example, a scribe might neglect to insert a number or word into the text he transcribed, as in the case of the omitted number in 1 Samuel 13:1.

Intentional changes account for a good number of textual variants, although the vast majority are attributed to unintentional errors. These intentional errors may have been motivated by good intentions, and no doubt they were, but nonetheless they were deliberate alterations of the text.

Among the factors involved in making intentional alterations in a biblical manuscript were the grammatical and linguistic variations. These *orthographic variations* in spelling, euphony, and grammatical form are abundant in the papyruses, and each scribal tradition had its own idiosyncracies. Within these traditions a scribe might tend to modify his manuscript in order to make it conform to them. Such changes include spelling of proper names, verb forms, smoothing of grammar, gender changes, and syntactical alterations.

*Liturgical changes* are widely observable in the lectionaries. Minor changes might be made at the beginning of a passage, and sometimes a passage might be summarized for liturgical use. On occasion some of these changes would creep into the biblical text itself, as in the case of the "doxology" of the Lord's Prayer (Mt 6:13). *Harmonizational changes* frequently appear in the gospels when one account is brought into agreement with its parallel passages (see Lk 11:2-4 and Mt 6:9-13), or in Acts 9:5-6 which was brought into more literal agreement with Acts 26:14-15. In the same manner some Old Testament quotations were enlarged in some manuscripts to conform more precisely with the LXX (cf. Mt 15:8 with Is 29:13, where the phrase *this people* is added). *Historical and factual changes* were sometimes introduced by well-meaning scribes. John 19:14 was changed in some manuscripts to read "third" instead of "sixth" hour, and Mark 8:31, where "after three days" was changed to read "on the third day" in some manuscripts. *Conflational changes* result from combining two or more variants into a single reading, as in the likely case of Mark 9:49 and Romans 3:22 (KJV).

*Doctrinal changes* constitute the last category of intentional scribal changes. Most of the deliberate doctrinal changes have been in the direction of orthodoxy, as is the reference to the Trinity in 1 John 4:7-8. Other alterations, while springing from good intentions, have had the effect of adding to the text what was not part of the original teaching at that point. Such is probably the case with the addition of "fasting" to "prayer" in Mark 9:29 and the so-called long ending to that gospel itself (Mk 16:9-20). But even here the text is not heretical. It is well to remember at this point that no Christian doctrine hangs on a debatable text, and that a student of the New Testament must beware of changing the text simply on the basis of doctrinal considerations.

When a comparison of the variant readings of the New Testament is made with those of other books which have survived from antiquity, the results are little short of astounding. For instance, although there are some 200,000 "errors" among the New Testament manuscripts, these appear in only about 10,000 places, and only about one-sixtieth rise above the level of trivialities. Westcott and Hort, Ezra Abbot, Philip Schaff, and A. T. Robertson have carefully evaluated the evidence and have concluded that the New Testament text is over 99 percent pure. In light of the fact that there are over 5,000 Greek manuscripts, some 9,000 versions and translations, the evidence for the integrity of the New Testament is beyond question.

This is especially true when some of the greatest writings of antiquity have survived in only a handful of manuscripts (see chap. 12). A comparison of the nature or quality of those writings sets the biblical text in bold relief for its integrity. Bruce M. Metzger made an excellent study of Homer's *Iliad* and the Hindu *Mahābhārata* in *Chapters in the History of New Testament Textual Criticism*. In that study he demonstrated that the textual corruption of those sacred books is much greater than the New Testament. The *Iliad* is particularly appropriate for this study because it has so much in common with the New Testament. Next to the New Testament the *Iliad* has more extant manuscripts than any other book (453 papyri, 2 uncials, and 188 minuscules for a total of 643). Like the Bible, it was considered sacred, and experienced textual changes and criticism of its Greek manuscripts. While the New Testament has about 20,000 lines, the *Iliad* has about 15,000. Only 40 lines (400 words) of the New Testament are in doubt, whereas 764 lines of the *Iliad* are in question. Thus the 5 percent corruption of the *Iliad* stands against the less than 1 percent of the New Testament text. The national epic of India, the *Mahābhārata*, has suffered even more corruption. It is about eight times as long as the *Iliad* and the *Odyssey* combined, roughly 250,000 lines. Of these, some 26,000 lines are textually corrupt, or just over 10 percent.

Thus, the New Testament has not only survived in more manuscripts than any other book from antiquity, but it has survived in a much purer form than any other great book, whether or not they are sacred works, a form that is over 99 percent pure. Even the *Koran*, which is not an ancient book since it originated in the seventh century A.D., has suffered from a large collection of variants that necessitated the Orthmanic revision. In fact, there are still seven ways to read the text (vocalization and punctuation), all based on Orthman's recension, which was made about twenty years after the death of Muhammad himself.

## THE PRINCIPLES OF TEXTUAL CRITICISM

The full appreciation of the arduous task of reconstructing the New Testament text from thousands of manuscripts containing tens of thousands of variants can be derived, in part, from a study of just how textual critics proceed about their task. They use two kinds of textual evidence: external and internal.

### EXTERNAL EVIDENCE

External evidence falls into three basic varieties: chronological, geographical, and genealogical. *Chronological* evidence pertains to the date of the text type rather than to the particular manuscript itself. The earlier text types have readings that are preferred over later ones by textual critics. *Geographical* distribution of independent witnesses that agree in support of a variant are preferred to those having closer proximity or relationship. *Genealogical* relationships between manuscripts follow the discussion presented in chapter 14. Of the four major textual families, the Alexandrian is considered to be the most reliable, although it sometimes shows a "learned" correction. Readings supported by good representatives of two or more text types are to be preferred to a single text type. The Byzantine text is generally considered to be the poorest. When the manuscripts within a given text type are divided in their support of a variant, the true reading is probably the reading of the manuscripts most generally faithful to their own text type, the reading that differs from that of the other text types, the reading that is different from the Byzantine textual family, or the reading that is most characteristic of the text type to which the manuscripts in question belong.

INTERNAL EVIDENCE

Internal evidence is classified in two basic varieties: transcriptional (depending on the habits of scribes) and intrinsic (depending on the habits of authors). *Transcriptional evidence* renders four general assertions: the more difficult reading (for the scribe) is preferred, especially if it is sensible; the shorter reading is preferred unless it arose from an accidental omission of lines because of similar ends (*parablepsis*) or intentional deletion; the more verbally dissonant readings of parallel passages is preferred, even if they are quotations of the Old Testament; and the less refined grammatical construction, expression, word, etc., is preferred.

*Intrinsic evidence* depends upon the probability of what the author is likely to have written. It is determined by the author's style throughout the book (and elsewhere), the immediate context of the passage, the harmony of a reading with the author's teaching elsewhere (as well as with other canonical writings) and the influence of the author's background.

In considering all the internal and external factors in textual criticism, it is essential to realize that their use is not merely one of science, it is also a delicate art. A few observations may assist the beginner in getting acquainted with the process of textual criticism. In general, external evidence is more important than internal, since it is more objective. Decisions must select internal as well as external evidence in textual evaluation, since no manuscript or text type contains all the correct readings in itself. On some occasions different scholars will come to conflicting positions, because of the subjective element in internal evidence.

Gleason Archer cautiously suggests the priority which should be utilized in the event that a textual variant is encountered: (1) the older reading is preferred; (2) the more difficult reading is preferred; (3) the shorter reading is preferred; (4) the reading which best explains the variants is preferred; (5) the widest geographical support for a reading makes it preferred; (6) the reading which conforms best with the author's style and diction is preferred; and (7) the reading which reflects no doctrinal bias is preferred.

## The Practice of Textual Criticism

The most practical way to observe the results of the principles of textual criticism is to compare the differences between the Authorized Version (KJV) of 1611, which is based on the Received Text, and the American Standard Version (ASV) of 1901 or the Revised Standard Version (RSV) of 1946 and 1952, which are based on the Critical Text. A survey of several passages will serve to illustrate the procedure used in reconstructing the true text.

### OLD TESTAMENT EXAMPLES

*Deuteronomy 32:8* provides another interesting exercise on Old Testament textual criticism. The Masoretic text, followed by the KJV and the ASV reads, "The Most High gave to the nations their inheritance. . . . He set the bounds of the peoples according to the number of the children of Israel." The RSV followed the LXX rendition: "According to the number of the sons [or angels] of God." A fragment from Qumran now supports the LXX reading. According to the principles of textual criticism indicated earlier, the RSV is correct because it (1) has the more difficult reading, (2) is supported by the earliest known manuscript, (3) is in harmony with the patriarchal description of angels as "sons of God" (cf. Job 1:6; 2:1; 38:7, and possibly Gen 6:4) and (4) explains the origin of the other variant.

*Zechariah 12:10* illustrates this same point. The KJV and ASV follow the Masoretic text: "They shall look upon me [Jehovah speaking] whom they have pierced." The RSV follows the Theodotian version (c. A.D. 180; see chap. 17) in rendering it, "When they look on him whom they have pierced." The Masoretic text preserves the preferred reading because it (1) is based on the earlier and better manuscripts, (2) is the more difficult reading and (3) can explain the other reading on the grounds of theological prejudice against the deity of Christ or the influence of the New Testament change from the first to the third person in its quotation of this passage (cf. Jn 19:37).

Some other important variants between the Masoretic and LXX texts were clarified with the Dead Sea Scroll discovery, and in these instances they tend to support the LXX. Among those passages are Hebrews 1:6 (KJV) which follows the LXX quotation of Deuteronomy 32:43, the famous Isaiah 7:14 rendition of "His name shall be called," instead of the Masoretic reading, "she shall call his name." The Greek Septuagint version of Jeremiah is sixty verses shorter than the Masoretic text, and the Qumran fragment of Jeremiah tends to support the Greek text. These illustrations should not be construed as a uniform picture of the Dead Sea Scrolls supporting the Septuagint text, since there are not many variants from the Masoretic text among the manuscripts found at the Dead Sea site. In general the scrolls have tended to confirm the integrity of the Masoretic text. The passages indicated here are merely indications of the problems and principles of textual criticism as they are practised by Old Testament textual critics.

NEW TESTAMENT EXAMPLES

*Mark 16:9-20* (KJV) produces the most perplexing of all textual problems. These verses are lacking in many of the oldest and best Greek manuscripts, such as ℵ (Aleph), B, Old Latin manuscript k, the Sinaitic Syriac, many Old Armenian manuscripts and a number of Ethiopic manuscripts. Many of the ancient fathers show no knowledge of it, and Jerome admitted that this portion was omitted from almost all Greek copies. Among the witnesses that have these verses, some also have an asterisk or obelus to indicate that they are a spurious addition to the text. There is also another ending which occurs in several uncials, a few minuscules, and several manuscript copies of ancient versions. The familiar long ending of the KJV and the Received Text is found in a vast number of uncial manuscripts (C, D, L, W, and θ [*Theta*]), most minuscules, most Old Latin manuscripts, the Latin Vulgate, and in some Syriac and Coptic manuscripts. In Codex W the long ending is expanded after verse 14.

A decision of which of these endings is preferred is still a moot point, since none of them commends itself as original because of the limited textual evidence, the Apocryphal flavor, and the non-Marcan style of the endings. On the other hand, if none of these endings is genuine, it is difficult to believe that Mark 16:8 is not the original ending. A defense of the Received Text (vv. 9-20) has been made by John W. Burgon, and more recently by M. van der Valk, although it is admittedly difficult to arrive at a solution about which text best represents the original. On the basis of known textual evidence, it appears more likely that the original end of the gospel of Mark was verse 8.

*John 7:53-8:11* (KJV) relates the story of the woman taken in adultery. It is placed in brackets in the ASV with a note that most ancient authorities omit it. The RSV places the passage in brackets at the end of the gospel of John, with a note that other ancient authorities place it there, at the end of John's gospel, or after Luke 21:38. The evidence that this passage is part of John's gospel is decidedly lacking because (1) it is not in the oldest and best Greek manuscripts; (2) neither Tatian nor the Old Syriac betrays any knowledge of it, and it is also omitted in the best Peshitta manuscripts, the Coptic, several Gothic, and Old Latin manuscripts; (3) no Greek writer refers to it until the twelfth century; (4) its style and interruption do not fit into the context of the fourth gospel; (5) its earliest appearance is in Codex Bezae (c. 550); (6) several scribes placed it in other locations (for example, following Jn 7:36; Jn 21:24; Jn 7:44 or Lk 21:38); and (7) many manuscripts which included it indicated doubts about its integrity by marking it with an obelus. As a result, the passage may well preserve a true story, but from the standpoint of textual criticism it should be placed as an appendix to John with a note that it has no fixed place in the ancient witnesses.

*First John 5:7* (KJV) is completely omitted in the ASV and RSV renditions without any explanation. There is an explanation for this omission, however, and it provides an interesting scene in the history of textual criticism. There is virtually no textual support for the KJV reading in any Greek manuscript, although there is ample support in the Vulgate. Thus, when Erasmus was challenged as to why he did not include the reading in his Greek New Testament of 1516 and 1519, he hastily responded that he would include it in his next edition if anyone were to find even one manuscript in its support. One sixteenth-century Greek minuscule was produced to support it, the 1520 manuscript of the Franciscan friar Froy, or Roy. Erasmus complied with his promise and included the reading in his 1522 edition. The KJV followed Erasmus' Greek text; and, on the basis of a single, late, and insignificant witness, all the weight and authority of all other Greek manuscripts were disregarded. In fact, the inclusion of this verse as genuine breaks almost every major canon of textual criticism.

On the basis of the above-mentioned case studies, it should be clear that textual criticism is both a science and an art. Not only is the Bible the most well-preserved book to survive from the ancient world, its variant readings of significance amount to less than one-half of one percent corruption, none of which affect any basic Christian doctrine. In addition, the textual critic has at his disposal a series of canons which for all practical purposes enables him to completely restore the exact text of the Hebrew and Greek autographs of the Scriptures—not only line for line, but even word for word.

# 16

# ARAMAIC, SYRIAC, AND RELATED TRANSLATIONS AND BIBLES

THE TRANSMISSION of the revelation from God to us centers about three significant historical developments: the invention of writing before 3000 B.C.; the beginnings of translation before 200 B.C.; the developments in printing before A.D. 1600. Earlier we looked into the matter of writing and copying the original manuscripts of the Bible as well as the role, method, and practice of textual criticism in preserving the text of those original writings. Here we shall direct our attention to the translation of God's Word.

The present chapter will be devoted to a study of the earliest of the translation efforts, and to those related to them by language. Before turning to these translations, however, certain technical terms involved in the history of Bible translation need to be clearly understood.

## DEFINITIONS AND DISTINCTIONS

There are more precise definitions of some of the basic words involved in Bible translation than are generally used in popular discussion. The careful student of the Bible should avoid confusing these terms.

### DEFINITIONS

*Translation, literal translation, and transliteration.* Those three terms are closely related. A translation is merely the rendering of a given literary composition from one language into another. For example, if the Bible were rendered from the original Hebrew and Greek into Latin, or from Latin into English, it would be a

187

translation. If these later translations were rendered back into the original languages, that too would be a translation. *The New English Bible,* NEB (1961, 1970), is a translation. A literal translation is an attempt to express, as far as possible, the exact meaning of the original words of the text being translated. It is a word-for-word rendering of the text. As a result, it is somewhat rigid. Such is the case with *Young's Literal Translation of the Holy Bible* (1898). A transliteration is the rendering of the letters of one language into the corresponding letters of another. Of, course, a complete transliteration of the Bible would be meaningless for one who did not understand Hebrew and Greek. However, transliteration of words such as "angel," "baptize," and "evangel" have been introduced into English.

*Version, revision, revised version and recension.* Again, these are closely related terms. Technically speaking, a version is a translation from (or with direct reference to) the original language into any other language, although common usage neglects this distinction. The key to this is that it involves the original language of a given manuscript. For all practical purposes, the NEB is a version in this sense of the term. *The Rheims-Douay Bible* (1582, 1609) and the *King James Version,* KJV (or AV, *Authorized Version*) (1611), both fail the test of being translated from the original languages. The Rheims-Douay was translated from the Latin Vulgate, itself a translation, while the KJV was the fifth revision of Tyndale's version. However, *The Revised Version,* RV or ERV (1881, 1885), *The American Standard Version,* ASV (1901), and *The Revised Standard Version,* RSV (1946, 1952), are all versions in the more common use of the word. Again, the crucial factor is that a version must be translated from the original language.

A revision, or revised version, is a term used to describe those translations, usually from the original languages, which have been carefully and systematically reviewed and critically examined with a view to correcting errors or making other necessary emendations. The KJV is an example of such a revision, as are the Rheims-Douay Challoner editions and the RSV. A recension is the critical and systematic revision of a text, although such works are generally and popularly called "revisions." The most outstanding example of a recent recension is the *New American Standard Bible*, NASB (1963, 1971).

*Paraphrase and commentary.* A paraphrase is a "free" or "loose" translation. It attempts to translate idea for idea rather than word for word. Hence, it is more of an interpretation than is a literal translation. In the history of Bible translation this format has been very popular. As early as the seventh century, for instance, Caedmon made paraphrases of the Creation. Recent paraphrases include J. B. Phillip's *New Testament in Modern English* (1958), the American Bible Society's *Good News for Modern Man: The New Testament in Today's English*, TEV (1966), and Kenneth Taylor's *The Living Bible* (1971). A commentary is simply an explanation of Scripture. The earliest example of such a work is the Midrash or Jewish commentary on the Old Testament. In recent years some Bible translations known as amplified or expanded translations have contained implicit, and sometimes explicit, commentary within the text of the translation itself. Two examples will suffice to illustrate this popular approach: Kenneth S. Wuest, *Expanded Translation of the New Testament* (1956-1959), which carried the same principles to various parts of speech; the Lockman Foundation made the fullest attempt at translating *The Amplified Bible* (1965) as a commentary by the use of dashes, brackets, parentheses, and italicized words.

DISTINCTIONS

In order to appreciate fully the role of Bible translations, it is important to understand that the very process of translation is itself indicative of the vitality the Bible has among the people of God. At first, translations were an integral part of the religious life of the ancient Hebrews. They set the tone for all later translations. In the early church, missionary activity was accompanied by diverse translations of the Bible into various languages. As time progressed, still another phase of Bible translation arose with the developments in printing. As a result, we should carefully distinguish between three general categories of Bible translations: the ancient, medieval, and modern translations.

*Ancient Translations and Bibles.* The ancient translations and Bibles contained portions of the Old Testament, and sometimes the New. They appeared before the period of the church councils (c. A.D. 350) and include such works as the Samaritan Pentateuch, the Aramaic Targums, the Talmud, the Midrash, and the Septuagint (LXX). Following the apostolic period, these ancient translations were continued in Aquila's version, Symmachus' revision, Origen's *Hexapla*, and the Syriac versions of the Old Testament. Translations of the New Testament into Aramaic and Latin also appeared prior to the Council at Nicea (325).

*Medieval Translations of the Bible.* Medieval translations of the Bible generally contained both the Old and the New Testaments. They were completed during the period 350-1400. During this period Bible translations were dominated by the Latin Vulgate of Jerome (c. 340-420). The Vulgate provided the basis for commentaries as well as thought throughout the Middle Ages. From it arose the paraphrases of Caedmon, the *Ecclesiastical History* of the Venerable Bede, and even the translation of the Bible into English by Wycliffe. The Bible continued to be translated into other languages throughout this period.

*Modern Translations.* Modern translations came into being about the time of Wycliffe and his successors. Following the example of Wycliffe, since his was the first complete English Bible, William Tyndale (1492-1536) made his translation directly from the original languages instead of the Latin Vulgate. Since that time multitudes of renderings have been produced containing all or parts of the Old and New Testaments. Following the development of movable typeset by Johann Gutenberg (c. 1454), the history of Bible transmission, translation, and distribution enters into a new era.

The translation of the Bible helped to keep Judaism pure during the last centuries before Christ, as our discussion of the Samaritan Pentateuch and the Targums will indicate. The translation of the Septuagint (see chap. 17) was translated into Greek at Alexandria, Egypt (beginning 280-250 B.C.), and it set the tone for such translations into Latin and other languages (see chap. 18). These translations were vital to the evangelization, expansion, and establishment of the church. Since the Reformation era, the dissemination of the Bible has resulted in translations into numerous other languages. The role of the English Bible has been paramount among modern translations (see chaps. 19 and 20). Our discussion will follow these general topical lines, beginning with the Aramaic, Syriac, and related translations.

## PRIMARY TRANSLATIONS

Early Bible translations had a twofold purpose that cannot be minimized: they were used to disseminate the message of the autographs to the people of God and assisted them in keeping their religion pure. Their proximity to the autographs also indicates their importance, since they take the Bible scholar back to the very threshold of the autographs.

### THE SAMARITAN PENTATEUCH

The Samaritan Pentateuch may be from the period of Nehemiah's rebuilding of Jerusalem; and, while it is not really a translation or version, it does indicate the need for careful study in tracing the true text of Scripture. This work was actually a manuscript portion of the text of the Pentateuch itself. It contains the five books of Moses and is written in a palaeo-Hebrew script quite similar to that found on the Moabite Stone, Siloam Inscription, Lachish Letters, and some of the older biblical manuscripts of Qumran. The textual tradition of the Samaritan Pentateuch is independent of the Masoretic text. It was not discovered by Christian scholars until 1616, although it had been known to such Fathers of the church as Eusebius of Caesarea and Jerome, and it was first published in the Paris Polyglot (1645) and then in the London Polyglot (1657).

The roots of the Samaritans can be traced back to the time of David. During the reign of Omri (880-874 B.C.) the capital was established at Samaria (1 Ki 16:24), and the entire northern kingdom came to be known as Samaria. In 732 B.C. the Assyrians, under Tiglath-pileser III (745-727), conquered the northeast portion of Israel and established a policy of deportation of inhabitants and importation of other captive peoples into the area. Under Sargon II (in 721 B.C.) the same procedure was followed when he captured the rest of Israel. Intermarriage was imposed by Assyria on those Israelites who were not deported in order to guarantee that no revolt would occur by automatically denationalizing and commingling the cultures of their captive peoples (2 Ki 17:24-18:1). At first, the colonists worshipped their own gods. By the time, or shortly after, the Jews returned from their own Babylonian captivity, these colonists seemed to want to follow the God of Israel. The Jews rebuffed the Samaritans who in turn opposed Israel's restoration (see Ezra 4:2-6; Neh 5:11-6:19). About 432 B.C., however, the daughter of Sanballat was married to the grandson of the high priest Eliashib. This couple was expelled from Judah and the event provided the historical incident for the break between the Jews and the Samaritans (see Neh 13:23-31).

The Samaritan religion as a separate system of worship actually dates from the expulsion of the high priest's grandson about 432 B.C. At this time, a copy of the Torah may have been taken to Samaria and placed in the temple built on Mount Gerizim at Shechem (Nablus), where a rival priesthood was established. This fifth-century date may account for both the palaeo-Hebrew script and the twofold categorization of the Samaritan Pentateuch into the Law and the noncanonical books. Samaritan adherence to the Torah and their isolation from the Jews resulted in a separate textual tradition for the Law.

The earliest manuscript of the Samaritan Pentateuch dates from the mid-eleventh century as a fragmentary portion of a fourteenth-century parchment, the Abisha scroll. The oldest Samaritan Pentateuch codex bears a note about its sale in A.D. 1149-50, although it is much older, and the New York Public Library owns another copy dating from about 1232. Immediately after it was discovered in 1616, the Samaritan Pentateuch was acclaimed as superior to the Masoretic text. After careful study, however, it was relegated to an inferior status. Only recently has it regained some of its former importance, although it is still regarded as less important than the Masoretic text of the law. The merits of the Samaritan Pentateuch text tradition may be seen in the fact that its approximately 6,000 variants from the Masoretic text are relatively few, mainly orthographic and rather insignificant. It does claim that Mt. Gerizim rather than Jerusalem is the center of worship, and adds to the accounts following Exodus 20:2-17 and Deuteronomy 5:6-21. Whenever the Samaritan Pentateuch and the Septuagint agree on a reading which differs from the Masoretic text, they probably represent the original reading of the text. Otherwise, the Samaritan Pentateuch reflects cultural trends in the Hebrew setting, such as sectarian insertions, repetition of God's commands, trends toward popularizing the Old Testament text, tendencies to modernize antique word forms, and attempts to simplify difficult portions of Hebrew sentence construction.

### THE ARAMAIC TARGUMS

*The Origin of the Targums.* There is evidence that the scribes were making oral paraphrases of the Hebrew Scriptures into Aramaic as early as the time of Ezra (Neh 8:1-8). They were not actually translations so much as aids in understanding the archaic language of the Torah. The individual involved in these paraphrases was called a *methurgeman,* and they played an important role in communicating the quaint-sounding Hebrew into the everyday language of the people. Before the birth of Christ, almost every book in the Old Testament had its own oral paraphrase or interpretation (Targum). During the next few centuries these Targums were committed to writing and an official text emerged.

The earliest Aramaic Targums were probably written in Palestine during the second century A.D., although there is evidence of some Aramaic Targums from the pre-Christian period. These early official Targums contained the law and the prophets, although unofficial Targums of later times also included the writings. Several unofficial Aramaic Targums were found in the Qumran caves, but they were superseded by the official texts of the second century A.D. During the third century, the official Palestinian Targums of the law and the prophets were practically swallowed up by another family of paraphrases of the law and the prophets, the Babylonian Aramaic Targums. Targums on the writings continued to be made on an unofficial basis.

*The outstanding Targums.* During the third century A.D., an Aramaic Targum on the Torah appeared in Babylonia. It was possibly a recension of an earlier Palestinian tradition, but may have originated in Babylonia, and has been traditionally ascribed to Onkelos (Ongelos), although the name is probably confused with Aquila (see chap. 17).

The Targum of Jonathan ben Uzziel is another Babylonian

Aramaic Targum which accompanies the prophets (former and latter). It dates from the fourth century and is a freer rendering of the text than Onkelos. Both these Targums were read in synagogues: Onkelos along with the Torah, which was read in its entirety, and Jonathan along with selections from the prophets (*haphtaroth*, pl.). Since writings were not read in the synagogues, no official Targum was made, although unofficial copies were used by individuals. During the middle of the seventh century the Pseudo-Jonathan Targum on the Pentateuch appeared. It is a mixture of the Onkelos Targum and some Midrash materials. Still another Targum appeared about 700, the Jerusalem Targum, but it survives in fragments only. None of these Targums is important on textual grounds, but they do provide significant information for the study of hermeneutics since they indicate the manner in which Scripture was interpreted by rabbinical scholars.

THE TALMUD AND MIDRASH

A second period of the Old Testament scribal tradition appeared between A.D. 100–500 known as the Talmudic period. *The Talmud* (lit., instruction) grew up as a body of Hebrew civil and canonical law based on the Torah. The Talmud basically represents the opinions and decisions of Jewish teachers from about 300 B.C. to A.D. 500, and it consisted of two main divisions: the Mishnah and the Gemara. The Mishnah (repetition, explanation) was completed about A.D. 200 as a Hebrew digest of all the oral laws since the time of Moses. It was highly regarded as the second law, the Torah being the first. The Gemara (completion) was an Aramaic expanded commentary on the Mishnah. It was transmitted in two traditions: the Palestinian Gemara (c. 200) and the larger, more authoritative Babylonian Gemara (c. 500).

*The Midrash* (lit., textual study) was actually a formal doctrinal and homiletical exposition of the Hebrew Scriptures written in Hebrew and Aramaic. About 100 B.C.–A.D. 300 these were gathered into a body consisting of the *Halakah* (procedure), a further expansion of the Torah only, and the *Haggadah* (declaration, explanation), being commentaries on the entire Old Testament. The Midrash actually differed from the Targums in that they were commentaries instead of paraphrases. The Midrash contains some of the earliest extant synagogue homilies on the Old Testament, as well as some proverbs and parables.

### SYRIAC TRANSLATIONS

The Syriac (Aramaic) language of the Old Testament, and indeed of the Gospels, was comparable to the Koine in Greek and the Vulgate in Latin. It was the common language of the market. Since Palestinian Jews of our Lord's time undoubtedly spoke Aramaic, the language to this entire region, it is reasonable to assume that the Jews in nearby Syria also spoke it. In fact, Josephus relates that first-century Jews proselyted in the areas east of ancient Nineveh, near Arbela. Following their example, early Christians went into the same area and then on into Central Asia, India, and even China. The basic language of this entire branch of Christianity was Syriac, or what F. F. Bruce has called "Christian Aramaic." Once the church began to move out from Syria in its missionary efforts, the need for a version of the Bible for that area became urgent.

*The Syriac Peshitta.* The Bible translated into Syriac was comparable to the Vulgate in Latin. It is known as the Peshitta (lit., simple). The Old Testament text of the Peshitta stems from a mid-second- and early-third-century text, although the name Peshitta dates from the ninth century. The Old Testament was probably translated from Hebrew, but it was revised to conform with the LXX. Where the Peshitta follows the Masoretic text, it gives valuable support to the text, but it is not too reliable as an independent witness to the Old Testament text.

The standard edition of the Syriac New Testament is believed to stem from a fifth-century revision by Rabbula, Bishop of Edessa (411-435). His revision was actually a recension of earlier Syriac versions which were brought closer to the Greek manuscripts then in use in Constantinople (Byzantium). This edition of the Syriac New Testament, plus the Christian recension of the Syriac Old Testament, has come to be known as the Peshitta. Following Rabbula's order that a copy of his recension be placed in every church in his diocese, the Peshitta had widespread circulation during the middle and late fifth century. As a result of this action, the Peshitta became the authorized version of the two main branches of Syriac Christianity, the Nestorians and the Jacobites.

*The Syro-Hexaplaric Version.* The Syro-Hexaplar text of the Old Testament was a Syriac translation of the fifth column of Origen's *Hexapla* (see chap. 17). Although it was translated about 616 by Paul, Bishop of Tella, it never actually took root in the Syrian churches. This was partly because it was an excessively literal rendering of the Greek text in violation of Syriac idiom. The literal character of its translation makes the Syro-Hexaplar text a valuable aid in determining the correct text of the *Hexapla*. Manuscript portions of it have survived in the Codex Mediolanensis, consisting of 2 Kings, Isaiah, the Twelve, Lamentations, and the Poetical books (except Psalms). The Pentateuch and historical books survived until about 1574, but they have subsequently disappeared. Like the Peshitta, the text of this version is basically Byzantine.

*The Diatessaron of Tatian (c. 170).* Tatian was an Assyrian Christian and follower of Justin Martyr in Rome. After the death of his mentor, Tatian returned to his native country and made a "scissors-and-paste" harmony of the gospels known as the *Diatessaron* (lit., through the four). Tatian's work is known mainly through indirect references, but it was a popular and widely used work until it was abolished by Rabbula and Theodoret, bishop of Cyrrhus in 423, because Tatian had belonged to the heretical sect known as the Encratites. Tatian's work was so popular that Ephraem, a Syrian father, wrote a commentary on it before Theodoret had all copies of it (about two hundred) destroyed. In its place, Theodoret presented another translation of the Gospels of the Four Evangelists.

Since the *Diatessaron* has not survived, it is impossible to determine whether it was originally written in Syriac or, more likely, in Greek and later translated into Syriac. Ephraem's commentary on the *Diatessaron* was written in Syriac, but it too has been lost. An Armenian translation of the commentary has survived, however, as have two Arabic translations of the *Diatessaron*. Although the original *Diatessaron* would bear heavily on New Testament textual criticism, its secondary witness from the translation and the commentary in translation add little additional weight to the text. One fact is observable, however: the *Diatessaron* was influenced by both the Eastern and Western texts of the New Testament.

*The Old Syriac Manuscripts.* The *Diatessaron* was not the only form of the gospels used among the Syrian churches. Among scholars there was a tendency to read them in one or another of several separate forms. Even before the time of Tatian, such writers as Hegesippus quoted from another Syriac version of the Bible. This Old Syriac text of the gospels was typical of the Western text type, and it has survived in two manuscripts. The first of these is a parchment, known as the Curetonian Syriac, and the second is a palimpsest, known as the Sinaitic Syriac. These gospels were called "the Separated Ones," because they were not interwoven in the manner of Tatian's *Diatessaron.* Although there are differences between the readings of these two texts, they both reflect the same version of a text dating from the late second or early third century. No Old Syriac texts of the remainder of the New Testament have survived, although they have been reconstructed on the basis of citations in the writings of the Fathers of the Eastern church.

*Other Syriac Versions.* Three additional Syriac versions require a comment even though they reflect later texts than those already discussed. In 508 a new Syriac New Testament was completed which included the books omitted by the Peshitta (2 Peter, 2 John, 3 John, Jude, and Revelation). This work was actually a Syriac revision of the entire Bible by Bishop Polycarp under the direction of Zenaia (Philoxenus), a Jacobite bishop at Mabbug in eastern Syria. This Philoxenian Syriac translation reveals that the Syrian church had not accepted the entire New Testament canon until the sixth century. In 616 another bishop of Mabbug, Thomas of Harkel (Heraclea), reissued the Philoxenian text, to which he either added some marginal notes or thoroughly revised in a much more literal style. His revision is known as the Harklean version, although the Old Testament portion was done by Paul of Tella, as indicated earlier. The critical apparatus of the Harklean Book of Acts is the second most important witness to the Western text, being surpassed in this respect only by Codex Bezae. The third

Syriac version is known as the Palestinian Syriac. No complete New Testament book from this translation exists. Its text probably dates from the fifth century and it survives in fragmentary form only, mostly from lectionaries of the gospels dating from the eleventh and twelfth centuries.

### SECONDARY TRANSLATIONS

Although the Samaritan Pentateuch, the Talmud, and the earliest Midrash manuscripts were written in Palaeo-Hebrew and Hebrew characters and thus do not even qualify as translations, they did provide a basis for later works of translation by making the Scriptures available for use by the people of God. The Aramaic Targums and various Syriac translations of the Bible further underscored this trend by placing them into the basic languages of Jewish and early Christian believers. From these basic versions arose several secondary translations. These secondary translations have little textual merit, but they do indicate the basic vitality of Christian missions and the desire of new believers for the Word of God in their own languages.

*Nestorian Translations.* When the Nestorians were condemned at the Council at Ephesus (431) their founder, Nestorius (died c. 451), was placed in a monastery as part of a compromise which brought many of his followers into the camp of his opponents. The Persian Nestorians, however, broke away and became a separate schismatic church. They spread into Central and even into East Asia and translated the Bible into several languages as they moved along their way. Among their translations are the so-called Sogdian versions. These translations were based on the Syriac Scriptures rather than the Hebrew and Greek Testaments. Scant remains of their work have survived, and all this is from the ninth, tenth, and later centuries. Textually speaking, none of these translations are significant, since they are translations of a translation. The devastating work of Tamerlane, "the Scourge of Asia," almost exterminated the Nestorians and their heritage toward the close of the fourteenth century.

*Arabic Translations.* Subsequent to the rise of Islam (following the *hejirah*, the flight of Muhammad in A.D. 622), the Bible was translated into Arabic from Greek, Syriac, Coptic, Latin, and various combinations of them. The earliest of the various Arabic translations appears to have stemmed from the Syriac, possibly the Old Syriac, about the time Islam merged as a major force in history (c. 720). Muhammad (570-632), the founder of 'Islam, knew the gospel story through oral tradition only, and this was based on Syriac sources. The only standardized Old Testament translation into Arabic was done by the Jewish scholar Saadia Gaon (c. 930). Similar to the Nestorian translations, the Arabic translations range from the ninth to the thirteenth centuries. Except for the Old Testament, Arabic translations are based on translations rather than the original texts, and thus offer little if any textual assistance.

*Old Persian Translations.* Two Old Persian translations of the gospels are known, but they are themselves translations of the fourteenth-century Syriac text and a later Greek text. The latter has some resemblance to the Caesarean text, but it is of little use in textual criticism.

# 17

# GREEK AND RELATED
# TRANSLATIONS

DURING THE CAMPAIGNS of Alexander the Great, Jews were shown considerable favor. As he moved on in his conquests, he established centers of population to administer his newly acquired territories. Many of these cities were named Alexandria, and they became centers of culture where Jews were given preferential treatment. Just as they had abandoned their native Hebrew tongue for Aramaic in the Near East, so they abandoned Aramaic in favor of Greek in such centers as Alexandria, Egypt.

Following the sudden death of Alexander in 323 B.C., his empire was divided into several dynasties by his generals. The Ptolemies gained control over Egypt, the Seleucids dominated Asia Minor, the Antigonids took Macedonia, and several minor kingdoms emerged. As far as the Bible is concerned, the Egyptian dynasty of the Ptolemies is of primary importance. It received its name from Ptolemy I Soter, the son of Lagus, who was governor from 323 to 305 and king from that time until his death in 285. He was succeeded by his son Ptolemy II Philadelphus (285-246), who married his sister Arsinoë after the example of the Pharaohs.

During the reign of Ptolemy II Philadelphus, the Jews received full political and religious privileges. It was also during this time that Egypt itself experienced a tremendous cultural and educational program under the patronage of Arsinoë. Included in this program were the founding of the museum at Alexandria and the translation of great works into Greek. Among the works which began to be translated into Greek at this time was the Hebrew Old Testament. It was, indeed, the very first time that it had been extensively translated into any language, as chapter 16 indicates. Our present discussion will center about this translation and those closely related to it.

## The Septuagint (LXX)

The leaders of Alexandrian Jewry produced a standard Greek version of the Old Testament which is known as the Septuagint (LXX), the Greek word for seventy. Although the term applies strictly to the Pentateuch, the only portion of the Hebrew Bible completely translated during the time of Ptolemy II Philadelphus, it has come to denote the entire Greek translation of the Old Testament. The Jewish community itself later lost interest in preserving their Greek version when Christians began to use it extensively for their own Old Testament Scriptures. Apart from the Pentateuch, the remainder of the Old Testament was probably translated during the third and second centuries B.C. Certainly it was completed before 150 B.C., since it is discussed in a letter of Aristeas to Philocrates (c. 130–100 B.C.).

This letter of Aristeas relates how the librarian at Alexandria persuaded Ptolemy to translate the Torah into Greek for use by the Jews in Alexandria. He goes on to report how six translators from each of the twelve tribes were chosen and that their work was completed in only seventy-two days. Although the details of this event are fictitious, they do indicate that the translation of the Septuagint for use by Alexandrian Jews is authentic.

The quality of the translation of the Septuagint is not consistent throughout, and this leads us to several basic observations. First, the LXX ranges from a slavishly literal rendition of the Torah to free translations of the writings. Second, there must have been a different purpose in view for the LXX from that of the Hebrew Bible, such as public readings in the synagogues as opposed to scholarly work by the scribes. Third, the LXX was a pioneer effort in translation of the Old Testament text and an excellent example of such an enterprise. Finally, the LXX is generally faithful to the reading of the Old Testament Hebrew text, as indicated in chapter 12.

One question that is raised by the Septuagint, however, comes from the fact that there are places where it differs from the

Masoretic text, and where the Dead Sea Scrolls agree with it as opposed to the Hebrew text. Several passages may be indicated which underscore this point, such as Deuteronomy 32:8; Exodus 1:5; Isaiah 7:14; Hebrews 1:6 (KJV), which quotes Deuteronomy 32:43. In addition, the Dead Sea Scrolls also contain some of the apocryphal books of the Old Testament, such as Psalm 151, which are known only through the LXX. From the available evidence about these variant readings between the texts, we are able to observe three basic textual traditions of the Old Testament: the Masoretic, the Samaritan (see chap. 16), and the Greek (LXX). On the whole, the Masoretic text is the best, but in several passages the LXX is better. The Samaritan Pentateuch reflects sectarian and cultural differences from the Hebrew text, and the LXX is itself a translation rather than the original text. Nevertheless, when the two agree against the Masoretic text, they probably witness to the original reading.

Having said this, however, it should be remembered that the LXX is generally faithful to the Masoretic textual readings, as are the Dead Sea Scrolls. A comparison of the variants in a given chapter of the Bible may be used to illustrate this point. In Isaiah 53, for example, there are 166 words, and only seventeen letters are in question. Ten of these letters are simply a matter of spelling, which does not affect the sense of the text in the least. Four other letters are the result of minor stylistic changes, such as conjunctions added by scribes. The three remaining letters comprise a single word, "light," which is added to verse 11 and does not affect the meaning greatly. Furthermore, this word is supported by both the LXX and the Dead Sea Scroll IA Is[b]. This example is typical of the entire Isaiah A manuscript. It compels the reader to note the dependability of the Old Testament text in such a way that he recognizes that all the variant readings do nothing to change our understanding of the religious teaching of the Bible.

As a result of this quality, the importance of the LXX is easily observable. It bridged the religious gap between the Hebrew- and Greek-speaking peoples, as it met the needs of the Alexandrian Jews. It also bridged the historical gap between the Hebrew Old Testament of the Jews and the Greek-speaking Christians who would take the LXX as their Old Testament and use it alongside their own New Testament Scriptures. In addition, it provided an important precedent for missionaries and Christian scholars to make translations of the whole Bible into various languages and dialects. On textual grounds, it bridges the gap between the Hebrew Old Testament and the great codices of the church (Aleph, A, B, C, et al.). Although the LXX does not have the excellence of the Hebrew text, it does indicate its purity.

### OTHER GREEK VERSIONS

It was as a result of Jewish criticism during the early centuries of Christianity that a reaction set in among the Jews against the Septuagint. Their reaction produced a new wave of translations of the Old Testament, such as the Greek translations known as Aquila's version and Symmachus' version, and even led to the first great work of textual criticism in the mid-third century, the *Hexapla* of Origen. All of these works play an important role in the study of textual criticism, since they are actually closer to the autographs than many of the Hebrew manuscript copies still extant.

F. F. Bruce has suggested that there are two basic reasons why the Jews rejected the LXX in the first centuries of the church. First, the LXX had been adopted by Christians as their own Old Testament text and freely used it in the propagation and defense of their faith. Second, a revised edition of the standard Hebrew text was established about A.D. 100. At first it included the Pentateuch and later on the rest of the Old Testament. The end result of this revision process was the establishment of the Masoretic text. Since there was no basic text acceptable to both Christians and Jews, Jewish scholars decided to correct the situation by making new Greek translations of their Scriptures.

*Aquila's Version* (c. A.D. 130-150). A new translation of the Old Testament was made for Greek-speaking Jews during the first half of the second century. It was done by Aquila, a man reported to have been a relative of the Emperor Hadrian who had moved to Jerusalem from Sinope as a civil servant. While at Jerusalem, Aquila was converted to Christianity, but found himself unable to extricate himself from his pre-Christian ideas and habits. He was publicly rebuked by the elders of the church, took offense and forsook Christianity for Judaism. As a Jewish proselyte he studied under the famed Rabbi Aqiba and translated the Old Testament into Greek.

Much of this story is undoubtedly fabricated, but Aquila was probably a Jewish proselyte from the area of the Black Sea who flourished during the first half of the second century. He did make a new translation of the Old Testament from Hebrew into Greek, and is the Aquila wrongly associated with the Targum Onkelos as mentioned in chapter 16. Aquila's version of the Old Testament was rigidly slavish translation of the Hebrew text. Although he used Greek words, the thought patterns and sentence structures followed Hebrew rules of composition. Nevertheless, Aquila's text became the official Greek version of the Old Testament used among non-Christian Jews. It has survived only in fragments and quotations.

*Theodotion's Revision* (c. 150-185). The next important Greek translation of the Old Testament is attributed to Theodotion. The exact place and date of this work is disputed, although it appears to have been a revision of an earlier Greek version: either of the LXX, possibly Aquila's, or perhaps of some other Greek version. The most feasible position about this work views it as having been done by Theodotion, a native of Ephesus, who was either a Jewish proselyte or an Ebionite Christian. His revision was much freer than Aquila's version, and in some instances he even replaced some of the older LXX renderings of the Hebrew text. Theodotion's translation of Daniel soon replaced the LXX version among Christians, and some of the early catalogs of the Scriptures. His rendition of Ezra-Nehemiah may have superseded the LXX version as well.

*Symmachus' Revision* (c. 185-200). Symmachus seems to have followed Theodotion in time as well as theological commitment, although some date this work prior to that of Theodotion. Jerome believed that Symmachus was an Ebionite Christian, but Epiphanius asserts that he was a Samaritan convert to Judaism. For our purposes, that disagreement makes little difference, since the purpose of Symmachus' work was to make an idiomatic Greek rendition of the text. As a result, Symmachus stands at the opposite pole from Aquila as a translator. He was concerned with the sense of his translation rather than the exactness of its meaning. With this in view, however, we should note that Symmachus exhibited high standards of accuracy which have had a profound influence on later Bible translators. His turning of Hebrew phrases into good and idiomatic Greek brings Symmachus nearer than any of his rivals to the modern conception of a translator's duty. Curiously, Symmachus had more influence on the Latin Bible than on later Greek translations, for Jerome made considerable use of him in his preparation of the Vulgate.

*Origen's Hexapla* (c. 240-250). The translations of the Hebrew Bible into Greek resulted in the four different textual traditions by the beginning of the third century A.D.: the LXX, Aquila's version, and the revisions of Theodotion and Symmachus. Such a muddled state of affairs opened the door for the first really outstanding attempt at textual criticism. This work was undertaken by Origen of Alexandria (185-254). Because of the many divergencies existing among the various manuscripts of the LXX, the discrepancies between the Hebrew text and that of the LXX, and the various attempts at revising the Greek translations, Origen seems to have decided to provide a satisfactory Greek text of the Old Testament for the Christian world. As a result, his work was essentially a recension rather than a version or a revision, since he corrected textual corruptions and attempted to unify the Greek and Hebrew texts. He had a two-sided objective: to show the superiority of the various revisions of the Old Testament over the corrupted LXX text, and to provide a comparative view of the correct Hebrew and the divergent LXX texts. He followed the notion that the Hebrew Old Testament was something of an "inerrant transcript" of God's revealed truth to man.

The arrangement of the *Hexapla* (sixfold) was in six parallel columns. Each column contained a particular version of the Old Testament, making it an extremely bulky work. In the first column Origen placed the Hebrew text. In column two was a Greek transliteration of the Hebrew text. The literal translation of Aquila was placed in column three, with the idiomatic revision of Sym-

machus in column four. Origen placed his own revision of the
LXX text in column five, and added Theodotion's revision in column six.

In his *Hexapla* of the Psalms, Origen added three further columns, but only two of them were different translations. He also
made a separate work called the *Tetrapla*, which was the *Hexapla*
with columns one and two omitted. Origen's tremendous work has
not survived the ravages of time, although Eusebius and Pamphilus did publish the fifth column (Origen's own translation of
the LXX) with additions. It has survived in the fourth or fifth
century Codex Sarravianus (G), which contains portions of Genesis through Judges. It is the only Greek edition of any significance
which has been preserved, although there is a Syriac translation
of the *Hexapla* dating from the seventh century, and some individual manuscripts have also survived.

The accomplishment of Origen is observable in what has been
discovered and disclosed about his techniques of textual criticism.
He had discovered many corruptions, omissions, additions, and
transpositions in the copies of the LXX of his day. Many of these
discoveries were made by comparing the various revisions of the
Greek Old Testament, but Origen was primarily concerned about
bringing the LXX texts into greater conformity with the Hebrew
text of column one of his *Hexapla*. He developed an elaborate
system of critical markings to disclose the problems he uncovered
in arriving at his own translation in column five. This enabled the
reader to see which corruptions had been corrected, which omissions and additions had been made, and where words had been
transposed among the various Greek texts.

Origen used an obelus (—), a horizontal stroke, to indicate
when a reading appeared in the LXX which was not in the Hebrew text. When a reading appeared in the Hebrew text but was
omitted in the LXX, Origen supplied the reading from Theodotion's revision and marked its beginning with an asterisk (※ or
⁜). He indicated the end of these corrections with a metobelus
(γ). Where short passages were transposed, Origen would leave
them where they appeared in the LXX and indicate them with a
combination asterisk-obelus sign (※ — or ⁜ —) at the beginning
and a metobelus at the close. In long transposed passages the

Hebrew order would be restored in an attempt to bring the LXX into closer conformity with the Hebrew text.

While Origen's task was of monumental significance, it is important for us to observe that his basic objective was different from that of the modern textual critic. His purpose was to produce a Greek version corresponding as closely as possible to the Hebrew text. The modern textual critic endeavors to recover the original text of the LXX itself as evidence for what the Hebrew text was before the development of the Masoretic text. The transmission of Origen's LXX text without the accompanying diacritical markings he supplied has led to the dissemination of a corrupted Greek Old Testament text rather than the production and preservation of a Septuagint version which conformed to the Hebrew text of that day. Had Origen's *Hexapla* survived, it would be a treasure beyond price, for it would provide us with a copy of the standard Hebrew text of the third century A.D., help solve the dispute over Hebrew pronunciation, and provide information about the Greek versions and translations of Origen's day. Only a translation of the fifth column had survived, largely through the work of Bishop Paul of Tella, in the Syro-Hexaplar text, in an eighth century copy which is currently housed in the museum at Milan.

*Other Recensions of the Septuagint.* Early in the fourth century, Eusebius of Caesarea and his friend Pamphilus published their own editions of Origen's fifth column. As a result, they advanced the version of the LXX which became the standard edition in many places. Two other scholars attempted to revise the Greek text of the Old Testament too. Hesychius, an Egyptian bishop martyred in 311, made a recension which is preserved only in the quotations from the text made by church writers in Egypt. The recovery of his work is dependent upon quotations of such writers as Cyril of Alexandria (d. 444). The works of Chrysostom (d. 407) and Theodoret (d. 444) may be used to recover still another recension of the Old Testament Greek text known as the Lucian Recension. Lucian was a resident of Samosata and Antioch who was also martyred in 311.

These two recensions, coupled with the works of Aquila, Theodotion, Symmachus, and Origen, provided Christians with the Old

Testament text in Greek in North Syria, Asia Minor, Greece, Egypt, and the regions of Jerusalem and Caesarea. All of this was accomplished before the time of Jerome. As far as the modern textual scholar is concerned, the various translations of the Old Testament provide valuable witnesses to the Hebrew text.

## TRANSLATIONS OF THE GREEK TEXT

Among the multitudes present in Jerusalem on the day of Pentecost were "Parthians, and Medes, and Elamites, and the dwellers in Mesopotamia, and in Judea, and Cappadocia, in Pontus and Asia, Phrygia, and Pamphilia, in Egypt, and in the parts of Libya about Cyrene, and strangers of Rome, Jews and proselytes, Cretans and Arabians" (Ac 2:9-11). These individuals would undoubtedly need the Scriptures in their own tongues if they were to be able to study them and use them to propagate their faith. We discussed the translation of the Old and New Testament texts into Syriac (Aramaic) in chapter 16 because of the close relationship those translations had with the translation of the Old Testament by Aramaic-speaking Jews. As a result, our attention here will be directed to other translations of the Greek text.

### COPTIC

Coptic is the latest form of ancient Egyptian writing. It followed earlier developments such as the hieroglyphic, hieratic, and demotic scripts (see chap. 11). The Greek language with seven demotic characters added to it became the written mode of Coptic by the beginning of the Christian era. This system of writing had several dialects into which the Bible was translated.

*Sahidic (Thebaic)*. The Coptic dialect of southern Egypt (Upper Egypt) was Sahidic (Thebaic). Its center was in the region of ancient Thebes, where it was used to translate virtually all of the New Testament by the beginning of the fourth century. Manuscripts in this dialect represent the earliest Coptic versions of the New Testament, which Pachomius (c. 292-346), the great organizer of Egyptian monasticism, required his followers to study diligently. The early date of the Sahidic version makes it an important witness to the text of the New Testament. It is basically related to the Alexandrian type text, although the gospels and Acts follow the Western text type.

*Bohairic (Memphic).* In Lower (northern) Egypt near Memphis in the Delta region, another Coptic was used alongside the Greek language. This was near Alexandria, and its central location and importance in early church history is reflected in that Bohairic Coptic became the basic dialect of the Christian church in Egypt. The nearness of this region to Alexandria, and the continued use of Greek in that center, probably accounts for the fact that Bohairic versions of the New Testament appeared later than their Sahidic counterparts. The only early Bohairic manuscript to have survived is the Bodmer papyrus manuscript of the gospel of John (Papyrus Bodmer III). It has a badly mutilated beginning, but its condition is much better following John 4. This manuscript casts important light on two textual problems: John 5:3b-4 and John 7:53–8:11 (see chap. 15). The Bohairic version appears to be closely related to the Alexandrian text type.

*Middle Egyptian Dialects.* A third area of Coptic dialects is that between the centers of Thebes and Alexandria. The Middle Egyptian dialects are classified as Fayumic, Achmimic and sub-Achmimic by J. Harold Greenlee. No entire New Testament book is extant in these dialects, although John is nearly complete. One fourth-century papyrus codex in the Fayumic dialect contains John 6:11–15:11. It is closer to Sahidic than to Bohairic, which places it in the Alexandrian type text. All of the Old Testament manuscripts in the Coptic dialects follow the Septuagint.

ETHIOPIC

As Christianity spread through Egypt into Ethiopia, a need arose for another translation of the Bible. Although no authoritative statement can be made about it, the Ethiopic translation of the Greek Old Testament seems to have been revised in light of the Hebrew text beginning in the fourth century. By the seventh century this translation was completed and the New Testament was then translated. The complete translation into Ethiopic was probably accomplished by Syrian monks who moved into Ethiopia during the Monophysite Controversy (fifth and sixth centuries)

and the rise of Islam (seventh and eighth centuries). Their influence was profound, as indicated by the fact that the Ethiopic
church continues to be Monophysite.

Two recensions of the Ethiopic New Testament have been made
in the fifth and the twelfth centuries. Its text was later influenced
by Coptic and Arabic translations, and it may actually have been
based on Syriac rather than Greek manuscripts. These manuscripts probably date from the fourth or fifth centuries, which
further reduces the importance of the Ethiopic Bible in terms of
textual criticism. The manuscripts that do survive reflect textual
admixture, but they are basically Byzantine in origin. The Old
Testament includes the noncanonical 1 Enoch (which is quoted
in Jude 14-15) and the Book of Jubilees. This indicates that the
Ethiopic church accepted a broader canon than the church at
large. Over one hundred manuscript copies of the Ethiopic Bible
have survived, but none are earlier than the thirteenth century.
While these manuscripts may deserve further study, they will
probably be neglected because of their late date.

GOTHIC

It is not clear exactly when Christianity moved into the area of
the Germanic tribes between the Rhine and Danube rivers. The
area was evangelized before the Council of Nicea (325), since
Theophilus, bishop of the Goths, was in attendance. The Goths
were among the chief Germanic tribes, and they played a significant role in the events of European history during the fifth century. The first of their tribes to be evangelized was the Ostrogoths,
in the region of the lower Danube. Their second bishop, Ulfilas
(311-381), the "Apostle of the Goths," led his converts into the
area now known as Bulgaria. There he translated the Greek Bible
into Gothic.

This enterprise was of great importance, especially if Ulfilas
actually accomplished the task attributed to him. He reportedly
created a Gothic alphabet and reduced the spoken language to
writing. Whether or not he actually accomplished this feat, he
did make a remarkably faithful translation of the Lucian recension
of the Old Testament into Gothic during the fourth century (c.
350). Very little remains of his Old Testament, and Ulfilas did not

translate all of it in the first place. He felt that the books of Samuel and Kings were too warlike to be transmitted to the Gothic tribes who were themselves quite warlike.

Much more remains of the Gothic New Testament translated by Ulfilas. It is the earliest known literary monument in the Germanic dialect, but it is not found in a single complete manuscript copy. The translation adheres almost literally to the Greek text of the Byzantine type. As such it tells little to the textual critic. The chief value of the Gothic version lies in the fact that it is the earliest literary work in the Germanic language group to which English belongs. Six fragmentary manuscripts have survived, including the Codex Argenteus, "the silver codex," written on purple vellum in silver and some gold letters. All other Gothic manuscripts are palimpsests except a vellum leaf of a bilingual Gothic-Latin codex. Gothic, like Coptic, is a language which took script form expressly for the writing of the Scriptures into the language of the people. All its manuscripts range from the fifth and sixth centuries.

ARMENIAN

As the Syrian churches carried out their evangelistic tasks, they contributed to several secondary translations of the Bible. These secondary translations are so called because they are derived from translations rather than manuscripts in the original languages. One of the foremost of these secondary translations is the Armenian, although not everyone agrees that it is a translation of a translation.

Two basic traditions about the origin of the Armenian translation are generally set forth. The first says that St. Mesrob (d. 439), a soldier turned missionary, created a new alphabet to assist Sahak (Isaac the Great, 390-439) in translating the Bible from the Greek text. The second tradition asserts that this translation was made from the Syriac text. Although both views have merit, the second best fits the actual situation, which stems from the nephew and disciple of Mesrob himself.

The earliest Armenian translations were revised prior to the eighth century in accordance with "trustworthy Greek codices" which were brought from Constantinople after the Council at

Ephesus (431). This revision rose to dominance by the eighth century and continues to be the most common Armenian text in use today. The oldest surviving manuscript of this revised text dates from the ninth century. Its late date and its closeness to the Caesarean or Byzantine text types makes it rather insignificant in matters of textual criticism. Although the matter is not settled, the text of the gospels tends toward the Caesarean type.

The first Armenian translation of the Old Testament was made in the fifth century and reveals a marked influence from the Syriac Peshitta. Its rendition of the Hexaplaric recension was revised in accordance with the Peshitta.

GEORGIAN (IBERIAN)

Georgia, the mountainous region between the Black and Caspian seas to the north of Armenia, received the Christian message during the fourth century. By the middle of the fifth century, it had its own translation of the Bible. Since Christianity spread into Georgia from Armenia, it is no surprise to learn that this was the same route taken by its Bible translation. Accordingly, if the Armenian Old Testament were translated from the LXX or the Syriac Peshitta and the New Testament were translated from the Old Syriac, they would be secondary translations. The Georgian translation was another step removed, since it was translated from Armenian. Even if the Armenian translations were from the original text, the Georgian would be a secondary translation.

The Georgian alphabet, like the Armenian and Gothic, was developed expressly for transmission of the Bible. In keeping with this cultural dependence, all the surviving manuscripts of the Georgian Bible indicate that it follows the Armenian textual tradition.

The continuation of Bible translations by the people of God, as they followed the precedent set by the Jews who had made Aramaic and Syriac translations of the Old Testament, brought about the first actual attempts to place the entire Old Testament into another language, Greek. The LXX was produced in the third and second centuries B.C. Although its quality as a translation varies, it provides the textual critic with invaluable information about the Hebrew text of the Old Testament. In addition, it was an example for other translators to follow as they sought means of transmitting God's Word. With the rise of Christianity, Jews turned away from the LXX and other translations, revisions, and recensions appeared. This culminated in the great work of Origen, the *Hexapla*. As Christianity continued to spread, additional translations were made. In order to accomplish this task, missionaries developed many new written languages. This fact alone made the translation of the Bible a major force in history. It also offers a reason why Bible translators did not make their secondary translations directly from the original languages of the Old and New Testaments.

# 18

# LATIN AND RELATED TRANSLATIONS

WESTERN CHRISTIANITY produced only one great translation of the Bible which was transmitted through the Middle Ages, the Latin Vulgate of Jerome. Once his translation emerged to its dominant position, it remained unchallenged for a thousand years. Others had translated the Scriptures into Latin before Jerome performed his task; and, in order for us to better understand his accomplishment, we will look at those earlier translations.

## THE OLD LATIN

Before an accurate picture of the Latin translations of the Bible can be presented, we need to have a grasp of the linguistic setting of the ancient world in general and the Roman Empire in particular. We will look at the linguistic and cultural aspects of life in the ancient world through its geographical structure before turning to the Old Latin translation itself.

### THE NEAR EAST

The fortunes of the Near East had been quite varied in terms of language, politics, and society by the time the New Testament was written. At any given moment in ancient times, several languages were spoken in the area around Palestine. Following the political fortunes of time, the official language of this region underwent radical shifts. The important languages of the Scriptures were discussed in chapter 11, but their periods of dominance need to be reviewed so we can have a sense of perspective on the overall process of the transmission of the Bible.

*Aramaic.* Following the Babylonian Captivity, the official language of Palestine became Aramaic. It was used by the Hebrew scribes as early as the time of Ezra (Neh 8:1-8). In fact, it was Aramaic that was used to write the Targums during the Sôpherim period (400 B.C.-A.D 200) and the Talmud and Midrash in the period between 100 B.C. and A.D 500 (see chap. 16). During New Testament times Aramaic was the language of Christ and his disciples.

*Greek and Latin.* After the campaigns of Alexander the Great (335-323 B.C.), Greek became the official language within the confines of his conquests. Much of this territory was later incorporated into the Roman Empire, including the Near East, and Hellenistic Greek prevailed as the dominant official language of both Egypt and Syria under the Ptolemaic and Seleucid empires, and even Palestine during the Hasmonean independence (142-63 B.C.). At the death of Attalus III (133 B.C.), the kingdom of Pergamum was bequeathed to Rome, and by 63 B.C. all of the East was incorporated into the Roman Republic. Accompanying this growth of the Roman state was the spread of Latin as the military language of the Near East.

GREECE

*Hellenic Dialects.* Hellenic Greek is applied to Greek culture of the Classical Age. It is derived from the Greek word for Greece: *Hellas.* The various dialects of Hellenic Greek were related to three waves of immigration into the southern part of the Balkan Peninsula during the second millennium B.C.: the Ionian, Achaean, and Dorian. In turn, the Ionians were pushed across the Aegean Sea, into Ionia, and other Greeks immigrated or founded colonies in the Near East, North Africa, and even in southern Italy and the islands of the Mediterranean. Although the Greeks were divided into a series of small states, they were united by their common language in its various dialects. The most famous of these dialects was Attic, which came into its own following the one great example of Greek unification when the Greek states united to oppose the Persians (490-80 B.C.), who were led by Darius I and his son Xerxes. During the next fifty years the Athenian Empire raised Greek culture to its most glorious heights. The The Peloponnesian

War (431-404 B.C.) brought about the defeat of Athens, and the Greek city-states struggled as they moved their separate ways. Philip II, king of Macedonia (359-336 B.C.), was succeeded by his son Alexander (356-323 B.C.), who realized his father's dream of reuniting the Greeks by crushing their revolts in 335. With his ascendancy the Hellenic Age shifts into what is commonly known as the Hellenistic Age.

*Hellenistic Greek.* Unlike Hellenic culture, which belongs to those peoples who spoke Greek as their native language, Hellenistic culture was superimposed upon these peoples whose language was not Greek, following the conquests of Alexander the Great. This intentional advancement of Greek culture and civilization used as its basic language a new and common speech (*koine dialektos*) derived from a blending of the various Greek dialects, although it was primarily derived from Attic. During the centuries following the death of Alexander, this Koine dialect became the official language of the Near East and Egypt as well as Greece and Macedonia. In fact, it was the dialect into which the Septuagint translation was made at Alexandria (see chap. 17). As the Romans moved into Greece and the Near East, and especially after the Battle of Actium (31 B.C.), Latin was the language used by military personnel as the Roman Republic was transformed into the Roman Empire by Octavian. Although the Greeks continued to expend their energies in independent activity, they were no longer in the place of leadership in the ancient world.

ITALY

During the first century B.C. and the centuries following, all roads truly led to Rome. Here was the greatest empire the West had ever seen. Its progress was continual from the tenth century B.C., before the city of Rome itself was founded (c. 753). About 509 B.C. the Tarquin kings were expelled from the city and the Roman Republic was born. From this time the chief city of Latium and its allies began to spread until a nearly three-hundred-square-mile territory along the Tiber River controlled most of the Italian Peninsula (c. 265) and Latin became the common speech. From 264 to 146 B.C. Rome came into conflict with Carthage, an African colony of Phoenicia, resulting in the Punic wars. Before these wars were half over, Rome became involved in the eastern Mediterranean area of Illyria and Macedonia (c. 229-148). By 148 B.C. Macedonia had become a Roman province, and in 133 Attalus III bequeathed his kingdom (Pergamum) to Rome. Rome had become enmeshed in the near East, and its intrusion brought Latin as the military and commercial, although not the official, language of the East.

In Italy, and especially Rome, the people were bilingual. The literary language of the upper classes was generally Greek, and even Latin literature followed the Greek models. Although both slaves and freedmen were bilingual, the military and commercial language was Latin. During the early years of the church, Christians in Rome were largely Greek speaking, as Paul's epistles and the epistles of Clement of Rome show. Only later on did Roman Christians begin to use Latin as the language of their writings. During the fourth and fifth centuries, the Germanic tribes used Latin instead of the more literary Greek as their written language. This is easily understood when it is recalled that the Germanic tribes came into more immediate contact with the Roman legions and merchants long before they did their literature.

AFRICA

The basic languages of North Africa were Greek and Latin. Greek was used in Egypt under the Ptolemies, and Alexandria was the center for translating the Hebrew Old Testament and other literary works into Greek. Farther west, Latin was the basic tongue within the Roman Empire, since it came under the influence of Roman military, commercial, and administrative contacts even before the Punic Wars. Latin was the native tongue of such early Christian writers as Tertullian (who wrote in both Greek and Latin), Cyprian, and others. The early church within the Roman Empire used Greek as its literary language, and only later did Latin and other languages become necessary and widespread.

THE OLD LATIN TRANSLATIONS

Although Latin was the official as well as the common language in the West, Greek retained its position as the literary language of

Rome and the West until the third century. By that time Old
Latin translations of the Scriptures were already circulating in
North Africa and Europe, indicating that Christians had already
begun to express their desire for a Latin translation of the Bible
in the second century.

*The Old Testament.* One of the earliest known translations of
the Hebrew Scriptures in the West was the Old Latin, composed
prior to A.D. 200. This translation was made from the LXX, arose
in North Africa, and had some Jewish influence exerted on the
translation itself. This Old Latin translation was widely used and
quoted in North Africa, and may have been the Old Testament
translation used by Tertullian and Cyprian during the second
century. The unrevised Apocrypha of this translation was apparently posthumously added to Jerome's Vulgate Old Testament. Apart from citations and fragmentary remains of the Old
Latin text of the Old Testament, nothing remains of this translation, its value to the textual scholar is minimal at best.

*The New Testament.* The Old Latin version of the New Testament is an entirely different matter. Some twenty-seven manuscripts of the gospels have survived, along with seven from Acts,
six from the Pauline epistles, and some fragments of the general
epistles and Revelation. These manuscripts date from the fourth
through the thirteenth centuries, but no codex copy is extant. This
evidence indicates that the Old Latin version continued to be
copied long after it had been displaced by the Vulgate.

The Old Latin New Testament, of early date, is among the most
valuable witnesses to the condition of the New Testament in the
West. It is represented by two, and possibly three, different texts.
The African text was used by Tertullian and Cyprian, a European
text appears in the writings of Irenaeus and Novatian and an
Italian (*Itala*) text is mentioned in the works of Augustine. In-
stead of regarding Augustine's text as a precursor to the Vulgate,
recent trends have been to indicate it as simply a reference to the
Vulgate itself. If this be the case, then there are only two different
Old Latin texts of the New Testament. The African is reflected in
Codex Bobiensis (k), and is a free and rough translation of the
Greek text dating from the second century. The European text is

represented in two codices: Codex Vercellensis (a), written by Eusebius of Vercelli before his death in 370-371, and Codex Veronensis (b), the basis of Jerome's translation of the Vulgate.

## THE LATIN VULGATE

The numerous texts of the Old Latin Bible that appeared by the last half of the fourth century led to an intolerable situation. As a result of this problem, Damasus, bishop of Rome (366-384), commissioned a revision of the Old Latin text. The product of this effort was the Vulgate.

### THE PURPOSE OF THE TRANSLATION

Damasus of Rome demonstrated a keen interest in the Scriptures as well as in scholars whom he befriended and patronized. He was quite concerned about the diversity of Bible versions, translations, revisions, and recensions in the fourth century and felt that a new and authoritative edition of the Scriptures was needed. This was especially true in light of the fact that the church in the West had always demonstrated an attitude toward outward conformity which was uncommon and almost unknown in the East. There are several reasons why Damasus saw the need for a new and authoritative edition of the Bible.

*Confusion of Latin Texts.* As indicated earlier, much confusion existed in the Latin texts of the Bible. This diversity was a product of the fact that the Old Testament in Latin was actually a translation of the LXX and the New Testament was translated on informal and unofficial occasions. An example of this may be seen in the Latin translation used by Tertullian. He was bilingual, being able to read and write in Greek as well as Latin, and used the African text of the Old Latin when he did not make his own translation as he went along. No end of problems was caused by such on-the-spot translations, especially if others tried to check on Tertullian's underlying textual authority.

*Many existing translations.* Many translations of the Scriptures existed, but Latin was rapidly becoming the official language of the church. In addition to those translations mentioned in chapters 16 and 17, there were the two basic Old Latin texts in the West.

There is little wonder that Damascus desired a new, authoritative translation upon which the official doctrines of the church could be based.

*Heresies and disputes.* Within the Roman Empire there were many disputes between Christians and Jews. Even within the church, there were numerous disputations which followed the emergence of such heretical groups as the Marcionites, the Manichaeans, and the Montanists, who based their doctrines on their own Bible canons and translations. The Arian controversy led to the councils at Nicea (325), Constantinople I (381), and Ephesus (431). The controversy surrounding Jerome's translation of the Old Testament from Hebrew reflects not only the conflicts between Christians and Jews, but the even more problematic notion that was held by many church leaders, including Augustine, that the LXX was actually the inspired and inerrant Word of God rather than a noninspired translation of the Hebrew originals.

*The need for a standard text.* Still other factors calling for a new and authoritative translation would include the demands by scholars for an authentic and authoritative standard text to carry out the teaching activities of the church, its missionary programs, and its defense of doctrines established at the great councils. The transmission of copies of the Scriptures to the churches in the Empire required a trustworthy (authentic) text, and the existing situation underscored the need.

THE AUTHOR OF THE TRANSLATION

Sophronius Eusebius Hieronymus, better known as St. Jerome (c. 340-420), was born to Christian parents at Stridon, Dalmatia. He was trained in the local school until he went to Rome at the age of twelve. For the next eight years he studied Latin, Greek, and pagan authors before becoming a Christian at the age of nineteen. Following his conversion and baptism, Jerome devoted himself to a life of rigid abstinence and service to the Lord. He spent many years pursuing a semiascetic and later a hermitic life. During the years 374-379 he employed a Jewish rabbi to teach him Hebrew while he was living in the East, near Antioch. He was ordained a presbyter at Antioch before going to Constantinople, where he studied under Gregory Nazianzen. In 382 he was summoned to Rome to be secretary to Damasus, bishop of Rome, and commissioned to revise the Latin Bible. Jerome was selected for his outstanding qualifications as a scholar. He probably undertook the project because of his devotion to Damasus, as he knew that the less educated would strongly oppose his translation.

### THE DATE AND PLACE OF THE TRANSLATION

Jerome received his commission in 382 and began his work almost immediately. At the request of Damasus he made a slight revision of the gospels, which he completed in 383. The Latin text he used for this revision is not known, but it was probably of the European type which he corrected in accordance with an Alexandrian-type Greek text. Shortly after his revision of the gospels was completed, his patron died (384), and a new bishop of Rome was elected. Jerome, who aspired to that position, had already completed a hasty revision of the so-called Roman Psalter when he returned to the East and settled at Bethlehem. Before his departure, however, he made an even more cursory revision of the remainder of the New Testament. Since the exact date of this revision is unknown, some scholars believe that he did not even do the work.

Back in Bethlehem Jerome turned his attention to a more careful revision of the Roman Psalter and completed it in 387. This revision is known as the Gallican Psalter, which is currently employed in the Vulgate Old Testament. It was actually based on Origen's *Hexapla*, the fifth column, and is only a translation instead of a version of the Psalms. As soon as he had completed his revision of the Psalter, Jerome began a revision of the LXX, although this had not been his original objective. While at Bethlehem he had begun to work on perfecting his knowledge of Hebrew so he could make a fresh translation of the Old Testament directly from the original language.

While his friends applauded his efforts, those more remote from him began to suspect that he might be Judaizing and even became outraged when he cast doubts on the "inspiration of the Septuagint." From this time he became more involved with his translation and the supervision of the monks at Bethlehem. He translated the Hebrew Psalter based on the Hebrew text then in use in

Palestine. This translation never actually surpassed the Gallican Psalter or the Roman Psalter in liturgical use even though it was based on the original language instead of a translation. Jerome kept on translating the Hebrew Scriptures in spite of opposition and poor health. Finally, in 405, he completed his Latin translation of the Hebrew Old Testament, but it was not readily received. During the last fifteen years of his life Jerome continued writing, translating, and revising his Old Testament translation.

Jerome cared little for the Apocrypha, and only reluctantly made a hasty translation of portions of it—Judith, Tobit, the rest of Esther, and the additions to Daniel—before his death. As a result, the Old Latin version of the Apocrypha was brought into the Latin Vulgate Bible during the Middle Ages over Jerome's dead body.

REACTION TO THE TRANSLATION

When Jerome published his revisions of the gospels, sharp reaction to them was heard. Since his work was sponsored by the bishop of Rome, however, the opposition was silenced. His reluctance to proceed with the revision of the remainder of the New Testament indicates that Jerome may have been aware of the approaching death of Damasus, his sponsor. The fact that Jerome left Rome just a year following his benefactor's death supports this notion, and the milder revisions he made when he did finally revise the remainder of the New Testament shows that he was concerned to win the approval of his critics. The adoption of the Roman Psalter by the church at Rome reveals that it was first used there and that Jerome's scholarship was already apparent. Since the Gallican Psalter was accepted by churches outside Rome, it seems that Damasus was not so influential over those critics of Jerome's earlier work.

When Jerome began to study Hebrew at Bethlehem, and when he had translated the Hebrew Psalter, sharp cries of accusation arose against him. He was accused of presumption, making unlawful innovations and sacrilege. Not being one to take criticism lightly, he used the prefaces of his translations and revisions as tools for counterattack. These items merely added fuel to the flames, and Jerome's translation was opposed by many of the outstanding leaders of the church. Among those critics was Augustine, who was outspoken against Jerome's Old Testament translation but wholeheartedly favored his New Testament revisions after 398.

Augustine's attitude provides us with a capsule view of what actually happened to the Vulgate Old Testament historically. During the early years of that translation, Augustine, and a large majority of influential church leaders, opposed the translation because it was not based on the LXX. In fact, Augustine and others used Jerome's New Testament revision while they urged him to make his translation of the Old Testament from the LXX which many held to be inspired.

Shortly after the great scholar's death in 420, his Old Testament translation gained a complete victory over other translations. Whether this fact is attributed to the sheer weight of the translation cannot be known with certainty, for the biting criticism and denouncing of his translation by its critics would scarcely be set aside merely on the basis of its merits. The Vulgate became the unofficially recognized standard text of the Bible throughout the Middle Ages. It was not until the Council of Trent (1546-1563), however, that it was officially elevated to that position by the Roman Catholic Church. In the meantime it was published in parallel columns with other translations as well as itself. When Latin became the dominant language of European scholars, other translations and versions faded and fell into the background behind the majestic Vulgate of Jerome.

THE RESULTS OF THE TRANSLATION

Of primary concern to the modern Bible student is the relative weight of the Latin Vulgate. As a result it must be considered in the light of history. As has been indicated, the Vulgate New Testament was merely a revision of the Old Latin text, and not a critical revision at that. The Vulgate text of the Apocrypha is of even less value, since it is simply the Old Latin text attached to Jerome's Old Testament translation, with minor exceptions. The Vulgate Old Testament is an entirely different matter, however, since it was actually a version made from the Hebrew text rather than simply another translation or revision. The Old Testament text is thus much more important to Bible scholars than the New.

It was inevitable that the Vulgate text would be corrupted in its transmission during the Middle Ages. Sometimes this corruption was the result of careless transcription and the intermingling of elements from the Old Latin text, with which it was often published. Throughout the Middle Ages several attempts at revision and recension of the Vulgate text were made in monasteries. This led to the accumulation of over eight thousand extant Vulgate manuscripts. Among these manuscripts the greatest amount of "cross-contamination" of text types is evident. Still, the Council of Trent issued a "Decree Concerning the Edition, and the Use, of the Sacred Books," which held "of all the Latin editions, . . . the said old and Vulgate edition, . . . [is] held as authentic."

It may be asked just which of the over eight thousand manuscript copies, and which particular edition of the Vulgate should be regarded as the ultimate authority. As a result, the Council of Trent ordered that an authentic edition of the Vulgate be prepared. A papal commission was committed with the task, but it was unable to overcome the many difficulties before it. Finally, in 1590, Pope Sixtus V published an edition of his own, just a few months before he died. This Sixtene edition was quite unpopular among scholars, especially the Jesuits, and was circulated for only a short time. Gregory XIV (1590-1591) succeeded to the papal chair and was immediately prepared to revise the Sixtene text drastically. His sudden death would have brought an end to the revision of the Sixtene text had it not been for the renewed interest of his successor, Clement VIII (1592-1605). In 1604 a new "authentic" Vulgate edition of the Bible appeared which is known as the Sixto-Clementine edition. It differed from the Sixtene edition in some 4900 variants, and became the dominant Vulgate text, surpassing even the Gutenberg edition printed at Mainz between 1450 and 1455. Since 1907 a critical revision of the Vulgate Old Testament has been undertaken by the Benedictine order. The New Testament underwent critical revision by a group of Anglican scholars at Oxford. It was begun by Bishop John Wordsworth and

Professor H. J. White between 1877 and 1926, and was completed by H. F. D. Sparks in 1954.

The consistency of the Vulgate text is quite mixed after the sixth century, and its overall character is rather faulty. Nevertheless, the influence of the Vulgate on the language and thought of Western Christianity has been immense, but its value to the textual critic is not nearly so high. When the text of Jerome is discovered from its own textual criticism, it reveals that Jerome's New Testament was a late fourth-century revision of the Old Latin, and his Old Testament was a late fourth or early fifth-century version of the Hebrew text then in use in the East. The Apocrypha shows that Jerome had little regard for it, since he only reluctantly translated four books, but that they were quite popular within the Roman Catholic Church. Only a few individuals acknowledged their error in accepting the LXX Old Testament as authoritative and inspired, and supported the accuracy of the Hebrew text underlying Jerome's Vulgate version. Among these was Augustine, bishop of Hippo, who would become the dominant voice in the next several centuries of church history. During those centuries the Vulgate became the dominant edition of the Bible in the Middle Ages. It also served as the basis for most modern Bible translators prior to the nineteenth century.

## Secondary Translations

In the middle of the ninth century a Moravian empire was formed in east-central Europe. This kingdom came under the sway of Christianity and its church leaders used Latin in their liturgy. The laity were not familiar with Latin, and Rostislav, the founder of the kingdom, requested that Slavonic priests be sent to conduct church services in the language of the people. At this time only Slavonic was spoken in this region of Europe.

In response to Rostislav's request, the Emperor Michael III sent two monks to Moravia from Byzantium (Constantinople). The monks were the brothers Methodius and Constantinus, natives of Thessalonica. Constantinus changed his name to Cyril when he entered the monastery. In order to accomplish their task the brothers devised a new alphabet, known as the Cyrillic alphabet.

It is comprised of thirty-six letters and is still the basis of Russian, Ukranian, Serbo-Croatian, and Bulgarian. The Cyrillic alphabet superseded the local alphabet, the Glagolithic, in the tenth century.

Shortly after their entry into the region, Cyril and Methodius began translating the gospels into Old Slavonic. Then these "Apostles to the Slaves" began translating the Old Testament. At one time it was believed that their translation was from the LXX, but recent evidence indicates that it was actually made from the Latin. The New Testament follows the Byzantine text, although it has many Western and Caesarean readings. Most of the known Slavonic manuscripts are lectionaries, and the first translation itself may have been in the form of a lectionary.

Of the other translations based on the Latin text, only the Anglo-Saxon and the Frankish translations demand a word of information. The Anglo-Saxon text will be discussed in chapter 19, and the Frankish translation appears in a bilingual edition. It is known from one fragmentary eighth-century manuscript containing portions of Matthew, facing a Latin text.

# 19

# EARLY ENGLISH TRANSLATIONS

THE CHAIN from God to us takes a new direction at this point. The Bible text in the original languages and early translations gives way to the particular transmission of the text in the English language. For although the Old Testament was recorded primarily in Hebrew, and the New was written basically in Greek, more modern translations of the Bible are in English than any other language.

## PARTIAL TRANSLATIONS IN OLD AND MIDDLE ENGLISH

English is a sort of tag-end dialect of Low German, which itself belongs to the West Teutonic branch of the Teutonic group of languages in the Indo-European family. In order to place it in its proper setting, it is necessary for us to sketch the background of the English language and the place of the Bible in it.

### THE LATE DEVELOPMENT OF THE ENGLISH LANGUAGE

Just how the English language developed is not known for certain, but most scholars follow the lead of the Venerable Bede (c. 673-735), who dates its beginning about A.D. 450. The period 450-1100 is called Anglo-Saxon, or Old English, because it was dominated by the influence from the Angles, Saxons, and Jutes in their various dialects. Following the Norman invasion of 1066, the language came under the influence of the Scandinavian dialects, and the period of Middle English appeared from 1100–1500. This was the period of both Geoffrey Chaucer (1340-1400) and John Wycliffe. Following the invention of movable typeset by Johann Gutenberg (c. 1454), English entered into its third period of development: Modern English (1500 to the present). This period of development was precipitated by the Great Vowel Shift during the century following the death of Chaucer and preceding the birth of William Shakespeare. With this background in mind, our survey of the various translations of the Bible into English should be more meaningful.

OLD ENGLISH PARTIAL TRANSLATIONS (450–1100)

At first only pictures, preaching, poems, and paraphrases were employed to communicate the message of the Bible to the Britons. The early translation of portions of the Scriptures were based on the Old Latin and Vulgate translations rather than the original Hebrew and Greek languages, and none of them contained the text of the entire Bible. Nevertheless, they do illustrate the manner by which the Bible entered into the English tongue.

*Caedmon (d. c. 680)*. The story of Caedmon is recorded in Bede's *Ecclesiastical History*. It involves an ungifted laborer at the monastery at Whitby in Yorkshire, Northumbria, who left a party one night for fear that he might be called upon to sing. Later that night he dreamed that an angel had commanded him to sing about how things were first created. Other paraphrases and poems sung by Caedmon included the full story of Genesis, Israel's exodus from Egypt, the incarnation, passion, resurrection and ascension of the Lord, the coming of the Holy Spirit, the teachings of the apostles, etc. His work became the basis for other poets, writers, and translators, for it became the popularized people's Bible of the day. As a result, Caedmon's songs were memorized and disseminated throughout the land.

*Aldhelm (640-709)*. Aldhelm was the first bishop of Sherborne in Dorset. Shortly after 700 he translated the Psalter into Old English. It was the first straightforward translation of any portion of the Bible into the English language.

*Egbert (fl. c. 700)*. Egbert of Northumbria became archbishop of York shortly before the death of Bede. He was also the teacher of Alcuin of York, who was later called by Charlemagne to establish a school at the court of Aix-la-Chapelle (Aachen). About 705, Egbert translated the gospels into Old English for the first time.

*The Venerable Bede (674-735)*. The greatest scholar in England, and one of the greatest in all Europe in his day, Bede was situated at Jarrow-on-the-Tyne in Northumbria. From there he wrote his famous *Ecclesiastical History* and other works. Among these works was a translation of the gospel of John, which was probably meant to be a supplement to the three translated by Egbert. According to traditional accounts, Bede finished his translation in the very hour of his death.

*Alfred the Great (849-901)* Alfred was a scholar of the first rank as well as being king of England (870-901). During his reign the Danelaw was established under the Treaty of Wedmore (878). The Treaty contained only two stipulations for the new subjects: Christian baptism and loyalty to the king. Along with his translation of Bede's *Ecclesiastical History* from Latin into Anglo-Saxon, he also translated the Ten Commandments, extracts from Exodus 21-23, Acts 15:23-29, and a negative form of the Golden Rule. It was during his reign that Britain experienced a revival of Christianity.

*Aldred (fl. c. 950).* Another element was introduced into the history of the English Bible when Aldred wrote a Northumbrian gloss between the lines of a late seventh-century Latin copy of the gospels. It is from the Latin copy of Eadfrid, bishop of Lindisfarne (698-721), that Aldred's work receives its name, the Lindisfarne Gospels. A generation later the Irish scribe MacRegol made another Anglo-Saxon gloss known as the Rushworth Gospels.

*Aelfric (fl. c. 1000).* Aelfric was bishop of Eynsham in Oxfordshire, Wessex, when he translated portions of the first seven books of the Old Testament. This translation, and other Old Testament portions which he translated and cited in his homilies, was based on the Latin text. Even before Aelfric's time the Wessex Gospels were translated into the same dialect. These items constitute the first extant independent translation of the gospels into Old English.

MIDDLE ENGLISH PARTIAL TRANSLATIONS (1100–1400)

The Norman Conquest (1066) came as a result of the dispute over the throne of Edward the Confessor. With it the period of Saxon domination in Britain came to an end, and a period of Norman-French influence exerted itself on the language of the conquered peoples. During this period of Norman domination, additional attempts were made at translating the Bible into English.

*Orm, or Ormin, (fl. c. 1200)*. Orm was an Augustinian monk who wrote a poetic paraphrase of the gospels and Acts with an accompanying commentary. This work, the Ormulum, is preserved in only one manuscript of 20,000 words. Although the vocabulary is purely Teutonic, the cadence and syntax show Norman influence.

*William of Shoreham (fl c. 1320)*. Shoreham is often credited with producing the first prose translation of a Bible portion into a Southern dialect of English, although there is some question about whether or not he was actually the translator of this 1320 work.

*Richard Rolle (fl. c. 1320-1340)*. Rolle is known as the "Hermit of Hampole." He was responsible for the second literal translation of the Scriptures into English. Living near Doncaster, Yorkshire, he made his translation from the Latin Vulgate into the North English dialect. His translation of the Psalter was widely circulated, and it reflects the development of English Bible translation to the time of John Wycliffe.

### COMPLETE TRANSLATIONS IN MIDDLE AND EARLY MODERN ENGLISH

Although there were no complete Bibles in English prior to the fourteenth century, several indications pointed to the fact that one would soon appear. The wide circulation of Rolle's literal Psalter at the very time the papal court was experiencing struggles associated with the so-called Babylonish Captivity (1309-1377). This event and its aftermath provided a backdrop for the work of other Bible translators.

#### FOURTEENTH AND FIFTEENTH CENTURY BIBLE TRANSLATIONS

*John Wycliffe (c. 1320-1384)*. Wycliffe, "the Morning Star of the Reformation," lived during the Babylonish Captivity, along with Geoffrey Chaucer and John of Gaunt. In his recoil from the spiritual apathy and moral degeneracy of the clergy in England, he was thrust into the limelight as an opponent of the papacy. Wycliffe cast aside scholastic Latin as a vehicle of communication and directed his appeal to the English people in their common language. His appeal was directed through the Lollards, an order of itinerant preachers also known as the "poor priests." These Lollards went throughout the countryside preaching, reading, and teaching the English Bible. In order to help them with their task, a new translation of the Bible was needed. The New Testament translation was completed in 1380, and the Old Testament appeared in 1388. Although this complete translation is attributed to Wycliffe, it was completed after his death by Nicholas of Hereford.

The translations were made from contemporary manuscripts of the Latin Vulgate. The manuscripts upon which these translations were based reflect a generally poor quality and textual tradition, but they provided the basis for the first complete translation of the Bible into English. With the Wycliffe Bible translation, a new epoch in the history of the Bible was opened. One of Wycliffe's basic principles was that laid down by Hampole, namely, that the translators would seek no strange English, and use the easiest and commonest English, which would be most like the Latin, so that those who knew no Latin might by the English come to many Latin words.

*John Purvey (c. 1354-1428).* John Purvey served as Wycliffe's secretary and is credited with making a revision of the Earlier Wycliffite Bible in 1395. This revision is commonly known as the Later Wycliffite Version, and the first as the Earlier Wycliffite Version, although the term *version* does not strictly apply to either.

Purvey's revision replaced many Latinate constructions by native English idiom. It also replaced the preface of Jerome by an extensive prologue written by Purvey. The net result was a continued weakening of papal influence over the English people. In broader form, the first complete English Bible was published, revised and circulated prior to the work of John Hus (c. 1369-1415) in Bohemia. It was also published before the invention of Johann Gutenberg (c. 1454), a revolutionary development which had a dampening effect on the spread of the Wycliffite translations.

### SIXTEENTH-CENTURY BIBLE TRANSLATIONS

The transformation of England, and all of Europe for that matter, followed the Renaissance and the feature accompanying it: the literary revival, the rise of nationalism, and the spirit of exploration and discovery. The resurgence of the classics followed the fall of

Constantinople in 1453, Johann Gutenberg (1396-1468) invented movable typeset, and cheaper paper was introduced into Europe. In 1456 the Mazarin Bible was published. Greek began to be studied publicly at the University of Paris in 1458, the first Greek grammar appeared in 1476, and a Greek lexicon was published in 1492. In 1488 the Hebrew Bible was published, the first Hebrew grammar came out in 1503, and the earliest Hebrew lexicon appeared in 1506.

Even prior to 1500 there were over eighty editions of the Latin Bible published in Europe, within a generation of the introduction of the new printing method into England by William Claxton in 1476. Indeed, the setting was such that a scholarly man was needed to fashion the Hebrew and Greek originals into a fitting English idiom, for no mere rendering of the Latin text would suffice to meet the demands of the situation.

*William Tyndale (c. 1492-1536).* William Tyndale was the man who could do what was needed, and he had the faith and courage to persist whatever the cost. Following unsuccessful attempts to do his translation in England, he sailed to the Continent in 1524. After further difficulties he finally printed the New Testament at Cologne in late February 1526. It was followed by a translation of the Pentateuch at Marburg (1530) and of Jonah at Antwerp (1531). The influences of Wycliffe and Luther were evident in Tyndale's work, and these kept him under constant threat. In addition, these threats were such that Tyndale's translations had to be smuggled into England. Once they arrived there, copies were purchased by Cuthbert Tunstall, bishop of London, who had them burned publicly at St. Paul's Cross. Even Sir Thomas More (1478-1535), the humanist Lord Chancellor of England under Henry VIII and author of the *Utopia*, attacked Tyndale's translation as belonging to the same "pestilent sect" as did Luther's German translation.

In 1534 Tyndale published his revision of Genesis and began work on a revision of the New Testament. Shortly after completing this revision, he was kidnapped in Antwerp and taken to the fortress at Vilvorde in Flanders. There he continued translating the Old Testament. In August, 1536, he was found guilty of heresy, degraded from his priestly office, and turned over to the secular authorities for execution. This was carried out on October 6. At the time of his execution Tyndale cried out, "Lord, open the King of England's eyes." At that very time events in England were working together to bring to pass the translator's last request.

*Miles Coverdale (1488-1569)*. Miles Coverdale, Tyndale's assistant and proofreader at Antwerp, became the key individual in printing the first complete English Bible in 1535. This work was barely a revision of Tyndale's translation with added insights from the German translations.

Coverdale introduced chapter summaries and some new expressions into the text of his translation. He also set the precedent of separating the Old Testament from the Apocrypha in those Bibles translated after the Latin Vulgate came into its position of dominance in the Western church. Coverdale's translation was reprinted twice in 1537, again in 1550, and once again in 1553. Nevertheless, the true successor to the 1535 edition was the Great Bible of 1539. This Bible will be discussed shortly.

*Thomas Matthew (c. 1500-1555)*. Thomas Matthew was the pen name of John Rogers, the first martyr of the persecutions under Mary Tudor. He too had been an assistant to Tyndale. In 1537 he published another English Bible by combining the Old Testament texts of Tyndale and Coverdale with the 1535 revision of Tyndale's New Testament. It was not published again until 1549 and 1551. In 1549 a slightly revised edition was also published, and in 1551 a Bible appeared which called itself "Matthew's" on the title page, but contained Taverner's Old Testament and the 1548 edition of Tyndale's New Testament.

John Rogers refused to attach his given name to work which had been done by others, even though he published it. Instead, he used a pen name, Thomas Matthew, and added copious notes and references. In addition to the editions of Tyndale and Coverdale, he borrowed heavily from the French editions of Lefèvre (1534) and Olivetan (1535). When he published his 1537 edition, he received a license to do so from Henry VIII. With its release, there were two licensed English Bibles in circulation within a year of Tyndale's execution. His assistants had carried on the work of their martyred associate, and others would follow in their train.

*Richard Taverner (1505-1575).* Taverner was a layman who knew Greek quite well. In 1539 he applied his talent to a revision of Matthew's Bible and produced a translation which made better use of the Greek article. Nevertheless, Taverner's work was soon to be surpassed by still another revision of Matthew's Bible, the Great Bible of 1539.

*The Great Bible (1539).* The notes and prologues to the two major translations of the printed English Bible in circulation in 1539, Coverdale's and Matthew's, gave much affront to so many groups in England that Henry VIII was frequently besought to provide a new translation free from interpretations. Thomas Cromwell (c. 1485-1540), Protestant Lord Chancellor under Henry VIII, was authorized to proceed with such an undertaking. With further approval by Thomas Cranmer (1489-1556), first Protestant archbishop of Canterbury, Miles Coverdale was willing to prepare a new text for it and to use the work of other men in preference to his own, which had been published but two years.

Under the direction of Coverdale, the Great Bible was offered as a means of easing the tensions stemming from the Bible situation in England. It received its name because of its great size and format, for it was larger than any previous edition and was elaborately decorated. Its title page was a fine woodcut attributed to Hans Holbein which depicts Henry VIII, Cranmer, and Cromwell distributing Bibles to the people who in turn cry, "Vivat rex" and "God save the King." The Bible contained no dedication and had only simple prefaces. In addition, the Apocrypha was removed from the remainder of the Old Testament text and placed in an appendix entitled "hagiographa" (holy writings). The situation was extremely awkward since most of the bishops of the church were still Roman Catholic. Although the Great Bible was authorized to be read in the churches in 1538, its delicate position was further threatened by the fact that it was neither a version nor a revision of a version, it was a revision of a revision.

*Cranmer's Bible (1540).* In April 1540, a second edition of the Great Bible was published. It contained a preface by Thomas Cranmer, then archbishop of Canterbury, and some further revisions based on Coverdale's earlier work. It was followed by five other editions before the end of 1541. These Bibles are called

Cranmer's because of the preface he wrote for them. In that preface is the statement, "This is the Byble apoynted to the use of the churches." The Bible of 1535 and Matthew's Bible of 1537 had been licensed, but this was definitely an authorized translation, which the translation of 1611 never was.

In the third and fifth of these six editions of Cranmer's Bible a notice was printed on the title page to the effect that bishops Tunstall and Heath had "overseen and purused" the edition. It is a curious irony that Tunstall as bishop of London had condemned Tyndale and his work. Now he officially authorized a Bible that largely contained Tyndale's translation and revisions of it. By 1547 Cranmer's Bible attained a predominate position in the churches. In 1549 and 1553 it was again reprinted, and Cranmer's order was not rescinded even during the brief and turbulent years of the reign of Mary Tudor (1553-1558).

*The Geneva Bible (1557, 1560).* During the persecutions under Mary Tudor many reformers fled to the Continent for safety. Among those who settled at Geneva were scholars and Bible lovers, like Miles Coverdale and John Knox (*c.* 1513-1572), who produced a revision that was to have a great influence on the people of England. In 1557 one of their group named William Whittingham, a brother-in-law to John Calvin, produced a stopgap revision of the New Testament. This was the first time the English New Testament had been divided into verses, although it had been so divided in the 1551 Greek Testament of Stephanus as well as earlier editions in Latin and Hebrew. Long prologues were added to the translation, along with chapter summaries and copious marginal notes. Italics were introduced into the translation to indicate where English idiom required words that were not in the original text.

Shortly after the New Testament was published at Geneva, work was begun on a careful revision of the entire Bible. In 1560 the Old Testament and a revision of the New were completed which included the latest textual evidence, and the long and eventful history of the Geneva Bible began. By 1644 the Geneva Bible had gone through 140 editions. It was so popular that it withstood the Bishops' Bible (1568) and the first generation of the so-called Authorized Version (1611). It was extensively used among the

Puritans, its text is quoted repeatedly in the pages of Shakespeare, and it was even used in the address from "The Translators to the Readers" in the 1611 translation. Although its notations were milder than those of Tyndale, they were too Calvinistic for either Elizabeth I (1558-1603) or James I (1603-1625).

*The Bishops' Bible (1568).* The Geneva Bible was not sponsored by the established church, but it quickly became the household Bible of the realm. Its immediate success made a new revision of the Great Bible, the authorized Bible of the churches. The work was given to a group of scholars including about eight bishops, hence the name the Bishops' Bible. They were to use the Great Bible as the basis of their revision and, while the intention was to make only slight alterations, some of the bishops went beyond their instructions. The revisers were better scholars in Greek than Hebrew, and their work in the New Testament is superior to that in the Old.

The Bishops' Bible was published in 1568 in London, "cum privilegio regiae majestatis." Its New Testament portion was published on thicker paper than the Old in order to withstand greater wear. It contained two prefaces, Cranmer's and one by Matthew Parker, then archbishop of Canterbury. Following the Great Bible, it had few marginal notes. The Convocation of 1571 ordered that copies be placed throughout the land, in the houses of every bishop and archbishop, each cathedral and every church if possible. From 1568 to 1611 this compromise translation was generally found in the churches. Nevertheless, the Geneva Bible had already won over the households of the land. Its insurmountable disadvantage, however, did not keep the Bishops' Bible from being the basis for the famous revision of 1611.

### STANDARD TRANSLATIONS OF THE BIBLE IN ENGLISH

While Protestants were busy making vernacular translations of the Bible for use in England, their Roman Catholic counterparts were beginning to sense a similar desire. After the death of Mary Tudor in 1558, Elizabeth I ascended to the throne and Roman Catholic exiles of her reign undertook a task similar to that of Protestant exiles at Geneva during Mary's reign. The multiplicity and diversity of translations was such that by the time James I ascended to the throne in 1603, a more unified translation was needed so the various groups within the church could appeal to a common authority in their theological discussions. As a result of the efforts then set into motion, the King James Bible, the most influential single translation of the English Protestants, was produced.

THE RHEIMS-DOUAY BIBLE (1582, 1609)

In 1568 a group of Roman Catholic exiles from England founded the English College at Douay in Flanders. They sought to train priests and others who would preserve their Catholic faith. William Allen (1532-1594), Oxford canon during Mary Tudor's reign, led in the founding of this college and in its move to Rheims, France, when political troubles arose in 1578. At Rheims the English College came under the direction of another Oxford scholar, Richard Bristow (1538-1581), who had gone to Douay in 1569. During this time Allen was called to Rome where he founded another English College and was later made cardinal. In 1593 the English College at Rheims returned to Douay.

The Roman hierarchy desired an English translation of the Latin Vulgate, and Allen expressed this wish in a letter to a professor at the college in Douay in 1578. Gregory Martin (d. 1582), still another Oxford scholar, undertook the task. Martin had received his M.A. in 1564. He then renounced his Protestantism and went to Douay to study. In 1570 he became lecturer in Hebrew and Holy Scripture. He proceeded with his translation of the Old Testament at the rate of about two chapters a day until his death in 1582. Just before his death, the New Testament was published with many notations. These notes were the work of Bristow and Allen. They were joined in their efforts by another Protestant-turned-Catholic, William Reynolds, although his role in the task is not certainly known.

While the Rheims New Testament translation (1582) was designed to counteract the existing English translations of the Protestants, it had some serious limitations. It was a poor rendition of the text into English and was based on still another translation rather than the original language of the New Testament. The translators guarded themselves "against the idea that the Scrip-

tures should always be in our mother tongue, or that they ought,
or were ordained by God, to be read indifferently by all." Not only
that, the translators made no secret that they were making a
polemic work, as their copious notes indicate. The New Testament
was republished in 1600, 1621, and 1633.

In the meantime, the Old Testament, which was actually translated before the New, was delayed in its publication. Financial
limitations and the appearance of several new editions of the
Vulgate text prevented publication of the Douay translation of the
Old Testament until 1609. Its second edition was released in 1635.
The actual translation was begun by Martin and probably completed by Allen and Bristow, with notes apparently furnished by
Thomas Worthington, although the details are so obscure that
these matters cannot be determined with certainty. It was based
on the unofficial Louvain Vulgate text (1547), edited by Henten,
but conformed to the Sixtene-Clementine text of 1592. The translation itself was uniform throughout, including the over-literal
use of Latinisms. The annotations were basically designed to
bring the interpretation of the text into harmony with the decrees
of the Council of Trent (1546-1563).

The Rheims New Testament was in circulation long enough to
have an important influence on the English Bible translators of
1611. The Douay Old Testament translation, however, was not
published in time to influence those translators. With a Protestant
queen on the throne and a Protestant king as her successor, the
Rheims-Douay Bible had little possibility of competing with or
replacing the Protestant translations already available. The scarcity of reprints of the Rheims-Douay Bible indicate that Catholics
had "no fear that the few available copies would be found in the
hand of every husbandman." After 1635 several reprints were
made, but the second revised edition did not appear until 1749-
1750, when Richard Challoner, bishop of London, made his significant contribution.

THE KING JAMES BIBLE (1611)

In January, 1604 James I was summoned to the Hampton Court
Conference in response to the Millenary Petition which he re-

ceived while on his way from Edinburgh to London following the death of Elizabeth I. Nearly one thousand Puritan leaders had signed a list of grievances against the church of England, and James desired to be peacemaker in his new realm and placed himself above all religious parties. He treated the Puritans with rudeness at the conference until John Reynolds, Puritan President of Corpus Christi College, Oxford, raised the question of having an authorized version of the Bible for all parties within the church. The king expressed his support for the translation because it would help him to be rid of the two most popular translations and raise his esteem in the eyes of his subjects. A committee was named, following the example of the Geneva Bible, which James regarded as the worst of all existing translations. It and the Bishop's Bible were the Bibles he hoped to replace in the church.

Six companies of translators were chosen: two at Cambridge to revise 1 Chronicles through Ecclesiastes and the Apocrypha; two at Oxford to revise Isaiah through Malachi, the gospels, Acts, and the Apocalypse; and two at Westminster to revise Genesis through 2 Kings and Romans through Jude. Only forty-seven of the fifty-four men chosen actually worked on this revision of the Bishops' Bible. Their instructions ruled that they should follow the text of the Bishops' Bible unless they found that the translations of Tyndale, Matthew, Coverdale, Whitchurche, and Geneva more closely agreed with the original text. That original text was based on few if any of the superior texts of the twelfth to the fifteenth centuries, since it followed the 1516 and 1522 editions of Erasmus' Greek text, including his interpolation of 1 John 5:7. Using the Bishops' Bible as its basis meant that many old ecclesiastical words would be retained in the new revision. In an unofficial way, the recent publication of the Rheims-Douay Bible would influence the reintroduction of many Latinisms into the text.

No marginal notes were affixed to the new revision, and the so-called Authorized Version was never actually authorized, nor was it actually a version. It replaced the Bishops' Bible in the churches because no editions of it were published after 1606. Being cast in the same format as the Geneva Bible gave the 1611 publication added influence, as did its use of precise expression.

In the long run the grandeur of its translation was able to successfully compete with and overpower the influence of the Geneva Bible of the Puritans, its chief rival.

Three editions of the new translation appeared in 1611. Further editions were published in 1612, and its popularity continued to call forth new printings. During the reign of Charles I (1625-1649), the Long Parliament established a commission to consider either revising the so-called Authorized Version or producing a new translation altogether. Only minor revisions resulted in 1629, 1638, 1653, 1701, 1762, 1769, and two later editions. These last three revisions were made by Dr. Blayney of Oxford. They varied in about 75,000 details from the text of the 1611 edition. Slight changes have continued to appear in the text as recently as 1967, in the text of the Authorized Version accompanying the New Scofield Reference Edition. In the meantime, attempts were being made to bring extensive alterations and corrections into English translations of the Bible as a result of the new textual discoveries and the changing character of the language itself.

# 20

# MODERN ENGLISH BIBLE TRANSLATIONS

THE BIBLE is the most publicized book in the world. One of the strongest evidences of this is the multitude of translations and variety of languages into which it has been translated. The entire Bible has been translated into over two hundred languages, and portions of it appear in more than a thousand languages and dialects. These translations provide ample illustration of the final link in the chain from God to us, but our primary concern and attention will be directed to the translation of the Bible into English. Our survey will center on those translations growing out of the Rheims-Douay and King James Bibles of the late fifteenth and early sixteenth centuries.

### ROMAN CATHOLIC TRANSLATIONS AND VERSIONS

The major English Bible translation for Roman Catholics during the Reformation era was the Rheims-Douay Bible of 1582, 1609 (see chap. 19). It began slowly but came to dominate the scene by 1635 and was published several times after that date. Nevertheless, it was not the only Roman Catholic translation of the Bible into English.

#### THE RHEIMS-DOUAY-CHALLONER BIBLE

Although several printings of the Rheims-Douay Bible were made after 1635, it was not until 1749-50 that Richard Challoner, bishop of London, published the second revised edition. It was little more than a new translation of the Bible into English, for it took advantage of several developments in Bible translation made during the eighteenth century. In 1718, for instance, a new translation of the Vulgate New Testament was published by Cornelius Nary. In 1730 Robert Witham, president of the English College at Douay, published a revision of the Rheims New Testament. It had some revisions which are attributed to Challoner, who had been an associate with Witham at Douay following his conversion from Protestantism. A fifth edition of the Rheims New Testament was published in 1738. It contained some revisions generally attributed to Challoner and was the first revised edition of this New Testament published in over a century (the fourth revised edition being published in 1633). In 1749 Challoner published his Revised Rheims New Testament, as he did again in 1750, 1752, 1763, and 1772. His revision of the Douay Old Testament was published in 1750 and 1763.

Since that time, further editions of the Rheims-Douay Bible have been made, but they are practically all based on the 1749-50 revision. As a result, Father Hugh Pope has correctly observed that "English-speaking Catholics the world over owe Dr. Challoner an immense debt of gratitude, for he provided them for the first time with a portable, cheap, and readable version which in spite of a few inevitable defects has stood the test of two hundred years of use."[1] There have been so many revisions and editions of this Challoner's Bible, which differs very much from the original Rheims-Douay Bible, that it is no longer accurate to identify his work by its predecessor's name. It is indeed Challoner's Bible translation.

THE CONFRATERNITY OF CHRISTIAN DOCTRINE BIBLE

The first Roman Catholic Bible published in the United States (1790) was a large quarto edition of the Douay Old Testament and a mixture of several of the Challoner revisions combined with the 1752 edition of the Rheims-Challoner New Testament text. This Bible was actually the first quarto Bible of any kind in English to be published in North America. In 1849-1860, Francis Patrick Kenrick made a new revision of the Challoner Bible in six volumes, although he claimed that he

---

1. As quoted by Luther A. Weigle, "English Versions Since 1611," in *The Cambridge History of the Bible* (New York: Cambridge U., 1963), 3:367.

had made his translation from the Latin Vulgate after it had been diligently compared with the Hebrew and Greek texts. From this time onward, other editions appeared on both sides of the Atlantic.

In 1936 a new revision of the Rheims-Challoner New Testament was begun under the sponsorship of the Episcopal Committee of the Confraternity of Christian Doctrine. They named a committee of twenty-eight scholars to work on the revision under the direction of Edward P. Arbez. It used the Latin Vulgate text as its basis, but made use of recent developments in biblical scholarship. Many of the archaic expressions of the earlier revisions were removed, as were many of the copious notes. The text was arranged in paragraphs and American spelling was employed. The St. Anthony Guild Press published the Confraternity New Testament in 1941, and it was quickly used by English-speaking Catholics around the world as a byproduct of World War II.

Pope Pius XII published an encyclical, *Divino Afflante Spiritu* ( 1943), stating that translations of the Bible could be based on the original Hebrew and Greek texts rather than merely on the Latin Vulgate. This was a sharp reversal of the position taken by the translators of the Rheims-Douay Bible (see chap. 19). After wartime restrictions were lifted, the Confraternity began to publish a new version of the Old Testament. Unlike any translation by Catholics in over a millennium and a half, this would be based on the original languages rather than some earlier Latin translation. By 1967 the four Old Testament volumes were completed and published. Work was then begun, under the direction of Louis F. Hartman, on a new version of the New Testament. In 1970 the New American Bible was published. It was based on the most recent developments of textual criticism and translated directly from the Hebrew and Greek texts.

THE KNOX TRANSLATION OF THE BIBLE

Just as the Confraternity of Christian Doctrine Bible is the official Roman Catholic Bible in the United States, the Knox translation is the official Roman Catholic Bible in Great Britain. It had been requested by Ronald A. Knox in 1939 when he, as a

new convert to Roman Catholicism, approached the English
hierarchy about making a new translation. Although there had
been a new English translation published in 1935 (*Westminster
Version of the Sacred Scriptures*), and a new Latin Vulgate
text appeared in 1945, following the encyclical of Pope Pius XII
of 1943, Monsignor Knox did not incorporate these materials in
his New Testament (1945) or Old Testament translations
(1949). Instead, he based his translations on the Sixto-Clementine Vulgate text of 1592. Still, in 1955 the Roman hierarchy
gave its official sanction to Knox's translation for English speaking Catholics. From the outset, Knox's translation rests on a
much weaker foundation than does the American Confraternity
Version, and its sequel the New American Bible. These are
based on more recent manuscript evidence as well as the texts
of the original languages. In addition, the Knox translation is
weaker textually and inferior as a translation than the *Westminster
Version of the Sacred Scriptures*, which remains an unofficial work.

MODERN SPEECH TRANSLATIONS FOR ROMAN CATHOLICS

The initial attitude of the Roman Catholic Church toward publishing the Scriptures for laymen was far from enthusiastic. Pope
Pius IX condemned Bible societies as pestilent sects in his famous
Syllabus of Errors (1864), some sixty years after the founding of
the British and Foreign Bible Society in 1804. He reflected the
attitude of the Roman Catholic hierarchy at large, but others felt
that the Bible should be placed into the hands of Catholic laymen.
As early as 1813, for instance, a group of enthusiastic churchmen
founded the Roman Catholic Bible Society and published the
Rheims-Douay Bible without notes. In 1815 the same group published another improved edition of the same translation.

Meanwhile, a host of editions of the Bible for Roman Catholics
appeared, including *Coyne's Bible* (1811), *Haydock's Bible* (1811-
1814), the *Newcastle New Testament* (1812), *Syer's Bible* (1813-
1814), *MacNamara's Bible* (1813-1814), *Bregan's New Testament*
(1814), and *Gibson's Bible* (1816-1817). Other Bibles were published throughout the nineteenth century both in England and
the United States. In 1901 a remarkable version of the gospels was

published by the Dominican Father Francis Spencer. He completed the rest of the New Testament just prior to his death in 1913, but it was not published until 1937. *The Laymen's New Testament* was first published in London in 1928. It contained the Challoner text of the Old Testament on the left page and polemic notes on the right. In 1935 an excellent new version of the New Testament was published under the general editorship of Cuthbert Lattey, S. J. This *Westminster Version of the Sacred Scriptures* was based on the original languages of the New Testament, but it did not receive the official sanction of the Roman Catholic hierarchy. Following the same principles, the first installment of the Old Testament was published. Work has continued, but been delayed, because of the death of Lattey in 1954. Because of the position of the Knox translation, it is difficult to imagine that the Westminster Version will come to official recognition in the church.

A fully Americanized edition of the New Testament appeared in 1941 as the first installment of the Confraternity of Christian Doctrine Version. In 1956 James A. Kliest and Joseph L. Lilly published still another translation entitled *The New Testament Rendered from the Original Greek with Explanatory Notes.* Probably the most significant recent translation in this category produced by Roman Catholic scholars is *The Jerusalem Bible.* Although it is translated from the original texts, it owes a great debt to *La Bible de Jerusalem* (1961), whose introduction and notes have been translated without substantial variation directly into the English text. These notes represent the work of the "liberal" wing of Catholic biblical scholarship, although the translation itself is basically literal and contemporary in style.

### JEWISH TRANSLATIONS AND VERSIONS

Although Jews have sought to preserve the study of Scripture in its original language (Hebrew), they have not always been able to do so. They have run into the same problems faced by Roman Catholics and the Latin Bible, as indicated by the very existence of the Septuagint (LXX). As early as the third century B.C., Jews found it necessary to translate their Bible into the vernacular lan-

guage of Alexandria. Their translation of portions of the Old
Testament into Aramaic further attests to the fact that they were
not always able to study the Scriptures in the Hebrew language.
Throughout the Middle Ages, the conditions under which Jews
lived were not conducive for scholarship of any kind. The attitude
of the church about their role in the crucifixion of Christ made it
even more difficult for them to openly participate in biblical
scholarship. Nevertheless, about 1400 they began to make new
and fresh translations of the Old Testament into various languages.
It was not for about four hundred years after these early vernacular translations, however, that Jews began to translate the Old
Testament into English.

In 1789, the year of the French Revolution, a Jewish version of
the Pentateuch appeared, claiming to be an emendation of the
King James Bible. In 1839 a similar work was published by Salid
Neuman. Between 1851 and 1856 Rabbi Benisch produced a
complete Bible for English-speaking Jewry. A final attempt at
amending the King James Bible for use by Jews was made by
Michael Frielander in 1884.

In 1853, Isaac Leeser made a marked departure from tradition
when he produced his version of *The Hebrew Bible*, a long time
favorite in British and American synagogues. Before the turn of
the century, however, the inadequacy of Leeser's work was felt;
and the Jewish Bible Society decided to revise it during its second
biennial convention in 1892. As the work of revision proceeded, it
became apparent that it would have to be little short of an entirely
new translation. After considerable time was spent in reorganizing
the project, the Jewish Publication Society finally released its new
version of the Hebrew Bible. Published in 1917, this revision
closely paralleled the American Standard Version (1901).

The Jewish Publication Society did not stop its work with the
publication of 1917. Following the release of the Revised Standard
Version and activity toward the publication of the New English
Bible, they began to publish a new translation of the Old Testament. In 1962 they published *The Torah*, and in 1969 they released *The Megilloth*. Both of these versions are based on the
Masoretic text of the Old Testament. In fact, the complete title
of the 1962 publication is enlightening in this regard: *The Torah:*

*A New Translation of the Holy Scriptures According to the Masoretic Text*. It does not claim to be a new version at all, and its preface bears out the title by stating that its purpose is "to improve substantially on earlier versions in rendering both the shades of meaning of words and expressions and the force of grammatical forms and constructions." In order to accomplish its task, the translators utilize the neglected insights from ancient and medieval Jewish scholarship as well as new knowledge from the Near East.

## PROTESTANT TRANSLATIONS AND VERSIONS

In keeping with their Reformation principle of private interpretation, Protestants have produced a greater number of private translations of the Bible than have Roman Catholics. Some of the earlier translations grew out of the discoveries of new manuscript materials, since none of the great manuscripts had been discovered at the time of the King James translation (see chap. 14) except Codex Bezae (D) which was used very little. Before turning to those private translations, we should look at some of the official attempts to bring the King James Bible into alignment with the manuscript discoveries.

### THE ENGLISH REVISED BIBLE

All of the revisions of the King James Bible mentioned in chapter 19 were made without official ecclesiastical or royal authorization. In fact, no official revision of it was forthcoming for over a century after the work of Dr. Blayney (1769). Some of the revisions that did arise were ill-advised, such as additions made like Ussher's chronology. Nevertheless, there were some excellent revisions in an unofficial capacity, as in the case of an anonymous edition of *The Holy Bible Containing the Authorized Version of the Old and New Testaments, with Many Emendations* (1841). In the preface of this unofficial revision of the King James Bible, the author mentions that he used manuscripts not available in 1611.

With advances in biblical scholarship during the nineteenth century, including the accumulation of earlier and better manuscripts, archaeological discoveries in the ancient world as a whole and changes in English society and its language, the revision of the King James Bible on a more "official" basis was becoming mandatory. Before this could be accomplished, however, a group of outstanding scholars published *The Variorum Edition of the New Testament of Our Lord and Saviour Jesus Christ* (1880). The editors of this work, R. L. Clark, Alfred Goodwin, and W. Sanday, made this revision at "his majesty's special command." Their task was to revise the King James Bible in light of the various readings from the best textual authorities. As a result, the *Variorum Bible* followed the tradition of Tyndale, Coverdale, Great, Geneva, Bishops', and the various editions of the King James Bible. In addition, however, it prepared the way for the English Revised Bible.

The widespread desire for a full-fledged revision of the Authorized Bible resulted in a convocation of the Province of Canterbury in 1870. Samuel Wilberforce, bishop of Winchester, proposed to revise the New Testament where Greek texts revealed inaccurate or incorrect translations in the King James text. Bishop Ollivant enlarged the motion to include the Old Testament and Hebrew texts. As a result, two companies were appointed. Originally there were twenty-four members in each company, but they were later enlarged to include some sixty-five revisers from various denominations. They began their work in 1871, and in 1872 a group of American scholars was asked to join the enterprise in an advisory capacity. Oxford and Cambridge University Presses absorbed the costs of the project with the provision that they have exclusive copyright privileges to the finished product. Over three million copies of the revision were sold in the United States and Great Britain in less than a year. The Old Testament was released in 1885, the Apocrypha in 1896 (1898 in the United States), and the entire Bible was published in 1898. While the text of the revision was much more accurate than the King James Bible, it would take several generations for acceptance of the altered words and rhythms.

Some of the rendering of the English Revised Bible were not completely favored by the American revision committee, but they had agreed to give for fourteen years "no sanction to the publication of any other editions of the Revised Version than those issued by the University Presses of England." In 1901 *The Ameri-*

*can Standard Edition of the Revised Version* was published, indicating that there had been some unauthorized or nonstandard editions of it published prior to that time. Further revisions were made by the American committee, such as changing the names *Lord* to *Jehovah* and *Holy Ghost* to *Holy Spirit.* Paragraph structures were revised and shortened, and short page headings were added. Slowly this American Standard Version (ASV) won acceptance in the United States and even began to be imported into Great Britain.

Like its English counterpart, the ASV lacks the beauty of the King James Bible, but its more accurate readings have made it quite acceptable to teachers and students of the Bible. In 1929 the copyright passed to the International Council of Religious Education and they revised the text again. Like the earlier translations building on the foundation laid by William Tyndale, the ASV was the work of many hands and several generations.

THE REVISED STANDARD BIBLE

Half a century after the English Revision of the King James Bible was published, the International Council of Religious Education expressed its desire to utilize the great advances in recent biblical scholarship. The Westcott-Hort text of the New Testament (see chap. 14) had been sharply modified as a result of the papyrus and new manuscript discoveries. In addition, the literary style and taste of the English language had continued to change so that a new revision was deemed necessary. In 1937 the International Council authorized a committee to proceed with such a revision.

The revision committee consisted of twenty-two outstanding scholars who were to follow the meaning of the American Standard Version unless two-thirds of the committee agreed to change the reading. Its use of the simpler and more current forms of pronouns except in reference to God and more direct word order were also used as their guidelines. Delayed by World War II (1939-1945), the New Testament did not appear until 1946, with the Old being published in 1952 and the Apocrypha in 1957. These publications followed a tremendous publicity campaign which set into motion almost predictable reactions. In contrast to the ASV, the RSV was accused of blurring traditional Messianic passages, such as the substitution of "young woman" for "virgin" in Isaiah 7:14. Criticism of the New Testament was not so sharp, although they were sharp enough. All the criticism notwithstanding, the Revised Standard Version provides the English-speaking church with an up-to-date revision of the Bible based on the "critical text" (see chap. 14).

THE NEW ENGLISH BIBLE

Not satisfied that the Revised Standard Version was a continuation of the long-established tradition of earlier English Bible translations, the General Assembly of the Church of Scotland met in 1946 to consider a completely new translation. A joint committee was appointed in 1947, and three companies were chosen: one each for the Old Testament, the New, and the Apocrypha. C. H. Dodd was appointed chairman of the New Testament panel and in 1949 was named director of the entire translation. The New Testament of *The New English Bible* appeared in 1961, with the Old Testament and Apocrypha being published in 1970.

The principles of translation for *The New English Bible* were aimed at presenting a genuinely English idiom which would be "timeless," avoiding both anachronisms and transient modernisms. The translators sought to make their version plain enough to convey its meaning without being bald or pedestrian, for they hoped to produce a translation which would be a second authoritative version alongside the King James Bible.

Over four million copies of the NEB were sold during its first year of publication. Differing greatly from both the English Revised and the Revised Standard editions which preceded it, its translators frequently departed from literal renderings of the text, especially when they felt the text permitted two possible interpretations. In addition, the NEB has been criticized for its Anglicisms and its concentration on intelligibility over literalness of meaning, as well as its critical rearrangement of some sections of the Old Testament. This undoubtedly reflects the influence of contemporary theology on the translation through the translators. All things being considered, however, this translation has continued the tradition of its English forebears and is a valuable work in its own right.

## THE NEW AMERICAN STANDARD BIBLE

During the 1960's still another revision of the American Standard Bible was attempted. This effort was undertaken by the Lockman Foundation in an attempt to revive as well as revise the ASV. Its translation committee set forth its fourfold purpose in the preface accompanying the New Testament (1963). In 1970 the entire Bible was published following the same fourfold objective. They sought to be true to the original Hebrew and Greek texts, be grammatically correct, be understandable to the masses, and give proper place to the Lord Jesus Christ.

The *New American Standard Bible* translators attempted to renew the American Standard Version, the "rock of biblical honesty." Although they have not equaled the literary work of other standard versions in the process of translation, they have produced a helpful and faithful heir of the ASV. Another more or less official translation is currently being made under the sponsorship of the New York Bible Society. This translation is tentatively entitled, *The Holy Bible: New International Version.* The New Testament portion was released in 1973, and the Old Testament is scheduled for 1976.

## EIGHTEENTH- AND NINETEENTH-CENTURY TRANSLATIONS

Alongside the official translations discussed above, there were a host of unofficial translations and versions published. In 1703, for example, Daniel Whitby edited a *Paraphrase and Commentary on the New Testament.* Edward Wells followed with a revised text of the King James Bible called *The Common Translations Corrected* (1718-1724). In 1745 William Whiston, known for his translation of Josephus, published a *Primitive New Testament;* and John Wesley made some 12,000 changes in the Authorized Bible text. Edward Horwood made a *Liberal Translation of the New Testament* in 1768 to round out the translations of the eighteenth century.

During the nineteenth century, efforts to translate the Old

Testament began to appear more frequently. The first of these was *The Septuagint Bible* published by Charles Thompson in 1808. In 1844 Lancelot Brenton followed it up by publishing his *Septuagint Version of the Old Testament*. The Unitarian scholar Samuel Sharpe published his *New Testament* in 1840 and his *Old Testament* in 1865. In the meantime, Robert Young produced his *Literal Translation of the Bible* (1862), and Dean Alford published his *Greek New Testament* and a revision of the Authorized Bible in 1869. John Nelson Darby, leader of the Plymouth Brethren, published a *New Translation of the Bible* (1871, 1890), while Joseph Bryant Rotherham was publishing *The Emphasized Bible* (1872, 1902). Thomas Newberry edited *The Englishman's Bible* during the 1890's. One of the best known examples of translations of portions of the Bible appears in W. J. Conybeare and J. S. Howson, *The Life and Epistles of St. Paul* (1964), where the translation is embedded in a commentary.

TWENTIETH-CENTURY TRANSLATIONS

The great profusion of English Bible translations did not occur until the present century, when the great manuscripts had been discovered, public sentiment sought colloquial translations, attempts were being made to make official translations, and additional textual evidence was discovered. From that time there has been a virtual parade of scholars and their translations. Arthur S. Way, a classical scholar, led the parade with his translation of *The Letters of St. Paul* (1901). The very next year witnessed the publication of *The Twentieth Century New Testament* based on the text of Westcott and Hort. A consultee for this translation, Richard Francis Weymouth, translated *The Resultant Greek Testament* which was published posthumously in 1903 and thoroughly revised by James A. Robertson in 1924.

Perhaps the most pretentious enterprise by one man was *The Holy Bible in Modern English* (1895, 1903) by Ferrar Fenton. It was based on Hebrew, Chaldee, and Greek manuscripts. James Moffat, an Oxford scholar, published *The New Testament* (1913) and *The Old Testament* (1924), which he later combined into *A New Translation of the Bible* (1928). Moffat's work is characterized by its Scottish tone, freedom of style and idiom, and his modernistic theological bias. The American counterpart to Moffat appears in Edgar J. Goodspeed's *The Complete Bible: An American Translation* (1927). G. W. Wade presented a fresh translation arranged in what he believed were the chronological order of books in *The Documents of the New Testament* (1934). *The Concordant Version of the Sacred Scriptures* (1926 f.) was based on the principle that every word in the original should have an English equivalent. In 1937 Charles B. Williams issued *The New Testament in the Language of the People*, in which he tried to convey the exact meaning of the Greek verb tenses into English. During that same year Gerald Warre Cornish's *St. Paul from the Trenches* was published posthumously. W. C. Wand produced *The New Testament Letters* in 1943 in the format of a bishop writing a monthly letter to his diocese. In another attempt to get the Bible into the hands of laymen, J. H. Hooks served as chairman of a committee which translated *The Basic English Bible* (1940-1949) using only one thousand "basic" English words. Charles Kingsley Williams attempted a similar work in *The New Testament: A Translation in Plain English* (1952).

A conservative attempt to produce a counterpart to the Revised Standard Bible was produced under the direction of Gerrit Verkuyl of Berkeley, California. This Bible translation was entitled *The Berkeley Version in Modern English* (1945, 1959) and more recently the *Modern Language Bible* (1971). In 1969 this work was revised and published as *The Holy Bible: The New Berkeley Version in Modern English*. After releasing several components, J. B. Phillips published *The New Testament in Modern English* (1958). His paraphrase was quite different from the Jehovah's Witness publications, under the name of the Watchtower Bible and Tract Society, *The New World Translation of the Christian Greek Scriptures* (1950) and *The New World Translation of the Hebrew Scriptures* (1953). A distinguished Jewish scholar, Hugh J. Schonfield, attempted to reconstruct the "authentic" New Testament Jewish atmosphere for Gentile readers in *The Authentic New Testament* (1955).

George M. Lamsa made his translation of *The Holy Bible from Ancient Eastern Manuscripts* (1933-1957) from the Syriac Peshitta (see chap. 16) instead of Greek manuscripts. Kenneth S. Wuest followed J. B. Phillips in publishing his *Expanded Translation of the New Testament* in several installments before it was finally combined in 1959. His work, along with the Lockman Foundation publication of *The Amplified Bible* (1958, 1964) followed the tradition of Charles B. Williams. In fact, *The Amplified Bible* is little short of a commentary.

In 1961 Olaf M. Norlis published *The Simplified New Testament in Plain English* and R. K. Harrison translated *The Psalms for Today* to accompany it. A year later Kenneth Taylor began publishing portions of *The Living Bible* as a paraphrase. The completed translation of *The Living Bible* was published in 1971, and it has had an amazingly wide circulation in the millions. In the meantime, F. F. Bruce added to this tradition of paraphrased translations by publishing *The Letters of Paul: An Expanded Paraphrase* (1965). The American Bible Society published its *Good News for Modern Man*, also known as *The New Testament in Today's English Version*, in 1966. By 1968 over ten million copies had been sold, and it has entered into its third edition as of 1971. In addition to the New Testament, the *Good News for Modern Man* (TEV) has published portions of the Old Testament, including Psalms, Job, and Proverbs.

### ECUMENICAL TRANSLATIONS AND VERSIONS

With the great profusion of Roman Catholic, Jewish, and Protestant Bibles being published, it was inevitable that in an ecumenical age there should be attempts made at producing ecumenical Bibles.

*The New Testament: Revised Standard Version Catholic Edition* (1965) falls into this category. Although it is really the text of the Revised Standard Bible, with about twenty-four basic changes (listed in an appendix) and notes added, it has been officially approved for use by Roman Catholics. Some of the textual changes include the change of "brothers" to "brethren," where the references are to the family of Jesus (Mt 12:46, 48), and "send her away" instead of "divorce her" with references to Joseph and Mary (Mt 1:19); the addition of "and fasting" to "prayer" in Mark 9:29; as well as the restoring of the long ending to the gospel of

Mark (16:9-20) and the incident of the woman taken in adultery in John 7:58—8:11 (see chap. 15).

The first attempt by a joint ecumenical committee to produce a common Bible is *The Anchor Bible* (1964). Under the general editorship of William F. Albright and David Noel Freedman, it claims to be international and interfaith in its scope. Specifically, it claims to encompass Protestant, Catholic, and Jewish scholars from many countries among the translators. Their effort is to make available to all English-speaking peoples all of the significant historical and linguistic knowledge which bears on the interpretation of the biblical record. It is being produced in separate volumes, each of which is to be accompanied by a complete introduction and notes.

A revised edition of the Revised Standard Bible was published as the New Testament portion of *The Common Bible* in 1973. Although it is too early to appraise the value of this translation or its success as an ecumenical venture, it is difficult to see how it can maintain its unity, since the individual volumes are being produced by individual scholars of such varied theological and cultural outlook. Even if its unity is maintained, one wonders what the net effect of the theological diversities will have upon the overall unity of the biblical message.

Even at a glance, however, this endless procession of modern translations is sufficient to indicate that the twentieth century, as no century before it in human history, possesses the greatest proliferation of translations of the Bible in both an official and an unofficial thrust. With this great diversity and multiplication of translations comes a greater responsibility than ever to understand and communicate the whole counsel of God contained in His inspired Book.